After Kieślowski

Contemporary Approaches to Film and Television Series

A complete listing of the books in this series can be found online at wsupress.wayne.edu

after kieślowski

After Kieślowski

The Legacy of Krzysztof Kieślowski

Edited by Steven Woodward

WAYNE STATE UNIVERSITY PRESS DETROIT

13 12 11 10 09 5 4 3 2 1

Library of Congress Cataloging-in-Publication Data

After Kieślowski : the legacy of Krzysztof Kieślowski / edited by Steven Woodward.
p. cm. — (Contemporary approaches to film and television series)
Includes bibliographical references and index.
ISBN 978-0-8143-3326-6 (pbk. : alk. paper)
1. Kieślowski, Krzysztof, 1941–1996—Criticism and interpretation. I. Woodward, Steven, 1964–
PN1998.3.K54A38 2009
791.4302'33092—dc22
2008037701

Designed and typeset by Maya Rhodes
Composed in Helvetica Neue and Minion Pro

For Wendy and Jamie

Contents

Acknowledgments

Tracing the global legacy of a filmmaker like Krzysztof Kieślowski would be impossible for a single, isolated critic. As the editor of a volume that has drawn on the much greater expertise of the other ten contributors, I thank every one of them for their very considerable work on this project. Many have contributed personal resources and channeled whatever institutional support they have (the ever-shrinking support for travel, for example) into the book. To take but one example of which I am aware, Renata Murawska flew to Poland from Australia for the purpose of conducting the interview with Jerzy Stuhr included in this volume. Beyond such considerable concerns of time and money, every one of the contributors has responded with dedication and grace to my editorial queries through what has proved to be a lengthy process.

Barry Keith Grant, general editor of the Contemporary Approaches to Film and Television Series for Wayne State University Press, was very helpful in identifying major weaknesses of the first draft of the manuscript, as were the anonymous expert readers who evaluated it for the press. Annie Martin, acquisitions editor at the press, has been constantly encouraging through the process of editing the book and tireless in responding to my reiterations of the same questions. Many others have helped turn manuscript into book, including Carrie Downes Teefey, Maya Rhodes, and Beth Ina.

For help with illustrations from Polish sources, we thank Małgorzata Cup of Telewizja Polska and Grzegorz Balski of Filmoteka Narodowa. I also thank Krzysztof Piesiewicz's agent, Nicole Cann, who very kindly provided me with the English translation of *Heaven* (2002). The cost of indexing the book was defrayed by a generous grant from the Research Committee of my employer, Bishop's University, for which I am very grateful.

Finally, I offer my deepest gratitude to my wife, Wendy Bontinen, on behalf of both myself and the other contributors. She has read through the manuscript many more times than I and has identified weaknesses and inconsistencies throughout that have simply eluded my calloused eye.

Introduction

Steven Woodward

This collection of essays investigates two aspects of the legacy of Krzysztof Kieślowski (1941–96): films produced after his death by other filmmakers using his scripts and ideas; and the prescient thematic, stylistic, and philosophical preoccupations particular to his oeuvre that have subsequently been developed in an extraordinarily wide variety of films and television serials in the years since his death. Unlike a filmmaker such as Alfred Hitchcock (d. 1980), whose influence is both pervasive and diffuse, Kieślowski has not been dead so long, and his work has not been seen so much. But it is precisely because of his premature death, coming at a moment when his films *were* beginning to be seen by large audiences internationally, that his legacy is worth investigating.

Since Kieślowski died unexpectedly on 13 March 1996 at the age of fifty-four, arguably at precisely the moment he had reached the height of his career with the critical success of the *Three Colors* (1993–94) trilogy, his critical reputation has become divided. On the one hand, he has been hailed as one of the greatest directors of all time, lamented at the time of his death as "one of the few European directors capable of measuring up to the giants of the past" (Malcolm 26) and elevated to the elect of world cinema alongside Jean Renoir, Robert Bresson, Federico Fellini, Ingmar Bergman, Yasujiro Ozu, Max Ophuls, and Andrei Tarkovsky. For his adulators, his movement from the early documentaries to the last feature films, from small-scale Polish documentaries on pointedly political subjects to lavish international coproductions probing metaphysical questions, marked the increasing depth and mastery of the maturing artist. On the other hand, his importance has been heavily qualified on a whole range of accounts. For some, particularly Polish critics, Kieślowski's work up until 1989 was motivated by and important within the Polish communist context, but his last four films, all international coproductions made largely outside Poland and predominantly in French, demonstrated a suspicious involvement with beautiful images and a dreamy disengagement from the messy substance of the world, even while purportedly maintaining a commitment to ethical and existential investigations. Perhaps this late work evidenced what Robert Stam has termed the "ephemeral, artificial, and polyglot style of transnational cinema" or Marek Haltof has labeled the self-important strategies typical of art cinema (Haltof, *Cinema* 111–14). For critics who adopt this attitude, Kieślowski had clearly lost his bearings in the postcommunist, extra-Polish context.

Still other critics question the value of all of Kieślowski's metaphysical films, including the Polish films, from *Blind Chance* (1981; released 1987) on. Perhaps most infamously, David Denby used the occasion of the release of *Three Colors: Red* (1994) to lament the state of the European cinema in general and to dismiss the importance of Kieślowski, its "current hero," in particular: "He's essentially a constructor of intricate puzzles; an artificer, perhaps, but not an artist" (85). Another curious class of critic begrudgingly admits Kieślowski's importance while finding the films almost unwatchable. David Thomson, for one, recognizes Kieślowski's mastery and connects him with such figures as Robert Bresson, but he also asserts that, "for me, Kieślowski frequently runs the risk of being precious, mannered, and so cold as to forbid touching . . . to see a Kieślowski film for me requires a steeling, as if I were going into torture or church" (468). How can we reconcile Thomson's response with Emma Wilson's description of Kieślowski as "a director of intimacy and interiority" (xv), and with the fact that many viewers of his films were so affected and engaged by them that they felt a deep connection with the taciturn filmmaker and profound grief when he died?

Whatever one feels about Kieślowski's own body of films, there can be no doubt that he has had an extraordinarily wide and overt influence on other filmmakers, during his life and even more so in the years since his death. This alone is incontestable evidence for his importance. However, the scholarly response to Kieślowski's importance has been focused on analyzing and evaluating his work rather than considering issues of reception. The question of his engagement with and influence on other filmmakers has barely been addressed, even in the most recent book-length studies, Joseph G. Kickasola's *The Films of Krzysztof Kieślowski: The Liminal Image* (2004) and Marek Haltof's *The Cinema of Krzysztof Kieślowski: Variations on Destiny and Chance* (2004). Annette Insdorf did offer a schematic overview of possible lines of Kieślowskian influence in the "Postscript" to her *Double Lives, Second Chances: The Cinema of Krzysztof Kieślowski* (1999), but this was necessarily brief and provisional. In the concluding chapter to her 2000 book on Kieslowski, "Conclusion: Home Movies," Emma Wilson offers the perfect rationale for a return to the issue of Kieślowski's legacy: "Evidently much work is still to be done . . . on the influence Kieślowski will have had on the future development of French national cinema. Such a prospective survey . . . might again open new ways of thinking about hybridity in film and about how national cinemas are always already open to infiltration and identificatory mechanisms whereby what is alien is absorbed, repeated, and reproduced" (118).

Just as Kieślowski absorbed French and other European cinemas in his last works, so filmmakers are now absorbing Kieślowski. Now, more than ten years after his death, an extended analysis of this influence can provide a more accurate measure of his true importance to filmmaking and his contribution to vitally important cultural discourses. Examining Kieślowski's legacy is a way of thinking about issues that remain at the heart of filmmaking and of cultural production in general. And since Kieślowski was a filmmaker deeply engaged with existing cinematic tradition—most obviously that of Poland but increasingly of Europe—thinking about Kieślowski's influence is also a way of identifying ongoing discursive lines of thought. In this sense, "after Kieślowski" is also before Kieślowski.

Kieślowski left an unusually large legacy to other filmmakers for at least three reasons. First, he came to international prominence only in the 1990s, although his career had begun in the late 1960s, and he died shortly after completing his most successful project, the *Three Colors* trilogy, which brilliantly embodied ruminations on the elusive meanings of liberty, equality, and fraternity in narrative form. Arriving on the international stage abruptly and to considerable dramatic effect, Kieślowski almost immediately died (like Weronika, the Polish protagonist of *The Double Life of Véronique* [1991]), compelling enthusiasts of his late work not only to meditate on the unusually complex aesthetics and powerful effect of that work but also to excavate and analyze the whole body of his earlier Polish films made within the government-funded and monitored film industry.

Second, Kieślowski's career as a filmmaker was by no means over at the time of his death. Although he had announced, after completing the *Three Colors* trilogy, that he would be retiring from filmmaking, that announcement seems to have been more a petulant reaction to his current exhausting project (and perhaps to the Cannes jury that gave the Palme d'Or to Quentin Tarantino's *Pulp Fiction* [1994] over *Red*) than a fully considered decision about his career. Indeed, shortly after his death, it was revealed that he had begun writing another trilogy of films, again working with his long-time collaborator Krzysztof Piesiewicz, this time using Dante's *Divine Comedy* as the inspiring and structuring force. At the time of Kieślowski's death, he and Piesiewicz had completed a treatment for only one part of the trilogy, *Heaven,* but Piesiewicz subsequently completed screenplays for all three parts. Rights for this new trilogy were bought by Miramax, though they produced only *Heaven,* directed by Tom Tykwer in 2002, before selling the rights for the other parts. The Bosnian director Danis Tanovic completed *Hell* (*L'Enfer*) in 2005, but *Purgatory* remains unproduced as of this writing (though many reviewers mistook

Nadzieja [*Hope*; Stanislaw Mucha, 2007], a film also scripted by Piesiewicz, as the final installment of the trilogy. In fact, *Nadzieja* is the first installment of a new trilogy centered around the concepts of faith, hope, and love). Furthermore, actors and assistant directors involved with Kieślowski have gone on to make films that develop his uncompleted projects or that are closely derived thematically and stylistically from his work.

Third, with the collapse of Polish communism in 1989, Kieślowski was forced to consider the question of transnational cultural production, now a major pragmatic concern for other filmmakers and an inescapable issue for cultural critics. As Haltof has observed, the problem facing all the cinemas of Central Europe after the collapse of communism in 1989 was "to find a new voice to adequately express the 'national' while incorporating other cinematic discourses" (*Polish* 182). While other Polish filmmakers like Andrzej Wajda and Krzysztof Zanussi struggled, in the post-1989 situation, to find not only funding but relevant subjects, Kieślowski capitalized on the French recognition of his achievement with *Decalogue* (1988) to make films that narrativize the extranational circumstances of production (most obviously in *The Double Life of Véronique* and *Three Colors: White* [1994]), even as they broaden the ethical and metaphysical investigations of the earlier films.

That Kieślowski's work was prescient in all kinds of ways, that he developed innovative narrative forms and stylistic methods to address pressing existential, moral, and political issues, is partly explicable with reference to his social context and the tensions and conflicts that surrounded him. Beginning his career with short black-and-white documentaries, ending it with sumptuous features; committed at first to the principles of realism, yearning to escape film's literalism at the end of his life; laboring under communist surveillance and censorship in pre-1989 Poland, selling himself and his work within the system of capitalist commodification in post-1989 Europe: Kieślowski was bound to be very conscious of the contingencies impinging on and choices placed before him as a filmmaker. On top of this, although living in one of the most devoutly Catholic countries in Europe, Kieślowski remained agnostic. Such circumstances go some way toward explaining why he developed an extraordinary ability to deepen and transform cinematic signification and why he remained committed throughout his career to examining the failures, deceptions, and possibilities of representation.

Some of the stylistic devices Kieślowski utilized in his late feature films—fades to black or white in the middle of a scene, insertions of apparently unmotivated shots and sounds (for example, elderly people depositing bottles in recycling bins, or pigeons cooing)—were developed during his documentary phase, where they served as the director's commentary on the events unfolding before him. Unwilling to actually intervene in those events or to comment on them in voiceover, Kieślowski used editing to punctuate these films. When he brought these same techniques to his feature films, he was able to create an extraordinary range of aesthetic effects that placed him among the most avant-garde of feature filmmakers. However, in refusing to limit himself in subject or stylistic approach, in increasingly addressing moral and metaphysical dilemmas that transcend the particular political and social circumstances of communism or capitalism, Kieślowski alienated many Polish critics, even while making his work more universally relevant.

The Polish Legacy

Nevertheless, Kieślowski has had a pronounced influence within Poland, and Marek Haltof's essay begins this collection with a survey of Kieślowski's legacy in three areas: the national, the critical, and the creative. The tenth anniversary of his death, 2006, was proclaimed the "Year of Kieślowski" in Poland, with exhibitions, conferences, and retrospectives organized throughout the country. However, despite being celebrated nationally as an important cultural hero, Kieślowski has a more divided reputation among Polish film critics themselves. While most are willing to acknowledge his legacy in the Kieślowskian metaphysics, characters, and images of other filmmakers, some key critics remain suspicious of the direction he took to achieve international fame, avoiding Polish history and mythology and abandoning the realism with which his career had begun. Some judge his stories increasingly contrived and pretentious, his characters and events improbable, and even the music, such a crucial element in the last three films, banal. Nevertheless, writers and filmmakers, former collaborators and students, continue to produce films rich in formal, stylistic, and thematic allusions to Kieślowski's work. Krzysztof Piesiewicz is collaborating with Michał Rosa on a series of films reminiscent of the *Decalogue.* Other filmmakers have made sequels to Kieślowski's *Camera Buff* (1979), *First Love* (1974), and *Talking Heads* (1980). The actor Jerzy Stuhr has moved decisively into directing with a range of films that bear the direct or indirect influence of his long-time colleague. And a number of talented filmmakers who were supervised by Kieślowski at the Katowice Film School are now making films that show their deep appreciation of, and the impression made on them by, their teacher. Even Jan Hryniak's *The Third* (2004), a kind of remake of *Knife in the Water* (1962), modulates Polanski's original scenario in a Kieślowskian, metaphysical direction by changing the original hitchhiker into an angel-like figure.

The broad contours of influence mapped by Haltof are complemented by the two following essays, which offer a detailed tracing of influence and divergence in the work of the director Krzysztof Zanussi and the actor/director Jerzy Stuhr, both of whom were key collaborators of Kieślowski. During the communist period, Polish cinema functioned partly as an antidote to the propaganda of state television, perhaps never more strongly than with the so-called Cinema of Moral Concern (sometimes referred to as the Cinema of Moral Anxiety) in the late 1970s, a loose grouping of blunt and stylistically unpolished films about social ills, the flow of which was eventually stopped by the imposition of martial law in 1981. That antagonism between cinema and television is the explicit focus of one of the key films of that period, Andrzej Wajda's *Man of Marble* (1976), the ending of which suggests that even television might eventually be turned to searching ethical examinations of the past with a goal toward charting a better future. As Sarah Cooper argues, both Kieślowski and Krzysztof Zanussi realized that goal in their television series: Kieślowski's *Decalogue* at the end of the 1980s and Zanussi's *Weekend Stories* (1997), a series with obvious thematic connections to Kieślowski's, almost a decade later. While Kieślowski thereby "lives on" through the work of his friend and former mentor, Zanussi, Cooper demonstrates that the connection between their series is extremely complex: Zanussi neither slavishly imitates nor, following Harold Bloom's pattern of anxious influence, purposely misreads Kieślowski's work. Drawing on Jacques Derrida's implied theory of influence from his essay "Survivre" and on Emmanuel Levinas's notion of ethics arising from a filial relation to the future, Cooper carefully traces the stylistic affinities between Kieślowski's and Zanussi's work, derived from the shared influence of anxiety, and argues instead that the relationship between *Decalogue* and *Weekend Stories* is an extension of the ethical investigations that form their narratives. In these, we see characters who cannot draw on an absolute moral code inherited from the past but must instead find an ethical path, inspired by but not restricted to such a code, if they are to live differently, to create a better future. Similarly, Zanussi's series cannot simply reiterate Kieślowski's: if Zanussi revisits similar ethical questions, his answers reflect his difference from Kieślowski (his Catholic faith, for example) and the changed sociopolitical context for his *Weekend Stories.*

Renata Murawska also extends Haltof's observations with her study of the nature of the relationship between the famed Polish actor Jerzy Stuhr and Kieślowski, a relationship that some critics see as unidirectional and determining all of Stuhr's recent directing projects. For Murawska, their working relationship was much more deeply symbiotic, with Kieślowski's increasingly complex control of feature filmmaking drawing on Stuhr's improvisational ability, scripting of dialogue, and evolving screen persona. If, after Kieślowski's death, Stuhr did direct at least two films with decisively Kieślowskian scenarios, he rendered them as fables or moral tales, eschewing the mystery and ambiguity that are the hallmarks of Kieślowski's late feature films. (In parallel with this, Stuhr sees the script, Kieślowski the process of editing, as the most essential element of filmmaking). Thus, while the general structure of *Love Stories* (1997) might seem to mark it as a clumsy reprise of *Blind Chance,* Stuhr's film has little stylistic resemblance to Kieślowski's work, and the fates meted out to Stuhr's four protagonists mark their stories as moral tales rather than metaphysical investigations. Similarly, although Stuhr's *The Big Ani-*

mal (2000) was based directly on Kieślowski's 1973 treatment (of Kazimierz Orłoś's short story), Stuhr's additions and modifications, as well as his stylistic approach, transform the story from a realistic tale with a sociopolitical focus (of the kind typical of the Cinema of Moral Concern) to a poetic, universal fable. Murawska concludes that Kieślowski and Stuhr's shared formative professional and artistic experiences inevitably informed the work of both and that the centripetal force of Kieślowski's vision attracted other directors and also conditioned audiences to perceive his themes and visual tropes in the work of others.

In his interview with Murawska, Stuhr provides more particular details of his essentially symbiotic relationship with Kieślowski. After an uninspiring first encounter at a time when Stuhr was a rising theater actor, Stuhr explains that, against his better judgment, he committed to acting in Kieślowski's first feature, *The Scar* (1976). He quickly discovered an extraordinary degree of freedom in the improvisational aspects of film acting. While Stuhr brought an ear for dialogue to Kieślowski's films and actually scripted much of the dialogue for his next film, *The Calm* (1976), Kieślowski tutored Stuhr in the cinema's unique rendering of character and world, in which small gestures and physical quirks can carry much meaning, like Fillip Mosz's hiccups in *Camera Buff*. Extraordinarily, Kieślowski's decision to change the ending of *Camera Buff* so that Mosz would direct the film camera at himself prefigured what Stuhr would do in the films he later directed. For Stuhr, unlike Kieślowski, would follow what Tadeusz Lubelski has called the strategy of the myth-biographer, transforming the matter of his own life into his film narratives (Lubelski 35).[1] In turning to directing, Stuhr would perhaps inevitably be seen as Kieślowski's epigone, given their collaboration through numerous films. But as Stuhr points out, his faith distinguished him from Kieślowski. While he may have learned much about the craft of directing from Kieślowski, he eschews the metaphysical tendencies of Kieślowski's cinema and tends to construct unambiguous moral tales. Thus, Stuhr's testimony is invaluable in helping to trace Kieślowski's own development as a filmmaker, in distinguishing the unique aspects of Kieślowski's cinema, and in providing a very lucid example of the way that Kieślowski has been a powerful influence even on filmmakers with very different aspirations.

The European Legacy

What Stuhr identifies as his crucial difference from Kieślowski—the latter's metaphysical tendency—is precisely what won Kieślowski an audience outside Poland, even before the collapse of communism in 1989. As Andrzej Wajda put it, "When we were lost and confused during martial law, he alone knew which path to follow" (Macnab). In writing the screenplays for the *Decalogue*, Kieślowski consciously avoided grounding the stories in contemporary Polish politics, for two reasons. For one, he was entirely disillusioned with politics and devoted to larger issues:

> During martial law, I realized that politics aren't really important. In a way, of course, they define where we are and what we're allowed to do, but they don't solve the really important human questions . . . In fact, it doesn't matter whether you live in a Communist country or a prosperous capitalist one as far as such questions are concerned, questions like, What is the true meaning of life? Why get up in the morning? (Stok 144)

Given the more universal and metaphysical direction of his interests, Kieślowski, along with Piesiewicz, also had a much more practical realization: "We'd begun to suspect intuitively that *Decalogue* could be marketed abroad. So we decided to leave politics out" (Stok 145). Creating the cycle of ten hour-long films for Polish television, Kieślowski also edited two of the films to feature length for theatrical release, with extraordinarily successful results outside Poland. *A Short Film about Killing* won the Fédération Internationale de la Presse Cinématographique (FIPRESCI) award and Jury Prize at Cannes in 1988. *A Short Film about Love* won three awards at the San Sebastian Film Festival in 1989: the FIPRESCI award, the Special Jury Award, and the Catholic Jury Prize (Haltof *Cinema*, 77). And this recognition was part of a much broader discovery and celebration of Kieślowski's work at film festivals in Europe and around the world. Thus, just as Poland and its film industry transitioned to a market economy, Kieślowski had created an audience for himself outside Poland, and his work began to have an influence on European filmmakers.

Indeed, the various Kieślowskian methods, both narrative and stylistic, of exposing the uncertainties of life, the impossibility of judging the actions and lives of others—what Kickasola has called Kieślowski's existentialist strain—have been appropriated by a number of other European directors. Kieślowski's *Blind Chance*, a meditation on the part contingency plays in determining human lives, has alone provoked a number of ripostes, including *Sliding Doors* (Peter Howitt, 1998) and *Run Lola Run* (Tom Tykwer, 1998). The Austrian filmmaker Michael Haneke's spare work, devoid of emotive cues, fractured in perspective, and built upon lengthy shots that tend to draw attention to the cluttered matter of reality, seems almost like an extension of Kieślowski's own Polish work.

Emma Wilson examines films by two of Kieślowski's former assistant directors, Emmanuel Finkiel and Julie Bertucelli, French filmmakers whose films redirect the tropes of cultural and linguistic difference and dislocation that were common in Kieślowski's work but particularly important in *The Double Life of Véronique* and *Three Colors: White*. As Wilson notes, where

Kieślowski's fictional imagining of nations and places seems ultimately designed to defy difference and emphasize the universality of existential situations, Finkiel's *Voyages* (1999) and Bertucelli's *Since Otar Left* (2003) employ these tropes toward a nuanced exploration of the migrant's experience of voyaging between nations and cultures, when fantasy and memory collide with actuality. These particular filmmakers' debt to and reinterpretation of Kieślowski's work is indicative of the scope of Kieślowski's influence, in Europe as a whole and particularly in France, since Finkiel and Bertucelli are representative of a new generation of filmmakers concerned with diasporic identities in a still-divided Europe.

The collapse of communism in Eastern Europe and the formation of the European Union might be thought to have heralded an increasing sense of unity across the continent. However, as Georgina Evans argues, the French films of both Kieślowski and the Austrian director Michael Haneke suggest the increasing isolation of the individual in an ever-more-fragmented Europe, while acknowledging the difficulty of adequately representing this situation through film. The directors' French work has a shared pedigree: they both made use of Juliette Binoche as a kind of icon of Frenchness, and both were supported, in their French filmmaking, by the Romanian-Jewish producer Marin Karmitz, who felt that the Central European identities of these directors would allow them particular insight into the idea of Europe. Indeed, as Evans shows, the two directors offer very similar insights, even if arriving at them by very different formal and stylistic means. Both *Red* and *Code Unknown* (2000) depict a populous Europe, but one where those with different identities—of class or ethnicity or career or age—come into contact with each other only through violence or accident. In this context, the camera self-consciously strains to construct a coherent narrative world: Kieślowski's camera becomes mechanized, avoiding adopting the characters' subjective views, and Haneke constantly reminds us of the limits of the camera's view both spatially and temporally. Their characters, too, are locked into separate perceptual worlds, even when standing next to each other, as both filmmakers indicate through clamorous environments in which the aural and the visual no longer coincide. But just as religions form communities of believers by offering a shared vision of the heavens, so both filmmakers indicate that a shared code might bring individuals together, as Kieślowski optimistically asserts in the final moments of his film and Haneke more ambiguously and tentatively suggests at the closing of his.

If Haneke, who was born less than a year after Kieslowski (b. 1941), can be seen as his longer-living peer, Tom Tykwer (b. 1965) might be seen as a filial successor. As already mentioned, Tykwer's *Run Lola Run* is clearly structurally derived from Kieslowski's *Blind Chance,* and Tykwer was impressed enough with the screenplay of *Heaven*—perhaps recognizing there thematic echoes of his own *The Princess and the Warrior* (2000)—that he brought the project to completion after Kieslowski's death. The next two essays in this volume, then, contemplate this lineage.

In comparing Tom Tykwer's *Run Lola Run* with Kieślowski's *Blind Chance,* Paul Coates effectively maps the trajectory of Kieślowski's work from the early documentaries through the essentially tragic visions of his narrative features. As Coates notes, the tripartite *Blind Chance* serves as a fulcrum, marking the point where Kieślowski balances the contingency-bound narratives of documentary against the narrative liberty of fiction. Tykwer certainly borrows Kieślowski's tripartite structure and makes many direct allusions to Kieślowski's film. However, where Tykwer adopts a game-like strategy of allowing repetitions of character and situation until the desired outcome is reached, Kieślowski's repetitions have metaphysical ramifications and ultimately assert a tragic vision: although the protagonist of the third repetition seems to have escaped from politics into a realm of peace, he cannot ultimately evade "the envious revenge of invisible gods." Thus, for Coates, Tykwer's film is not a remake of Kieślowski's, as Slavoj Žižek assumes in praising Tykwer's supposedly more perfect form, but a play on Kieślowski's film with entirely different implications. Coates closes by noting that *Heaven,* the film scripted by Kieślowski and Piesiewicz but directed by Tykwer, could actually be seen as an extension of *Blind Chance,* the protagonist's missing fourth story, in which Kieślowski, like the aging Shakespeare who turned to romances, allows his protagonist salvation, enabling him to find peace through a heavy injection of artifice.

My own essay in this volume also considers *Heaven* as an extension of, and fulfillment of implications in, Kieślowski's earlier work. However, I argue that, as such, the film is also the final note of a response to Jean-Luc Godard. While most critics have glossed over the allusion to Godard's *Contempt* (*Le Mépris,* 1963) that occurs early in *White,* and Kieślowski himself denied its import, even a summary review of Godard's film reveals an extraordinary number of coinciding features with *White* and the rest of Kieślowski's *Three Colors* trilogy. Indeed, the most provocative connection between the two filmmakers is their use of marriage as a metaphor for cinematic signification. In *Contempt,* the increasing alienation of a husband and wife as they are drawn into the production of a transnational film project figures cinema's divorce from a world it purports to present. *White* begins with the literal divorce of a Polish hairdresser and his French wife, but precisely through the interplay of voyeurism and exhibitionism, those crucial practices of mainstream narrative cinema, the estranged couple are brought back together, even if they remain trapped in a spectatorial spatial relationship at the film's conclusion. Kieślowski eventually offered a narrative solution to this impasse, though posthumously, in the film directed by Tykwer. *Heaven* charts the increasingly ethereal connection between an English schoolteacher guilty of planting a bomb in a Milan office building and the Italian policeman who is one of her captors. Concluding with the couple ascending from the earth (albeit by helicopter), disappearing into a blue sky, and thereby inscribing heaven with their presence, the film's final shot answers that of *Contempt,* a sea and sky devoid of human or divine presence. Thus, by taking on Godard and by engaging more generally with the extra-Polish cinematic tradition, Kieślowski was able, through Tykwer's agency, to reassert cinema's power to connect self and other, to transcend the visible, and to evoke the supersensible. Tykwer's relatively limited changes to the Kieślowski/Piesiewicz screenplay and his inscription of *Heaven* with his own stylistic hallmark—most notably the kinetic camera that pervades all his work and carries its own connotations of a fateful mechanism working steadily and inexorably—do not substantially alter these implications of the film's ending.

The Global Legacy

The manner in which Kieślowski engaged with the cultural discourses and adapted to the market forces of European cinema, even while maintaining the unique signature of his Polish work, ensured that he appealed to European, and particularly French, audiences, but also that his work could escape the potentially narcissistic nature and fate of European art cinema and appeal to a global audience. As Paul Coates has noted in *Cinema, Religion and the Romantic Legacy: Through a Glass Darkly,* "As the spiritual impulses [of East European filmmakers] waned in tandem with the rusting of the Iron Curtain, they migrated ironically into an American cinema nearer the end of the capitalist road the East Europeans and Russians were entering" (178). Kieślowski's increasing visibility outside Europe, particularly with *Decalogue* and the subsequent transnational productions, coincided with the rise of the new American spirituality. As an avowed agnostic from devoutly Catholic Poland who brooded on the possibility of god, Kieślowski was like a salve to the West, where the secular had blanched the spiritual out of life. Miramax acted as a conduit for his work, distributing his last four films, the European coproductions, in North America. In fact, Harvey Weinstein arranged for *The Double Life of Véronique* to open the 1991 New York Film Festival (and it was Miramax again that stood behind the production of *Heaven*). As a result of growing American recognition of Kieślowski's achievement, *Decalogue* was finally given theatrical and video release in the United States in 2000. Furthermore, this delayed recognition of Kieślowski's importance in the United States has meant that he has continued to have a direct influence on American film and television into the first decade of the new millennium.

Charles Eidsvik demonstrates that no small part of this influence is visual rather than narrative or thematic. Kieślowski employed a wider range of cinematographers than directors like Bergman or Bertolucci, but he was nevertheless able to turn the distinctive visual styles and techniques of such cinematographers as Sławomir Idziak, Piotr Sobociński, and Edward Kłosiński to the articulation of a consistent, coherent, but cinematically dynamic visual world. Inspiring his cinematographers to work very closely with his art directors, fusing documentary and fiction-film techniques and conventions, Kieślowski created films that seem to unfold in the present tense. Eidsvik enumerates the many techniques that combine in this hybrid style, including images of characters watching and watched; an alternation between a predictive and a trailing camera; detailed attention to the sense of space, color, and texture of the sets; careful control of relation of character to background through both contrast and color; and the use of key images, visually intense moments resembling still photographs in their condensation of the action and meanings of the film. While none of these elements is unique to Kieślowski, their combination creates his unique visual signature, the direct influence of which Eidsvik traces in the Indian film *The Terrorist* (Santosh Sivan, 1999), in a number of films shot by Idziak, including *Men with Guns* (John Sayles, 1997) and *Black Hawk Down* (Ridley Scott, 2001), sporadically in Gonzalez Iñárritu's films such as *21 Grams* (2003), which are obviously heavily narratively and thematically influenced by Kieślowski, and finally in recent work by Julian Schnabel, especially *The Diving Bell and the Butterfly* (2007). However, Eidsvik concludes that Kieślowski's visual legacy is likely to become much greater in the future, if more diffuse, as his techniques are now almost universally known by young filmmakers through DVD and as digital filmmaking technology makes it economically feasible for these filmmakers to attempt variations on Kieślowski's hybrid visual form.

Joseph G. Kickasola then explains how Kieślowski's probing of metaphysical questions through what Kickasola terms multivalent narratives—multiple-plot films whose stories interweave and intersect with each other in unpredictable but suggestive ways—undoubtedly presaged, if not directly influenced, American cinema from 1990 on. Mosaic narratives (or what David Bordwell calls "network narratives"), forking-path stories, and films of "multivalent consciousness" (in which one person inhabits two lives simultaneously, as in Kieślowski's *The Double Life of Véronique*) inevitably raise the question of whether events unfold according to chance or design. While Kieślowski's response to this question was to maintain a dialectical tension, to dwell in "existential possibility," the extraordinary number of American filmmakers who have recently employed multivalent narratives take varied positions. Robert Altman's mosaic narratives (which he first began to use in the 1970s), no matter what patterns they seem to reveal, ultimately arrive only at a bleak contingency. Quentin Tarantino's apparent mosaics depend on the filmmaker's clever shuffling of narrative events rather than leading to any deeper revelation of cosmic order. At the other extreme, filmmakers like P. T. Anderson insist on the uncanny, if not miraculous, nature of coincidence. Most recently, though, a number of filmmakers have appeared who maintain Kieślowski's dialectical tension, such as Paul Haggis and Iñárritu. Kieślowski's pessimistic disposition may have clashed with the contrary quality in Americans, but the form and nature of his metaphysical probings have now proved prescient of, and deeply relevant to, American cultural discourse.

While Kieślowski's connection with other Slavic and Scandinavian metaphysical filmmakers is self-evident, the similarity of his work (and the arc of his career) with that of the Iranian filmmaker Abbas Kiarostami is a fruitful focus for John Caruana. Seeing the work of both as a challenge and antidote to the moral and spiritual vacuity of the postmodern, Caruana adopts André Bazin's and Siegfried Kracauer's notion of realism, reasserting the cinema's potential to probe beyond the purely phenomenal world, and he celebrates Kieślowski's and Kiarostami's success in doing so. Both filmmakers adopt an expanded, Aristotelian notion of politics that encompasses metaphysical inquiry, and a Levinasian notion of ethics that calls into question their own personal investments in the cinematic process, as they do in self-reflexive moments in their films. Kiarostami, like Kieślowski, returns obsessively to the subject of death, not for dramatic effect or emotional weight, but as the ultimate, inaccessible mystery, the negative force that gives weight and point to life, that returns us to a world we share with others.

For Sean O'Sullivan, the sophistication of recent American television serials like *Six Feet Under* and *Lost* is perhaps the most prominent indication of Kieślowski's American legacy, even if unremarked by other critics. Indeed, Kieślowski's critics have failed to note his formal innovations of television serial narrative with the ten episodes of *Decalogue,* which they typically describe as *films,* while critics commenting on the recent renaissance of American television have often been blind to influences beyond the Anglo-American. Although Kieślowski implied that he had failed to follow the "correct" conventions of television with his series, O'Sullivan argues that it is precisely as television serial that *Decalogue* is most productively discussed and its relationship with recent American television becomes clear. Kieślowski's concern with metaphysical issues in his work—with the undecidable tension between the fated and the accidental—finds an ideal form in the serial narrative, with its structural tension between the formulaic and the unpredictable, but Kieślowski deploys that tension in much more dynamic and strikingly meaningful ways than previous serials. O'Sullivan identifies three crucial ingredients of Kieślowski's serial form—"the collision of accident and design, the manufacture of doubt, and . . . the 'absent middle' [the narrative solution that gives unity and meaning to previous diegetic information]"—and traces their deployment in *Decalogue* and in *Six Feet Under* and *Lost,* which share *Decalogue*'s interest in depicting the subjects of religion, death, and memory as lived anxieties. All three series demand that the audience forgo narrative resolution and instead approach them with negative capability, that mode of consciousness that Keats identified as central to lyric poetry.

Beyond any of the specific arguments offered in this book, and because of film's status within popular culture, the precise scope of Kieślowski's legacy is impossible to delimit, as it is diffused through and integrated into that culture. At times, of course, it becomes very obvious. Take, for example, Kieślowski's contribution to the screen persona of one of his stars. The makers of the film *Bee Season* (2005), Scott McGehee and David Siegel, cast Juliette Binoche as Miriam in their adaptation of Myla Goldberg's novel. In a film that follows four major characters, each of whom is on a journey of personal redemption, Miriam is a detached mother, the reason for her distraction apparently lying in her childhood when she witnessed a car crash that killed her parents. In flashbacks, we see her approaching a shattered car and picking up a pair of broken spectacles. We later discover that as an adult, she collects small objects from apartments and houses, fragments of other people's lives, and assembles them into mobile-like arrangements on strings in a secret storage locker. Later, she is hospitalized for her mental illness. Clearly, Miriam recalls and refigures Binoche's character, Julie Vignon, in *Three Colors: Blue* (1993): Julie has not only lost her daughter in a car crash but preserves her memory through a mobile made of blue crystals. Julie visits her mother in a nursing home, who uses the television as her connection to a lost world, just as we see Miriam doing at the end of *Bee Season,* watching her daughter perform in the national spelling bee.[2] More often, though, Kieślowski's influence is much more indefinable, felt as a haunting presence in the images and tropes of other filmmakers' work, like Patrice Leconte's *L'Homme du train* (*Man on the Train;* 2002) and Sergio Castellito's *Non ti muovere* (*Don't Move;* 2004). Both films seem to carry Kieślowski's metaphysical strain as they explore the way that chance meetings result in the transfer of qualities between people. Furthermore, Leconte's film uses the trope of the train as a way of figuring the contingency of existence, as in *Blind Chance,* and Castellito's makes use of a desolate apartment complex that is reminiscent of that in *Decalogue.* Even Jens Lien's darkly comic *Den Brysomme Mannen* (*The Bothersome Man;* 2006), about forty-year-old Andreas (Trond Fausa Aurvaag), a man who commits suicide twice under a subway train in his efforts to find a meaningful and fulfilling existence, seems to refract many aspects of Kieślowski's work, though in an absurdist vein.

Indeed, the numerous retrospectives and conferences commemorating Krzysztof Kieślowski ten years after his death attest to his lingering presence, to our efforts to listen for the "unheard music," the persistence of his images and ideas long after his unexpected demise. In addition to the numerous events in Poland celebrating the "Year of Kieślowski," outlined by Haltof, retrospectives of his work played in cities around the world in 2006: in Boston, Chicago, Hartford, New York, Seattle, and St. Louis in the United States; in Montreal and Vancouver in Canada; and worldwide in Hong Kong, London, Singapore, and Yerevan, Armenia. A Kieślowski retrospective was also part of the "Fourth Caravan of the Euro-Arab Cinema" that played in Cairo and Alexandria, Egypt, in August 2006.

That Kieślowski is a filmmaker who haunts those who know his work may well have to do with the nature of his last films, as Insdorf has noted: "If Kieślowski still seems so present to many of us, maybe it's because of the transcendence in which he seemed to believe, his 'impression that there must be more things beyond what we can see'" (qtd. in Przylipiak 231). This volume gives body to that presence and reanimates those images and ideas by tracing them in the work of living filmmakers.

Notes

1. Lubelski's typology of narrative strategies helps to chart the distinctions between Polish filmmakers and to track changes in the general ethos of Polish cinema. He cites Kieślowski as the preeminent example of the tale maker, one whose stories are inspired by real-life events but who injects those events with allegorical, instructive, or philosophical purpose (Lubelski 34).

2. The filmmakers seem to have reflected not only these particular circumstances and tropes from Kieślowski's film; we could say that their theme is precisely the one at the heart of the *Three Colors* trilogy. Kieślowski never approached that theme so directly, though. In *Bee Season,* Saul Naumann is a professor who announces to his students, in the film's first act, that the world is broken and that it is the task of every human to try to make it whole again. One of the filmmakers' previous films, *Suture* (1993), is built on the premise of brothers who are practically doubles. *The Double Life of Véronique* had opened the New York Film Festival in September 1991.

Works Cited

Coates, Paul. *Cinema, Religion, and the Romantic Legacy: Through a Glass Darkly.* Aldershot: Ashgate, 2003.

Denby, David. "The Feminine Mystique." *New York* 28 November 1994: 85.

Haltof, Marek. *The Cinema of Krzysztof Kieślowski: Variations on Destiny and Chance.* London: Wallflower, 2004.

———. *Polish National Cinema.* New York: Berghahn, 2002.

Insdorf, Annette. *Double Lives, Second Chances: The Cinema of Krzysztof Kieślowski.* New York: Miramax Books, 1999.

Kickasola, Joseph G. *The Films of Krzysztof Kieślowski: The Liminal Image.* New York: Continuum, 2004.

Lubelski, Tadeusz. "A Difficult Return to Freedom Cinema." *The New Polish Cinema.* Ed. Janina Falkowska and Marek Haltof. Trowbridge: Flicks Books, 2003. 24–36.

Macnab, Geoffrey. "Heaven Can't Wait." *Guardian* 24 May 2002. http://arts.guardian.co.uk/fridayreview/story/0,,735400,00.html.

Malcolm, Derek. Obituary for Krzysztof Kieślowski. *Manchester Guardian Weekly* 24 March 1996, Cinema section: 26.

Przylipiak, Mirosław. "The *Decalogue.*" *The Cinema of Eastern Europe.* Ed. Peter Hames. London: Wallflower, 2004. 224–34.

Stam, Robert. "Commentary." Disc 1. *Contempt.* Dir. Jean-Luc Godard. DVD. Criterion, 2002.

Stok, Danusia, ed. *Kieślowski on Kieślowski.* London: Faber and Faber, 1993.

Thomson, David. "Kyrzysztof Kieślowski." *The New Biographical Dictionary of Film.* New York: Knopf, 2002. 468.

Wilson, Emma. *Memory and Survival: The French Cinema of Krzysztof Kieślowski.* London: Legenda, 2000.

I. The Polish Legacy

1

Still Alive

Kieślowski's Influence on Post-Communist Polish Cinema

Marek Haltof

During his last public appearance, on 24 February 1996, Krzysztof Kieślowski commented on the reasons behind his self-imposed retirement from filmmaking, which had been officially announced earlier, during the making of the *Three Colors* (1993–94) trilogy:

> I stopped making films for a number of reasons. I think that one of the reasons was that I was tired. I made a number of films in a short period of time, perhaps too many. There was undoubtedly a lot of bitterness involved and the feeling that I tried too hard and never achieved what I really wanted. Apart from that, I started to live in a fictional world that I imagined, and was artificial. I ceased participating in real life and started in the one that I invented either alone or with my colleague [Krzysztof] Piesiewicz. And since it happened from film to film, essentially without a break, to be honest, I lost the feeling that I was communicating with the world. I drove myself into some fictitious world; I removed myself from those near and dear to me because fictitious problems started to become extremely important . . . Then I started to think that enough is enough. (Hendrykowski and Jazdon 11–12)

Despite Kieślowski's frequent remarks that his early retirement from filmmaking was due to fatigue and health problems, his premature death on 13 March 1996 following heart-bypass surgery came as a profound shock for the Polish filmmaking community. He died at the age of fifty-four, at the peak of his artistic powers and, despite his much-heralded retirement from filmmaking, while embarking on a new project with his long-time collaborator, the scriptwriter Krzysztof Piesiewicz.

The year 2006, marking the tenth anniversary of the director's death, was proclaimed in Poland as the "Year of Krzysztof Kieślowski." The celebration opened earlier, in October of 2005, with a series of events, including a biographical retrospective exhibition at the Museum of Cinema in Łódź, which was organized with the help of Kieślowski's former film unit TOR and the Skorpion publishing house, the latter headed by Stanisław Zawiśliński, the film critic who has published extensively on Kieślowski. The Łódź exposition, titled "Kieślowski—Signs and Memory" ("Kieślowski—ślady i pamięć"), featured film posters, film stills, film reviews, catalogues, books, fragments of documentary films, and interview footage about him, as well as other archive materials showing the director at work on his early short films. Also in October of 2005, several other events were held under the label "In the Circle of Kieślowski" ("W kręgu Kieślowskiego"). For example, during the international conference in Katowice called "The Cinema of Kieślowski—The Cinema after Kieślowski," Stanisław Zawiśliŋski launched his biography of Kieślowski, the well-researched *Kieślowski: What Matters Is to Keep Going . . .* (*Kieślowski. Ważne, żeby iść . . .*). The Katowice conference, organized by the film unit TOR, Silesia Film, and the Katowice Film School, attracted several Kieślowski scholars, filmmakers, and critics who discussed the director's legacy.

The official opening of the "Year of Kieślowski took place once again in Katowice, on 10 March 2006, with a four-day congress titled "Kieślowski—In Memoriam." The event consisted of film screenings, concerts featuring music from Kieślowski's films, scholarly seminars, and informal discussions with Kieślowski's friends and collaborators. On 14 March, as if reflecting on Kieślowski's legacy in Poland, Polish Television (Channel 2) also aired Maria Zmarz-Koczanowicz's new full-length documentary on Kieślowski, titled *Still Alive.*[1] Another Polish Television channel, "Kultura" (Culture), showed all of Kieślowski's works (including documentaries, feature films, and television plays) from 10–13 March. In addition to that, numerous retrospectives of Kieślowski's works, organized in movie theaters across Poland, leave no doubt that the arguably best-known contemporary Polish filmmaker has not been forgotten in his native country.

Given the scope of the above commemorations, the answer to the question of what Kieślowski's legacy has been in Poland seems easy at first glance, reinforced by numerous other signs of devotion to his cinema. Kieślowski's importance manifests itself in areas other than the cinema as well: high schools in Warsaw, Kraków, Łódź, Zielona Góra, Gorzów Wielkopolski, and Mieroszów (where he lived as a child) have been named after him. Perhaps more important, in the year 2000, the Katowice Film School, established in 1978 as the second film school in Poland (originally for the television industry exclusively), was named after Kieślowski, who taught there from 1979 to 1982.[2] Among several other indicators of Kieślowski's posthumous fame is the establishment of the Krzysztof Kieślowski Award by his Polish friends and collaborators, awarded to an actress or actor whose work continues the ideas propagated by Kieślowski himself. The award was given for the first time to Irène Jacob at the 2002 Festival of the Art of Cinematography, "Camerimage," in Łódź. Later recipients have included Charlize Theron (2004), Ralph Fiennes (2005), and Julia Ormond (2006). There is also a screenplay competition—Prix Kieślowski—organized for the first time in 1997 by the film unit TOR and the Łódź Film School, which concerns short (maximum five-minute-long) films.[3]

Looking at the large-scale program of events commemorating the tenth anniversary of Kieślowski's death, one may get the impression that his career has been mythologized to a certain extent, elevated to suit nationalist needs. Polish critics and viewers are talking about Kieślowski's "legend" and his impact on world cinema; they trace his presence in films made by other directors, particularly those who had been involved in the production of his films, and they often discuss other contemporary films by referring to "Kieślowski's metaphysics," "Kieślowski's characters," or "Kieślowski's images."

The reception of Kieślowski's films in Poland, however, was and still is anything but one-dimensional, despite the elevated tone and grand proportions of recent national celebrations, unprecedented in the Polish setting. The debates over Kieślowski's cinema and his influence on contemporary film practice polarize viewers and critics in Poland. For example, it is widely known and well documented that some prominent Polish critics considered Kieślowski's move to international coproductions and his growing critical recognition abroad as suspicious.[4] The majority of them clearly favoured "Kieślowski the realist" over the "mature, metaphysical Kieślowski." They supported him when, at the beginning of his career, he operated on a smaller scale, "in depth rather than breadth," as he put it in the title of his 1981 statement expressing belief in the power of faithful and detailed representations of reality (Kieślowski, "In Depth," 67). They were disappointed when he moved from realistic, documentary-like observations of people and places to films infused with what they saw as false tropes, episodic plots, and often-enigmatic scenes of apparently little consequence to the storyline. Even those who had previously supported Kieślowski were troubled by the "superficial metaphysics" and alleged banality of his "French films." They were also troubled by the fact that he achieved international fame atypically for a Polish filmmaker—without referring to Polish history and mythology.

As I have noted elsewhere (Haltof 125), the semantic richness of Kieślowski's *Three Colors* trilogy was not taken by all Polish scholars and critics as a sign of art. Although, by and large, they praised the visual aspect of the trilogy, they also pointed out its alleged emptiness, superficiality, and pop metaphysics ("metaphysics for the poor"). For example, Mariola Jankun-Dopartowa claimed that *Three Colors* cannot be described within the existing boundaries of art cinema and that it is somewhere between the domain of Bergman's cinema and "pretentious European production." She accused Kieślowski of telling stories familiar from numerous soap operas and "magazines for thinking women," promoting the "religion of blind chance," abandoning his earlier film poetics, and bordering on kitsch sensibility (Jankun-Dopartowa 4–7). The kitschy aspect of Kieślowski's trilogy, wrote Jankun-Dopartowa, involves a number of psychological and existential improbabilities that give the illusion of complexity while ultimately remaining trivial (6). Another critic, Tadeusz Sobolewski, who strongly supported Kieślowski's early films and the Cinema of Distrust movement in the late 1970s, spoke of "artful calligraphic form," "a *schmaltzy* finale," and "a banal musical score" when discussing the *Three Colors* trilogy ("Pani Bovary" 135). Furthermore, even some of Kieślowski's close friends and collaborators, for example the cinematographer Jacek Petrycki, did not appreciate his rejection of realistic description (Petrycki 177–85).

Similar opinions are being expressed today regarding Kieślowski's legacy. They range from voices praising Kieślowski's accomplishments, proud of his elevated status, and situating him in the pantheon of renowned European auteurs, to comments expressing disenchantment and questioning his influence, if any, on modern cinema. Representing the latter camp, Sobolewski writes bluntly about Kieślowski's legacy in his regular column in the monthly *Kino:* "I think that there is no mystery left. What is left is the paralysing cult and kitsch, supposedly inspired by him" ("Pani Bovary" 94).

Like film critics elsewhere, Polish writers on cinema look at Kieślowski's films through the prism of the director's life and his untimely death. His films have gained new meanings and have become saturated with his biographical legend. Kieślowski's "French films" in particular, as Sobolewski writes, give the impression of "postmortem films, as if there is present the awareness of one's death" ("Twarzą" 4). In a similar manner, contemporary viewers look at the last scene of Krzysztof Wierzbicki's classic documentary, *I'm So-So* (1995, Denmark), depicting Kieślowski on an evening ferry that takes him across the river, as if he is crossing the Jordan.

Krzysztof Piesiewicz and Kieślowski's Projects

Before his death, Kieślowski was embarking on a new project with his longtime collaborator Krzysztof Piesiewicz. They started working on another trilogy of films titled *Heaven* (*Raj*), *Hell* (*Piekło*), and *Purgatory* (*Czyściec*), which were published in Poland in *Dialog*, a monthly on drama, and in book form in 1999. It is likely that Kieślowski never intended to direct the new trilogy but to supervise the project. He wrote the first part, *Heaven*, together with Piesiewicz. The next two parts were written by Piesiewicz after the director's death. Tom Tykwer's *Heaven* (2002) (discussed in chapters 7 and 8 of this book), first shown at the 2002 Berlin Film Festival, also polarized Polish film critics, who, by and large, discussed the film in terms of its degree of fidelity to the spirit of Kieślowski's cinema and considered Tykwer almost as a director working on behalf of Kieślowski. According to the majority of these critics, although Tykwer's film had several recognizable elements of Kieślowski's last works (slow pace, art-film atmosphere, ambiguous ending, lyricism, hypnotic photography, and a story about deadly choices, among others), it did not duplicate the earlier experience. Danis Tanovic's second part of the trilogy, *Hell* (*L'Enfer,* 2005), was also treated harshly by Polish critics, who emphasized its imitative nature, stressing its intellectual emptiness and the recycling of Kieślowskian scenes and visual motifs.

In 1998, Piesiewicz, with the assistance of Agnieszka Lipiec-Wróblewska, his new collaborator, also authored another trilogy in the spirit of Kieślowski: *Faith-Hope-Love* (*Wiara-Nadzieja-Miłość*). The first two parts of this new trilogy, initially written for the Italian television channel RAI, were published in *Dialog* (Piesiewicz "Nadzieja" and "Wiara"). Stanisław Mucha (b. 1970), a Polish actor and director who has resided in Germany since 1995, directed the trilogy's first part, *Faith,* which was shown at the 2007 annual Festival of Polish Films in Gdynia.

The careful reader of Polish film journals and Internet sites will note that Piesiewicz's continuation of his screenwriting career after Kieślowski's death comes as a surprise to some Polish critics, who, perhaps, expected to close that chapter of Polish cinema. Asked by the monthly *Kino* interviewer whether he considered remaining silent after Kieślowski's death, Piesiewicz (surprised by the question) answered that thanks to his meeting and collaboration with Kieślowski, thinking in terms of images has become an integral part of his life: "Everything that I do now is predestined by my meeting with Kieślowski. . . . Definitely, I am shaped by a certain way of thinking and responding, the way I am moving through the visible and invisible world, the way I work on my protagonists—all this I have learned from working with Kieślowski" (Zarębski, "Zatrzymać" 21).

In the late 1990s Piesiewicz started collaborating with a younger film director, Michał Rosa (b. 1963), a 1992 graduate of the Katowice Film School. At the time of their meeting, Rosa was known chiefly for his early realistic films, such as the medium-length *Hot Thursday* (*Gorący czwartek,* 1993) and the feature *Paint* (*Farba,* 1997). *Hot Thursday,* scripted and directed by Rosa, offers a realistic depiction of young delinquent boys from the impoverished parts of Silesia. It portrays their mundane reality, marked by unemployment, poor living conditions, and lack of perspective. His work received the Best First Film award at the 1994 Festival of Polish Films in Gdynia. He followed this success with another well-received film, the road movie *Paint,* about young people searching for meaning in life, looking for their own identity. The girl nicknamed Paint (Agnieszka Krukówna) tries to find her grandmother, accompanied by an accidental fellow-traveller nicknamed Cyp (Marcin Władyniak).

The collaboration between Piesiewicz and Rosa resulted in the production of *Silence* (*Cisza,* 2001), based on Piesiewicz's script, a film that was well received by the judges at the 2001 Festival of Polish Films in Gdynia, where it received the Best Director Award and the Best Actress Award for Kinga Preis, but which failed at the box office.[5] The film also received the Best Actress award for Kinga Preis and the Ecumenical Jury Award at the 2002 Karlovy Vary International Film Festival.

Silence opens with brief scenes set during Easter Monday in 1978 in Łódź and introduces a young boy who, while playing pranks with his friends, unintentionally causes a deadly car accident. The action then moves to the summer of 2000 and focuses on Szymon (Bartosz Opania), the boy responsible for the accident twenty-two years ago, who befriends Mimi (Kinga Preis), the girl who survived the car crash, in which both her parents were killed. Szymon, whose guilty conscience prevents him from living a "normal life," is unable to get over the past. For many years he acts like a "silent angel," watching Mimi and trying to help her. Not surprisingly, one Polish critic titled his review "The Protective Angel from the City of Łódź" (Rudziŋski 25).

The film juxtaposes two different characters living worlds apart. Working for a dynamic international cosmetic firm, Mimi is portrayed as an almost stereotypical successful businesswoman. She has the trappings of the new Polish managerial class: a nice apartment, car, and clothes, and a lifestyle for which she sacrifices her personal life. Living a "successful modern life" means that she has no time for love or for her young daughter, who is staying with her grandmother. Mimi is portrayed as cold on the surface, showing no emotions, relaxing in dance halls playing techno music, and preferring casual sex. Unlike Mimi, Szymon lives a modest existence as a railroad engineer of cargo trains. As depicted in the film, he most probably missed the speedy Polish transformation after 1989. The chance meeting of the two characters shapes their lives. Thanks to the encounter with Szymon, Mimi's repressed memories from her childhood come back. The encounter forces Mimi to reconsider her life, to search for her roots and for continuity in her life, and to take care of her daughter. She embarks on a journey of self-discovery, which is emphasized by the way she changes her appearance and attitudes toward coworkers, and how she embraces her motherhood. Meanwhile, Szymon surrounds himself with a collection of Mimi's family photographs, as well as her mother's diary, which he took from the site of the accident (like the young boy from *Three Colors: Blue* who took the cross from the scene of the car crash). He is also collecting a dossier on Mimi, and he meddles in her private life. This is Szymon's way of paying the debt for his deed from childhood.

Is Szymon's character really a patient and understanding angel, a sinner trying to save his and his "victim's" soul, or is he perhaps a stalker infatuated with Mimi? Unimpressed by the film, the critic Andrew James Horton writes that it "depicts a victim of stalking who uncovers the obsessive relationship

In Michał Rosa's *Silence* (2001), cowritten with Krzysztof Piesiewicz, Szymon (Bartosz Opania) tries to assuage his guilt by watching over Mimi (Kinga Preis), the survivor of the childhood calamity for which he was responsible. (Copyright Stopklatka Sp. z.o.o.)

after a chance friendship turns out to have more intense and premeditated origins." Remarking that the film is trying to "cast itself as a successor to Krzysztof Kieślowski's own cycle of moral inquiry, *Dekalog* [1988]," Horton concludes that "its portrayal of a woman falling in love with her stalker will be morally sickening and insensitive and outweigh Piesiewicz's otherwise worthy aims." Perhaps the same can be said, however, about other Kieślowski and Piesiewicz characters, for example, the voyeur Tomek in *A Short Film about Love* (1988) and the manipulative puppet-master Alexandre in *The Double Life of Véronique* (1991).

Silence aspires to the metaphysics of *The Double Life of Véronique.* Photographed by one of Poland's new talents, Arkadiusz Tomiak, the film is abundant with metaphorical images that stress the role of mystery and fate. The music by Tomasz Stańko, a noted Polish jazz trumpeter and composer, also contributes greatly to the film's overall tenor.

According to Piesiewicz's comment from 2001, *Silence* begins an ambitious eight-part series of feature films called *Predestined* (*Naznaczeni*), which "attempt to synthesize the last twenty years in Polish history" (Zarębski, "Zatrzymać" 21). The title of the series, perhaps intended as a sequel to *Decalogue* (1988), refers to the beatitudes in the New Testament (Matthew 5:3–12). Piesiewicz's expressed goal in the series, the Polish critic Zarębski writes, is reminiscent of that of *Decalogue*: to refer loosely to this "universal, immortal program to achieve happiness" in order to analyze the nature of human relationships and the contemporary crisis of culture ("Zatrzymać" 21).

After Rosa made *Hot Thursday* and *Paint,* his name became associated with detailed, painstaking observations of everyday reality, adeptly captured on camera by his cinematographer, Mieczysław Anweiler. Rosa's collaboration with Piesiewicz on *Silence* indicated a possible shift of emphasis—on a road similar to the one travelled by Kieślowski—from works uncovering reality to works saturated with metaphysical ingredients. That collaboration proved to be an enormous artistic opportunity for Rosa, as well as a daring effort on his part: in the Polish context, any attempt to collaborate with Piesiewicz is unavoidably taken as an arrogant appropriation of Kieślowski's status. At this stage it is not certain whether *Silence* will be followed by the other parts of the intended series and who the director(s) will be. The film's mixed critical reception in Poland, combined with box office failure and the disappointing reception beyond Polish borders (despite the Karlovy Vary success), most probably will delay the other instalments.[6]

The careers of several other collaborators of Kieślowski are also intimately linked with him. For example, several Polish papers reported in May 2001 that there would be a sequel to Kieślowski's celebrated *Camera Buff* (*Amator,* 1979). Stanisław Latek, Kieślowski's assistant on *Three Colors: White* and *Blue,* and the director of the second unit on *Three Colors: Red,* was planning to direct a *Camera Buff 2.*

In addition, some earlier films directed by Kieślowski have been the source of sequels in recent years. Krzysztof Wierzbicki, Kieślowski's close collaborator and friend, known chiefly for his definitive television documentary *I'm So-So,* continued Kieślowski's classic documentary *First Love* (*Pierwsza miłość,* 1974) in *Horoscope* (*Horoskop,* 2000), a forty-seven minute film made for Channel 2 of Polish Television. The film by Kieślowski documents nine crucial months in the life of two young Warsaw inhabitants—the seventeen-year old Jadźka and her boyfriend, the twenty-year old Romek—as they work and complete high school. The camera follows them from the moment Jadźka discovers that she is pregnant to the birth of their daughter, Ewa, and the film ends with a scene of Jadźka and Romek beside their baby girl's crib, pondering her future. As the Polish critic Andrzej Kołodyński writes, the initiative to continue the project came from the Documentary and Feature Film Studio in Warsaw (WFDiF), which owns footage not used by Kieślowski in the original film (Kołodyński 4).

Wierzbicki took on Kieślowski's idea of documenting the first twenty years of the life of Ewa, the baby girl from the classic documentary. He moved with his crew to Kelowna, Canada, where Kieślowski's protagonists were then living, although they were preparing for their next move, this time to Chicago. They talk to the camera about their life, which in a sense is characteristic of their generation: in the 1980s they left Poland for Germany, and then, after a couple of years, emigrated to Canada. Ewa, now a mother herself at the age of twenty and living in Edmonton, Alberta, watches Kieślowski's film with her mother; both women are visibly moved. Wierzbicki also employs some footage by Kieślowski, who originally planned this sequel as a film about Ewa from her childhood to adulthood (working titles: *Ewa, Ewunia,* and *Horoscope*), by revisiting her every three or four years to document her life. He halted this project, however, afraid that his film might be used against the protagonists.[7]

Another film by Wierzbicki, *Talking Heads 2* (*Gadające głowy 2,* 2004), refers to Kieślowski's classic sociological inquiry, *Talking Heads* (*Gadające głowy,* 1980), and was produced with the assistance of the cinematographer Jacek Petrycki, who worked with Kieślowski on the original film and on several other projects. Kieślowski employed a television style in the film, which was much criticized at that time and characterized by the disapproving term "talking heads"—subjects in medium close-ups talking directly to the camera. He interviewed forty people, representing a spectrum of Polish society, beginning with a toddler born in 1979 and ending with a hundred-year-old woman, asking the same elementary questions: "When and where were you born?" "Who are you?" "What matters most to you?"

Twenty-four years later, Wierzbicki revisits some of the characters from the original film and asks them to comment on their lives. Wierzbicki also talks to the children of some of the original interlocutors who have passed away, and also interviews new characters in the hope of providing a portrait of the psychological conditions in a new epoch. Although several interviewees express the same desires for sincerity, tolerance, and self-fulfilment, the tone of Wierzbicki's film is much darker than that of Kieślowski's. The hundred-year-old woman, barely hearing Kieślowski's question but answering that she would like to live longer, certainly helped to add an optimistic note to the pessimistic diagnosis of Polish society under communism. Wierzbicki's film, with its clear emphasis on new problems that are associated with the Polish post-communist life, such as unemployment and homelessness, conveys disappointment with the long-awaited political freedom.

Wierzbicki's film is not the first continuation of Kieślowski's *Talking Heads. Questionnaire* (*Kwestionariusz*), the 1997 documentary made by students of Polish philology at Warsaw University (Anna Kaplińska, Iwona Kurz, Jacek Łagowski, Emilia Sadowska, Aleksandra Sekla, and Teodor Sobczak), closely follows Kieślowski's film and asks the same questions.

Kieślowski's Inspirations

Although Kieślowski's films are unique in the Polish context, several critics see the legacy of his cinema in recent films directed by one of his favorite actors, Jerzy Stuhr (discussed in detail in chapter 3 of this book): *A Week in the Life of a Man* (*Tydzień z życia mężczyzny,* 1999), *The Big Animal* (*Duże zwierzę,* 2000), based on Kieślowski's treatment, and *Tomorrow's Weather* (*Pogoda na jutro,* 2003). The spirit of Kieślowski is also undoubtedly present in another Stuhr film, the winner of the Festival of Polish Films in Gdynia, *Love Stories* (*Historie miłosne,* 1997): Kieślowski helped with the script and the film is dedicated to him. Furthermore, Stuhr employs an "art-film atmosphere," down-to-earth characters facing moral choices, and mysterious, otherworldly figures such as the "Master-Pollster" (played by Jerzy Nowak) who questions the four protagonists about the true nature of their choices. *Love Stories* resembles a morality play permeated with the very metaphysical ingredients that are so characteristic of Kieślowski's final films (though some crucial differences between the two filmmakers are discussed in chapter 3 of this book). In addition, a number of films made in Poland in the mid-1990s seem to owe their inspiration to Kieślowski's cinema. They include, for example, *Weekend Stories* (*Opowieści weekendowe,* 1996–1997), a series of television films produced by Kieślowski's mentor, Krzysztof Zanussi, the head of the film unit TOR. *Weekend Stories* are similar in spirit to *Decalogue* (and are discussed in detail in chapter 2).

In the mid-1990s, Kieślowski acted as an artistic supervisor on three short films made at the Łódź Film School. Although he was not officially teaching there, he certainly imprinted his mark on *Missy* (*Paŋcia,* 1995), directed by Iwona Siekierzyńska (b. 1967); *Before the Sunset* (*Przed zmierzchem,* 1995), directed by Grzegorz Zgliński (b. 1968); and *Late Afternoon* (*Późne popołudnie,* 1996), directed by Gilles Renard (b. 1963). His influence can be seen in these films' stylistic as well as thematic choices. When asked about their reminiscences of Kieślowski, these directors always emphasize his enormous impact on their filmmaking careers. For example, the Polish-Swiss director Greg (Grzegorz) Zgliński comments that he divides his own films into two groups, the ones made before and the ones made after Kieślowski, and he attests that meeting Kieślowski helped him to become a more conscious film director who knows what filmmaking is all about (Zarębski, "Każdy").

Polish critics sometimes suggest that Iwona Siekierzyńska's first major film, *My Roast Chicken* (*Moje pieczone kurczaki,* 2002), a sixty-three-minute television production, is a feminist version of Kieślowski's *Camera Buff.* Although at first glance this conclusion may seem exaggerated, there are several characteristics that justify such a comparison. In the center of Siekierzyńska's film is a young female protagonist with a camera, Magda (Agata Kulesza), trying to impose her cinematic perspective on the world that surrounds her, attempting, in a distinct style, to tell the story about the psychological condition of her own (as well as Siekierzyńska's) generation of thirty-somethings. Although narrated differently from Kieślowski's classic, Siekierzyŋska's film revolves around similar subjects, among them the finding of self-fulfilment through filmmaking. The film deals with the marital crisis of a couple who have just returned to Poland following an unsuccessful attempt to settle permanently in Canada, and who struggle with everyday problems, such as the inability to find employment, lack of money, and, as a consequence, homelessness (they stay with Magda's mother). Unlike Filip in *Camera Buff*, who ultimately turns the camera on himself, thus retreating from socially committed observations, Magda in *My Roast Chicken* overcomes her difficulties by observing external reality—she begins making a documentary film about her husband, Wojtek (Adam Nawojczyk).

In Siekierzyńska's film, Polish cinema buffs often notice conspicuous references to Kieślowski's cinema, for example, when Magda and her husband talk about their kettle ("it was blue," "no it was red"). The connection, however, as discussed before, goes much deeper. Commenting on the similarities between her cinema and that of Kieślowski, Siekierzyńska once stated that "there are no direct traces of the master–student relation." Instead, her film becomes "a discussion and polemic with his movies, and moreover an attempt to make his way of looking at the world more contemporary" (qtd. in Kosmala 7).[8] The modern, dynamic narration of Siekierzyńska's film, with its set of problems pertinent to post-communist Poland, helped this film to become one of the prime examples of what Polish critics describe (or perhaps overstate) as the new Polish cinema made by the "Generation 2000" (Pokolenie 2000).

Another filmmaker often discussed in the context of Kieślowski's legacy is the director of documentary and feature films Paweł Łoziński (b. 1965), the son of the acclaimed Polish documentarist Marcel Łoziński. Paweł Łoziński worked as an assistant to Kieślowski on his *Three Colors* trilogy. His debut, the medium-length television film *The Manhole* (*Kratka*, 1996), was based on Kieślowski's idea and was made under his artistic supervision. The story revolves around a fierce competition between a ten-year-old boy, Sebastian (Michał Michalak), and a retired man, Eugeniusz (Jerzy Kamas), for a 500-franc banknote found near a central Warsaw hotel. Both characters notice the banknote at the bottom of a manhole and try to retrieve it by competing and then collaborating with each other. The film, however, is not so much about the struggle for the banknote—which, owing to strange circumstances, takes almost the whole day—as their developing understanding and friendship. For his debut film Łoziński received an award at the 1996 Festival of Polish Films in Gdynia, and two of the film's actors, Kamas and Michalak, also received awards for their performances.

References to Kieślowski

Given Kieślowski's international status and the fact that he occupies a unique position within Polish cinema, it is perhaps expected that many Polish films would contain references to Kieślowski's cinema. As early as 1993, Rafał Wieczyński (b. 1968) wrote, directed, and produced a film whose very title bluntly refers to Kieślowski's preoccupations: *A Truly Short Film about Love, Killing and One More Commandment* (*Naprawdę krótki film o miłości, zabijaniu i jeszcze jednym przykazaniu,* Polish-French coproduction). Wieczyński's film, an unconvincing parable loosely referring to Kieślowski's *Decalogue* and two related "short" films, narrates the story of the relationship between a small group of characters: two men and a woman. The thematic and stylistic concerns of the film, which is set in a small town in 1989, border on unsophisticated and intentional parody of Kieślowski's cinema.

Although direct references to Kieślowski films (pastiches, parodies, sequels) have not been frequent in contemporary Polish cinema, several films produced in Poland in recent years either thematically or stylistically evoke Kieślowskian cinema, or cannibalize it to the point of parodying its characteristic features. In first films made by several young filmmakers, the viewer may find reminiscences of Kieślowski's early attempts to uncover the grey, yet somehow photogenic, aspect of communist Poland. For example, Leszek David's short film produced by the Łódź Film School, *My Place* (*Moje miejsce,* 2004), may be discussed in the context of Kieślowski's *Personnel* (1975).

The cinematic spirit of the late Kieślowski, full of metaphysical associations, can be found in films such as *The Third* (*Trzeci,* 2004), directed by Jan Hryniak (b. 1969), which at first glance deliberately refers to Roman Polanski's *Knife in the Water* (*Nóż w wodzie,* 1962). The reworking of the Polanski classic, however, replaces the young hitchhiker with an angel-like figure played by Marek Kondrat ("the third" of the title), who accompanies a young, financially successful couple on their yachting vacation. He helps Paweł (Jacek Poniedziałek) and Ewa (Magdalena Cielecka), sometimes against their will, to overcome their marital crisis and meddles in their private affairs. This intriguing film by Hryniak, while remaking Polanski's canonical work, moves it to the realm of Kieślowski's Polish-French-Swiss coproductions.[9]

References to Kieślowski bordering on parody of his aesthetic choices may be found interestingly in films made by his former actors. For example, in *Boys Don't Cry* (*Chłopaki nie płaczą,* 2000), directed by Olaf Lubaszenko (b. 1968), the director known outside of Poland mostly for his breakthrough role of Tomek in Kieślowski's *Decalogue 6* and its theatrical version, *A Short Film about Love,* quotes the ending of *White* in one of the final scenes: the bandit behind prison bars is exchanging mysterious signs with his girlfriend, who is standing outside of the prison. Earlier she had given him a hand-knitted red sweater. *Super Production* (*Superprodukcja,* 2003), a film directed by Juliusz Machulski (b. 1955), who played the main role in *Personnel,* features another clear reference to Kieślowski. In this bitter comedy, which targets the Polish film industry, an uncompromising young film critic, Yanek Drzazga (Rafał Królikowski), is forced to direct a film, an epic super production, for mafia

Jan Hryniak's *The Third* (2004) reworks Polański's first feature, *Knife in the Water* (1962), in a metaphysical, Kieślowskian direction by replacing the young hitchhiker with an angel-like figure. (Copyright Stopklatka Sp. z.o.o.)

bosses. Artur Barciś, the actor known for his role as the enigmatic angel-like character who appears in some decisive scenes of *Decalogue,* comes into view several times when the main protagonist is about to make an "important decision," such as calling or not calling an escort agency. Also, in another scene, when the film critic sends a negative review as an e-mail attachment, the camera frantically follows the electronic impulse, mirroring the psychedelic speeded-up opening of *Red.*

Conclusion

The recent celebrations of the tenth anniversary of Kieślowski's death clearly indicate that he is still not only remembered but also highly respected in his own country. Although it is difficult to talk about a "Kieślowski school of cinema" in Poland, the international stardom that he achieved in the art-house world will serve, without doubt, as an inspiration for younger Polish filmmakers for many years to come. He will also serve as an inspiration for those who believe in the concept of auteurism in cinema. Kieślowski is "still alive" in Poland, and abroad he remains the most visible representative of post-communist Polish cinema. The overall tone of the critical discussions in Poland, despite the infrequent dissenting voices questioning Kieślowski's legacy, shows the longing for a filmmaker who will fill the empty space left by the director.

Notes

1. *Still Alive,* the English title of the Polish documentary, refers to Kieślowski's habitual response to the customary "How are you?" Another phrase often used by Kieślowski—"I'm so-so"—provided the title for the 1995 Danish-Polish television film on him, directed by Krzysztof Wierzbicki (*I'm So-So*). Other recent Polish films about Kieślowski include *Krzysiek Kieślowski* (2001, TV, 26 minutes), produced by Wojciech Malinowski, and *Kieślowski i jego Amator* (1999, TV, 25 minutes), produced by Krzysztof Wierzbicki.

2. The Katowice Film School—popular name of the Krzysztof Kieślowski Faculty of Radio and Television at the University of Silesia in Katowice (Uniwersytet Śląski, Wydział Radia i Telewizji im. Krzysztofa Kieślowskiego w Katowicach).

3. Information from *Reżyser* (supplement to monthly *Kino*) 9 (1998): 8.

4. See Mirosław Przylipiak's essay on the reception of Kieślowski's films in Poland: "Filmy fabularne Krzysztofa Kieślowskiego w zwierciadle polskiej krytyki filmowej"; see also his "Monter i studentka."

5. The main award at the 2001 Festival of Polish Films, the Golden Lion, was given to the outstanding film *Hi, Tereska* (*Cześć Tereska*), directed by Robert Gliński.

6. *Silence* was listed fourteenth in the monthly *Kino* ranking of Polish films shown at the 2001 Polish Film Festival in Gdynia.

7. According to the often-cited comment by Kieślowski, "documentary films shouldn't be used to influence the subject's life either for the better or for the worse. They shouldn't have any influence at all" (Stok 68).

8. For more information on Siekierzyńska's film, see also Ewa Mazierska, "The Motif of Escape in Recent Polish Films."

9. Incidentally, Jan Hryniak is married to Marta Kieślowska, Krzysztof Kieślowski's daughter.

Works Cited

Haltof, Marek. *The Cinema of Krzysztof Kieślowski: Variations on Destiny and Chance.* London: Wallflower Press, 2004.

Hendrykowski, Marek, and Mikołaj Jazdon, eds. "Fragmenty spotkania z Krzysztofem Kieślowskim (24. II. 1996)." *Kino* 5 (1996): 11–12.

Horton, Andrew James. "Inhaling a Unique Atmosphere—Central and East European Film at the 37th Karlovy Vary." *Senses of Cinema* 22 (September–October 2002). http://www.sensesofcinema.com/contents/festivals/02/22/karlovy37.html.

Jankun-Dopartowa, Mariola. "Trójkolorowy transparent: Vive le chaos!" *Kino* 6 (1995): 4–7.

Kieślowski, Krzysztof. "In Depth Rather than Breadth." *Polish Perspectives* 24.6–7 (1981): 67–71.

Kieślowski, Krzysztof, and Krzysztof Piesiewicz. "Raj." *Dialog* 3 (1997): 5–33.

———. *Raj, Piekło, Czyściec*. Warsaw: Wydawnictwo Skorpion, 1999.

Kołodyŋski, Andrzej. "Jadźka i Romek." *Kino* 3 (2001): 4.

Kosmala, Katarzyna. "Cinema Is Yet a Deadly Serious Matter." *Kieślowski dziś: studenckie wydawnictwo okolicznościowe* 1 (21 November 2005): 5.

Mazierska, Ewa. "The Motif of Escape in Recent Polish Films." *New Cinemas: Journal of Contemporary Film* 3.1 (2005): 17–28.

Petrycki, Jacek. "Kiedy jeszcze lubiliśmy rejestrować świat." *Kino Krzysztofa Kieślowskiego*. Ed. Tadeusz Lubelski. Kraków: Universitas, 1997. 177–85.

Piesiewicz, Krzysztof. "Piekło. Nowela filmowa." *Dialog* 5 (1997): 5–31.

Piesiewicz, Krzysztof, and Agnieszka Lipiec-Wróblewska. "Nadzieja." *Dialog* 11 (1998): 5–32.

———. "Wiara. Nowela Filmowa." *Dialog* 3 (1998): 5–28.

Przylipiak, Mirosław. "Filmy fabularne Krzysztofa Kieślowskiego w zwierciadle polskiej krytyki filmowej." *Kino Krzysztofa Kieślowskiego*. Ed. Tadeusz Lubelski. Kraków: Universitas, 1997. 213–47.

———. "Monter i studentka." *Kino* 3 (1997): 6–9, 50.

Rudziński, Kamil. "Anioł stróż z miasta Łodzi." *Kino* 10 (2001): 25.

Sobolewski, Tadeusz. "Pani Bovary to ja." *Kino* 9 (2005): 94.

———. "Peace and Rebellion: Some Remarks on the Creative Output of Krzysztof Kieślowski." *Polish Cinema in Ten Takes*. Ed. Ewelina Nurczyŋska-Fidelska and Zbigniew Batko. Łódź: Łódzkie Towarzystwo Naukowe, 1995. 123–37.

———. "Twarzą w twarz." *Kino* 3 (1997): 94.

Stok, Danusia, ed. *Kieślowski on Kieślowski*. London: Faber and Faber, 1993.

Zarębski, Konrad J. "Ciągłość" [interview with Michał Rosa]. *Kino* 10 (2001): 23–24.

———. "Każdy mój film jest poszukiwaniem." *Kino* 10 (2005): 72.

———. "Zatrzymać się w ciszy" [interview with Krzysztof Piesiewicz]. *Kino* 10 (2001): 20–22.

Zawiśliński, Stanisław. *Kieślowski. Ważne, żeby iść . . .* Warsaw: Skorpion, 2005.

2

Living On

From Kieślowski to Zanussi

Sarah Cooper

Perhaps the most nebulous but all-pervasive phenomenon that underwrites creative bonds between artists of any kind is that of influence. Yet, what or whom writers, poets, painters, or filmmakers may recognize consciously as having a formative effect on their work may be entirely different from the traces of unconscious connections that others may discern when considering the complex ties that bind one artist's work to another's. The borderline between the implicit and the explicit in this territory is fluid, then, and it is within this mutable space that I wish to locate my own reading of the links between Krzysztof Kieślowski's *Decalogue* (1988) and Krzysztof Zanussi's *Weekend Stories* (1997). In the first instance, my reading will engage critically with Harold Bloom's and Jacques Derrida's models of artistic influence and will seek to transpose their concern with literary relations into the realm of film. At its most vital, this will be a tale of mutual friendship and collegiality that predates the two film series under discussion and spans careers in which the positions of mentorship and support oscillate continually between the two filmmakers. However, my discussion will also reach beyond the limits of such a lifelong bond to consider how Kieślowski lives on through Zanussi's work after the former's premature death in 1996. Zanussi's *Weekend Stories* establishes an indirect, interfilmic dialogue with Kieślowski's *Decalogue* across the boundaries of faith, as well as life and death. Through cinematographic echoes, themes, and structures that recall, without duplicating, Kieślowski's earlier series, Zanussi shows how the other filmmaker's vision fissures and informs his own from the very outset. The specter of ethical responsibility, which weaves in and out of both series as a principal concern, will also be seen to haunt this particular encounter between these two filmmakers. In temporal terms, this responsibility, which extends outward to others beyond the end of one lifetime, is akin to the temporality of the filial model of ethics offered in the work of Emmanuel Levinas. By bringing together theoretical discussion of Bloom and Derrida with the work of Levinas, the aim of this article is to explore and interrogate filial models of influence and ethics through the films of these signal Polish directors.

The Influence of Anxiety

Within a film and media context, influence is addressed conventionally with reference to varied questions of intertextuality, mimesis, homage, parody, and pastiche, in which a bond is suggested, from the respectful to the mocking, between films and filmmakers. Studies of genre especially are necessarily indebted to such discussion. It is, however, to the literary realm that I wish to turn for my own theoretical points of reference in this article, adopting and adapting them in line with my filmic argument. One of the best-known articulations of a theory of influence in literary circles, very much from within the confines of a particular genre, is that of Harold Bloom in *The Anxiety of Influence: A Theory of Poetry.* However, his notion of the creative mind's "desperate insistence on priority" (Bloom 13) in which one poet is understood deliberately to misread another in order to assert his originality, brings out a wholly antagonistic bond between the poet "father" and "son." Transposing this into the filmic realm, a loose filial metaphor of connection may indeed apply to the relation between Kieślowski and Zanussi, but the Bloomian antagonism is not borne out through their encounter, nor do we remain here within one particular genre or style of filmmaking. Zanussi's is emphatically not a filmic allegory of misreading that reasserts his priority after Kieślowski's death. In an inverted relation to Bloom's anxiety of influence, it is the influence of a period of anxiety within Polish history that sows the seed for the filmmakers' shared and nonconflicting concerns with morality from the 1970s onward.

The connection between Kieślowski and Zanussi dates back to the 1960s when both graduated from the Łódź Film School. This was cemented during the period of filmmaking in the late 1970s and early 1980s known as the Cinema of Moral Concern (or Moral Anxiety). As with the formation of the Polish School of the 1950s, the most prominent directors in this later movement were graduates of the Łódź Film School. The films of this later period, although diverse, were united by a sense of moral crisis in the face of sociopolitical problems generated by state socialism. Stylistically, the filmmaking emerged from the documentary tradition but took shape subsequently in both fictions and documentaries. Cinema assumed the role of reflecting critically on the very things that the propagandistic media—especially television and, particularly after December 1981, when General Wojciech Jaruzelski declared martial law—were suggesting were fine or improving. Both directors were active in this period, but Zanussi's films were more central: his *Camouflage* (1977) and Andrejz Wajda's *Man of Marble* (1977) are cited as two of the key films that epitomize this time. Kieślowski's *Camera Buff*, of 1979, features Zanussi playing himself and suggests Kieślowski's debt to the acclaimed talent of this filmmaker who, by then, was also a friend. In keeping with perceptions of their relationship at this time, Dina Iordanova characterizes Kieślowski as a "Zanussi epigone" at the outset of his career but continues by stating that he "went on to become one of the most widely acclaimed Polish filmmakers and by far surpassed the popularity of his mentor, thus giving the cinema of moral concern a powerful continuation at a higher level" (109). The television series *Decalogue* and *Weekend Stories* both continue the concerns of the Cinema of Moral Anxiety, but they offer a revised relation to Polish society in the light of the intervening years.

Decalogue comprises ten hour-long films, each of which bears a loose but important relation to a corresponding number of the Ten Commandments. In spite of the Judeo-Christian resonance of this relationship, the underlying values of the Biblical reference points do not pin the series to an illustration of any one religion. Indeed, Kieślowski was a self-proclaimed agnostic, and the idea of making films on this theme came from Krzysztof Piesiewicz, Kieślowski's co-screenwriter, who is a Christian. This split between belief systems at the level of scriptwriting is an initial indicator that the films do not set out to present univocal religious proclamations but are more concerned with the way in which the ethical principles underneath the Commandments relate to all people's lives, however much they may be diluted almost out of existence in some contexts. Zanussi was the director of the TOR film unit at the time Kieślowski was thinking about *Decalogue*, and Kieślowski was his deputy, ensuring that the house ran smoothly, since Zanussi was frequently away. Zanussi was linked to the series through both funding and production concerns, since TOR assisted with the costs of filming the two expanded films from the *Decalogue*, *A Short Film about Killing* and *A Short Film about Love*, which developed from *Decalogue 5* and *6*, respectively. Zanussi served as Kieślowski's supportive and inspirational figure behind the scenes, both before and throughout the making of *Decalogue*, and Kieślowski's background influence on *Weekend Stories* is no less significant.

Zanussi wrote, directed and coproduced *Weekend Stories*, which comprises eight films, each lasting roughly fifty minutes and each reflecting on accepted moral values, even though these do not have the progressive numerical coherence of the Ten Commandments. The series bears the traces of Zanussi's Catholic faith, which emerges explicitly at times (for example, in *Little Faith*, *The Dilatory Line*, and *Hidden Treasure*, the third, fourth and eighth films, through one or more of the films' characters), but this is never imposed dogmatically on the viewer. Josephine Woll suggests that this series is Zanussi's version of, or, more tentatively, his "response" to, Kieślowski's series (1). In an interview, however, when asked where *Weekend Stories* came from, Zanussi makes no mention of *Decalogue*. He just states that he aimed to apply experience from the past and take us back explicitly to the Cinema of Moral Anxiety: "In the 70s in Poland we made many films examining moral standards of Polish Communist society. I thought we should apply the same approach to the modern society of Free Poland" (Privett 1). He goes on to say that the people who used to see his films during the earlier period had stopped going to the cinema, since admissions were too expensive, so the impetus behind the television format was largely because he wanted to reach these people in their homes.

In comparison with his films of the 1970s, the *Weekend Stories* are unabashed in their optimistic conclusions. Zanussi explains that this pursuit of a happy ending is driven by the fact that moral issues in the political climate of the late 1990s could have a positive outcome, or a solution, that contrasted with the inevitability of moral compromise in the earlier period. The way in which Zanussi sets up these films is, then, in dialogue with himself as a filmmaker from the period of moral anxiety and with the history of that time, along with the audience he had then and was seeking once again to reach some twenty years on in free Poland. The explicit address is not to Kieślowski, although the resonance of both series when placed in interrelation is rich. In 1996, before the existence of Zanussi's television series, Christopher Garbowski cites Eric Rohmer's *Moral Tales* as one of the few film projects that could be compared to the *Decalogue* series (71) because of Rohmer's concern with moral issues across a series of films. Zanussi's *Weekend Stories* offers an even closer comparison since Garbowski wrote these words, working as it does in the same medium of television and reflecting on morality in an episodic manner.

In the light of signalling a move forward, as well as a continuing reflective relationship to times past, Kieślowski's decision to turn to Polish state television for the *Decalogue* series was as significant as Zanussi's, albeit for different reasons. As Jessie Labov writes, "Kieślowski was stepping outside of the accepted arena for cultural production, in order to gain access to the artistic freedom that the late 1980s promised" (127). This is also an appropriation of a medium previously associated with the antithesis of a questioning moral conscience. Indeed, both Kieślowski and Zanussi are reinvesting television with the ability to recognize moral concerns and choices, rather than disguise them, as in the propaganda machine it was seen previously to be. Television has an almost constant presence in *Weekend Stories,* which is pivotal in some of the films. It is solely responsible for triggering a past trauma in *A Woman's Business.* In *The Soul Sings,* it serves as the possible route to fame, which risks turning to humiliation (self-referentially, Zanussi's name features in bold on the poster advertising the concert that is to establish the main protagonist's reputation; he also appears in a cameo role toward the end of this film). In *The Dilatory Line,* television is presented as a powerful means through which truths might be recognized and injustices corrected. Zanussi and Kieślowski appear united in a desire to use this medium positively but also to unsettle any sense that the moral dimension had suddenly become a straightforward one in the intervening period. The turn to television also throws up some shared formal matters for both directors. They each have to conceive their cinematic training, consciousness, and sensibility to express a vision on the small screen. However, Kieślowski observes differences between television and cinema that are significant to the consideration of both series. The more restricted funding available for television means that staging is more straightforward and shots are closer, rather than wider, as a result (Stok 154). It is with this sense of relational proximity, both to the subject matter that each filmmaker is addressing and between the work of each filmmaker, that I would now like to consider the two series in more detail. Bloomian questions of poetic influence are revised here in nonantagonistic terms, but the relationship between the series also takes us beyond the confines of one particular style of filmmaking. It is with a view to exploring, but also questioning, the likenesses between Kieślowski's and Zanussi's styles in each series that we now need to proceed in filmic terms.

Borderlines

It is no accident that the essay to which the title of this article alludes questions the demarcation of boundaries between genres, already intimating that influence needs to be thought about on the edges of genre, if not through the deconstruction of this very term. My own influence in this regard is Jacques Derrida's essay, published in English as "Living On: Borderlines."[1] "Living On" is the translation of a play on the French verb *survivre,* which means survival in its most literal sense, but also, when split into its components, "sur vivre" (on or about life). Thus, the article is to be read as being concerned with life and with living, not, or not solely, with what might lie beyond this. The text, itself functioning as a split screen, is divided horizontally. The upper level performs a reading of Shelley's "The Triumph of Life" and Maurice Blanchot's *La Folie du jour* and *L'Arrêt de mort,* in which these latter texts constitute, in Derrida's view, and in spite of the apparent lack of any explicit relation between them, "translations" of Shelley's piece. The lower level is a running note to the translator, dated as a ship's logbook. This performative writing both asks about and enacts an overspill: Derrida is interrogating where the edges of a text lie and how texts regularly overflow their boundaries. He adopts a more feminine motif than Bloom's filial lineage suggests, but ultimately his article also only interrogates the bonds that link one male writer's text to the next. He uses the term *invagination* (or double invagination) to refer to the turning inside out of the border separating one text from another. Derrida's terminology is no less controversial than Bloom's masculinist antagonism, and does not displace the male lineage that Bloom initiates, but the conjunction of these two theorists allows me to ask how the bond between the two male filmmakers under discussion here appears in their film series. Without adopting the vocabulary of Derrida's double invagination, I do however want to show how images overflow their containment in one series, sketching out a filmic borderline readily transgressed and transcended in cinematographic terms.

To return momentarily to the genre that concerns Bloom in his literary study—poetry—of the many terms that have been used to describe Kieślowski's later work, of which *Decalogue* is seen as a harbinger, *poetic* seems vaguely appropriate. Seeking to capture his interest in abstraction while linking material reality to the metaphysical arena, the transcendent lyricism of his vision is grounded nonetheless in keen observation of people and objects. He remarks that it is the interior that concerns him more in the *Decalogue* than the exterior (Stok 146), referring in part to his interest in people or families at home, rather than the public sphere. Zanussi's series is more rooted in political issues that concern people beyond the more intimate encounters we have with them, but it is through these people, and through the relation to their home, that these broader issues come to light, so he too could be thought, on this level, to be more interested in the internal than the external world. Both directors take advantage of the constraints of the televisual form to focus on interiors and intimate details. Stylistically, however, the two filmmakers' approaches differ. Zanussi strives toward the objective filming of his protagonists, while Kieślowski allows us to encounter them through their subjective vision. While both are concerned with filming situations that give rise to ethical dilemmas, Kieślowski's style can itself be seen to embody the very transcendence for which he strives on a thematic level, whereas Zanussi's films are focused thematically on transcendence but employ a style more rooted in realist concerns.

In *The Films of Krzysztof Kieślowski: The Liminal Image,* Joseph G. Kickasola, when considering transcendence in relation to Kieślowski's work, takes some distance from its association with the Holy (in scholarship such as Paul Schrader's *Transcendental Style in Film*, for example), associating it, rather, with an abstract, poetic style that expresses the immaterial and aims to stimulate what he terms "metaphysical consideration" (44) in the audience. Kickasola notes that the term "abstract" could apply to images that emphasize form over "realist" indexicality (44), and he traces this style eloquently through *Decalogue* and the later *Three Colors* trilogy (1993–94). In keeping with Kickasola's association of abstraction with poetry, and immateriality with transcendence, my own reading of *Decalogue* sees these films as calling attention to the surface and form of the image. In a metaphor whose sense will be rendered literal in the discussion that follows, the image is more than just a window on a transcendent world, whether that of the Holy or some essence of the real. In this, Kieślowski departs from the phenomenological sense of cinema as defined by J. Dudley Andrew in *The Major Film Theories* (242–53) in relation to the work of the film theorists Amédée Ayfre and Henri Agel, in which the screen and image become windows to a transcendental beyond. In accordance with Kickasola's concern with Kieślowski's privileging of form over realist indexicality, in *Decalogue* it is the places in which this so-called window becomes literally something to be looked at rather than looked through that are the loci of a transcendent perspective. Although Zanussi takes up a concern with the window motif and places it at the start of each of his films, this serves a different purpose from the concern just outlined with regard to Kieślowski's work: instead, it becomes the marker of an influential link between the two filmmakers that serves fluidly, deconstructively even, also as a key marker of difference. The window represents the boundary between the protagonists' private lives and the public sphere, and because of both directors' interest in the interior, these windows serve frequently to reflect the protagonists back on themselves. Windows are connected to the ethical dimension of both directors' films, because they serve as a figure of the complex relationship between self and other, along with forming the boundary between the internal and external worlds.

The window serves as a borderline between the interior and the exterior, which separates the inside from the outside but allows each to be visible to the other. *Decalogue 1* begins with the foreknowledge of the tragedy that is going to unfurl in the film: the death of a child, Pawel, who appears ghostlike on a television screen above the head of his tearful aunt, a reaction presaged in the first few frames by the series' otherworldly figure, played by Artur Barcis, gesturing likewise as if to wipe a tear from his eye. But the camera then tracks up the building to a window in the otherwise anonymous Warsaw *blok*. The vertical move takes us back in time to where we see Pawel faintly behind the glass, watching a pigeon eating crumbs he has laid out, before we enter the interior space of the flat he shares with his father, Krzysztof. It is through glass, from the outside looking in, that we first encounter one of the main protagonists of this tale, and that, in flashback, we then enter the opening narrative of the *Decalogue* series. Echoing this, each of Zanussi's films in *Weekend Stories* features an opening static camera shot of a window, different in each case, since the films are unified through their focus on events in the lives of disparate people that happen over a weekend, not by featuring characters who live in the same building, as in *Decalogue*.

The properties of the window are an important element in Kieślowski's series, yet sometimes less so for the clarity of vision they provide than for their reflective capacity, as, in keeping with a critique of a phenomenological perspective, they become surfaces to be looked at as well as to be looked through. This focuses our attention on the cinematic image itself as well as the narrative it conveys. The glass of the post-office window counter through which Tomek addresses Magda in *Decalogue 6* is as reflective of her image at times as it is transparent at others. Polished surfaces also serve this same purpose as people stand before them as if before a mirror. *Decalogue 5* is emblematic in both regards. The midpoint of the series and the bleakest in terms of its reflections on murder and capital punishment, it suggests parity between these two acts through cross-cutting between the murderer, Jacek, and his future victim, the taxi driver, while returning occasionally to the lawyer, with whom the film opens and closes. Mirroring thus becomes a formal structuring principle in terms of the relation it suggests between Jacek's crime and the state's revenge, which undermines any sense of the moral rectitude of the latter. The cross-cutting technique establishes a continuum that permeates the line between the two, muddying any clear-cut delineation and echoing the uncertain boundaries between interior and exterior, reality and image suggested in the film's attention to glass, mirrors, and other reflective surfaces. The lawyer's words are heard first in voice-over during the opening credit sequence, and when we then encounter him, we do so in a reflection, in a mirror first of all. Jacek is also seen for the first time through his reflection in glass. The muted, drained color as an effect of the green lenses used by Sławomir Idziak, the cinematographer, along with the slightly clouded edge of each image, adds to the uncertain distinction between the crime, its punishment, and a lawyer who stands in an uneasy relation to both. In Zanussi's series, the division between visual clarity and obscurity manifests itself differently. From an opening shot of a window, we are thrown back continually to the interior, both of the home and the people's lives concerned, but in a different way from Kieślowski's concern with the reflective properties of this transparent surface.

The windows of Zanussi's opening shots appear veiled with blinds (*A Woman's Business, Little Faith, The Soul Sings*) or a net (*Unwritten Law*), though they are sometimes naked (*Deceptive Charm, The Dilatory Line, The Last Circle,* and *The Hidden Treasure*). The final film begins with the main protagonist, Roza, opening the windows of her attic flat in Paris in order to close the shutters before she returns to her native Poland for a week, signalling the closure of the entire series. One example serves to illustrate Zanussi's contrasting relation to Kieślowski's concern with reflective or transparent surfaces. The window at the outset of Zanussi's *The Dilatory Line* has a criss-cross design reminiscent of lead lights but also wiring, suggesting slightly obscured and constrained vision, which relates to the insecurities of the male protagonist. This opening shot, through which the street on the outside is visible, then appears in racked focus against which the feet and then hands of the female protagonist are foregrounded before we are introduced to the lovers in bed with one another. The explicit focus, in spite of the twists and turns of this narrative, is made obvious in these opening shots through cinematographically obscuring the window and what we are able to see beyond it, and we return to this couple in the end, reunited in spite of the test their relationship undergoes in the world beyond the bedroom during the course of the film.

Kieślowski remarks that there must be something akin to a spirit of a screenplay, since in spite of the different crew used for the *Decalogue* series, and especially the use of nine different cinematographers (Piotr Sobociński was the only one to be used twice, in *Decalogue 3* and *9*), the films look as though they belong together (Stok 156). Zanussi discovered a similar spirit in *Weekend Stories,* since, although he used three different cinematographers with the eight episodes, the films have a similar internal coherence. One person links the two series, however: Edek Kłosinski was cinematographer for *Decalogue 2* and for four of the *Weekend Stories,* the first, second, third, and final films: *A Woman's Business, Deceptive Charm, Little Faith,* and *The Hidden Treasure. Decalogue 2,* with its close-ups of faces, slow camera movements, and the importance of angles and color correspondences creating symmetries within and between shots as well as associations with warmth and coldness, has echoes, albeit distant and distorted, in the *Weekend Stories.* Choosing Kłosinski as the first cinematographer for his series establishes the visual link back to *Decalogue* that runs from start to finish: the resonance of the opening shot of *A Woman's Business,* the rich filming of color correspondences of *Deceptive Charm*—crimson red, white and brown is the scheme that returns, with a brief dash of yellow—and the importance of camera angles to the shooting of all of the films make this apparent. Zanussi's films pay less attention to the surface, and to a concomitant concern with formal abstraction, than Kieślowski's, however.

A Woman's Business begins with an oblique shot of part of a rectangular window, covered with slatted blinds, seen from the perspective of a room flooded with light, which allows us faintly to glimpse the street outside. There are lush green plants on the sill, one of which is a rubber plant. As the camera pans to the left, Zofia, the main protagonist in this tale, which asks her to make a choice between revenge or forgiveness of someone who ruined her life under communist rule, then walks into the shot and looks out of the window. We do not see from her perspective at this point but see her looking, and this sets the tone of our relation to her story, since the key to her present unhappiness is provided principally from the outside, by others (Dorota and Anna, her friends), rather than being revealed from her point of view. Indeed, it is more generally the case throughout the *Weekend Stories* that we view situations more objectively, and this opening scene from *A Woman's Business* can be contrasted with Kieślowski's filming of a woman at a window in *Decalogue.* Associatively, Zanussi's scene recalls Dorota in Kieślowski's *Decalogue 2,* who looks through the slats of the blinds midway through the film to watch the doctor leave the *blok* in which they both live, before turning to a rubber plant in front of her on the windowsill. We see her looking out of the window before we view through her eyes as she watches the doctor. We then see her twisting all of the leaves off the rubber plant. The film cuts again to a shot of the doctor, which is objective this time, as we watch him from the same height but not obscured by the blinds. We return to a close-up of her hands on the plant's stalk, which is left bent in half but still intact. The destruction of the plant expresses Dorota's frustration and distress, seeing through the blind the partial and distant vision of the man who is cold to her at this stage but who ultimately saves the life of her unborn child. Subsequently, the camera remains focused on the bent stalk of the plant in a manner that seems momentarily to detach it from the surrounding narrative and weight of significance that interpretation makes it carry. By luxuriating in this vision of the object in its own right and for its own sake, Kieślowski suggests a further difference between the two filmmakers: the rubber plant is just another plant on the sill of Zofia's flat, passed over with others that form the opening mise-en-scène, whereas Dorota's plant expresses but then stands apart from her painful situation, as object and image are presented to be looked at instead of looked through in order to find meaning. Rather than rematerializing Kieślowski's work and thus cutting it off from notions of transcendence, this attention to form and, elsewhere, abstraction is the very locus of transcendence.

Zanussi's filming tends more toward the linear, cause-and-effect narration that Kieślowski modulates. *The Soul Sings,* for example, begins with blinds being alternately opened and then closed, offering fleeting glimpses of

Through cinematographic echoes, Zanussi shows how Kieślowski's vision fissures and informs his own from the very outset. Zofia (Joanna Szczepkowska) looks through a slatted window in *A Woman's Business,* the first installment in Zanussi's *Weekend Stories* (1997), recalling the identical gesture of Dorota (Krystyna Janda) in Kieślowski's *Decalogue 2* (1988).

a road and traffic outside, and as the opening credit music ends, it reveals that a little girl has been playing with them. Thus, a far more transparent causal connection between child and activity is apparent here than in *Decalogue 7*, which begins with a child's cries, but cries that are separated visually and temporally from the upset child herself. The child of *The Soul Sings* is not the focus of the ensuing narrative in which her father has a choice to make between his career and helping out a neighbor, but she opens this film with play, in a sense affirming the life that was so fragile in the earlier film of the series, *Little Faith*, even though the sick child of this film recovers in the end. There are thematic echoes here of the switch from the death of the child in *Decalogue 1* to the survival of the unborn child in *Decalogue 2*, suggesting each series' acknowledgement of the arbitrariness of how sickness and survival manifest themselves, even though the style of Kieślowski's work differs from Zanussi's.

In spite of their different approaches, neither filmmaker allows us unequivocally to view their various images as windows to a transcendent space beyond themselves: rather, this transcendence lies within the image itself and, importantly, cannot be pinned down to any one coherent expression of religious belief. Where Zanussi orients our focus in realist terms toward an interior set of choices for individuals to make, while not permitting us to view things through their eyes, Kieślowski does so by more abstract means. This is not to deny that Zanussi's Catholicism is present within his series (in *Little Faith*, *The Hidden Treasure*, and *The Dilatory Line*, at least one of the key protagonists mentions and advocates this belief system explicitly). Religion, and Catholicism in particular, is as much a part of Zanussi's series as it is Kieślowski's (pictures of Pope John Paul II appear in *Decalogue 1* and, in a more irreverent fashion, in *Decalogue 9*). The protagonists of *Weekend Stories* recognize right from wrong, what they should do, as opposed to what they might want to do, and this is what leads to happy endings. The "unwritten law" that serves as a title to one of the *Weekend Stories* is an appropriate designation for the ways in which people relate to these values that they may have forgotten but that are still a part of the ways in which they live. It is in this sense that we move beyond morality and toward ethics in both Kieślowski's and Zanussi's filmmaking.

Living On

Slavoj Žižek observes that what interests Kieślowski in *Decalogue* is ethics and not morality, stating that it is by breaking the moral code in each film that an ethical path is to be found (137). In a crucial sense, then, this is how the concerns of the Cinema of Moral Anxiety might be thought to live on through the work of the two directors: through a form of ethical questioning as opposed to the imposition of a strict moral code based in religious principles. In Bloom's (and Derrida's) text-based examples within their theories of influence, survival into the future is based in a succession of male writers. Very much within the Judeo-Christian lineage of the filmmakers' concerns under discussion, Emmanuel Levinas's postphenomenological ethics builds on the filial connections of these literary theorists: it is through the son that the father bears an ethical relation to the future, surviving himself through the body of his offspring, who is engendered by him but still separate from him. As Levinas writes: "The son resumes the unicity of the father and yet remains exterior to the father" (279). Although I differ from Levinas in conceiving of this ethical relation to the future along filial lines, I believe that the affirmation of life, of living somehow beyond physical death, and of the priority of the other in the life of the self, is an important facet of the ethics of influence that is at work in the relation between Zanussi and Kieślowski. Indeed, Zanussi's series, in relating back to Kieślowski but taking his own work forward in a distinct way, actually suggests a new direction for the future.

How people might live alongside one another is one of the key issues that *Weekend Stories* raises from the outset. Neither it nor *Decalogue* is entirely able to abandon its social or religious markers of morality, but Zanussi's films retain these more explicitly than Kieślowski's do. Critical remarks are made about the old state socialism from the first film and its corrupt official, Lukowska, who could grant or deny travel visas and passports as she saw fit. The Count criticizes Karol, in *Deceptive Charm,* for his attitude to money in this regard. Furthermore, the former system of rule that led to the exile of Witold Crac (the ballet dancer in *The Last Circle*) and Roza (the former aristocrat in *The Hidden Treasure*) is also exposed for criticism. At base, the benevolent attitudes of the victims toward their victimizers in these films suggest that there is a concern for one's neighbor that surfaces beyond feelings of vengeance, animosity, or hatred, gesturing to a new way forward. This concern for one's neighbor is rendered literal in *The Soul that Sings* when the opera singer chooses, against his better judgment, to help his elderly neighbor. Such behavior is not dictated to him but, as is so for the other protagonists of this series (and in *Decalogue*); it is dependent on his/their response to the other who creates an unavoidable ethical demand, and dilemma, for the protagonist. Each film, without celebrating the present as entirely rosy, does give people a choice as to how they might live differently. This element of choice is governed partly by belief systems that transcend an existentialist sense of self-definition, and in Zanussi's work as in Kieślowski's, the presence of a religious reference point is incontestable. Zanussi, at times, is the more normative in this regard. His work explicitly endorses the sanctity of the family throughout, and *Deceptive Charm* risks homophobia in its casting of the gay Count as the devil incarnate who tries but finally fails to split up the young couple. Even such problematic normativity is not conveyed unambiguously, however, and it becomes subject to question. Beyond the imposition of a religious code of reference that would constitute a stable moral code, we have in the work of both filmmakers the creation of a form of ethical questioning, permanently unsettling, in Levinasian fashion, the subject who has to respond to his or her neighbor's exorbitant demands, but who responds nonetheless in order to look forward to the promise of a different future. In spite of the fact that Kieślowski and Zanussi have different beliefs, their series are strikingly similar in the uncertainties they portray.

Even though Zanussi's films are couched explicitly in the Catholic faith, this absolute reference point becomes as loose as superstition in some cases. In *The Soul Sings,* for example, the old woman says that the opera singer's good deed will be rewarded, while he says that they will be punished: both prophecies end up coming true, but the power cut that saves his career ultimately could be divine intervention or just pure chance. The chance event or act of divine intervention in *The Soul Sings* stands in contrast to the tragic outcome of *Decalogue 1,* but the reason for the event that caused Pawel to drown is left just as open in Kieślowski's film. In *Decalogue 2,* in contrast, a child is saved by human decision, while ambiguity surrounds the survival of Dorota's husband, previously thought to be dying of cancer and then miraculously on the mend: again the question is raised of whether this is a fluke recovery or the act of a higher power. Likewise, in Zanussi's *Little Faith* there is an ostensible miracle in the recovery of Karol, the child, who has suspected but unconfirmed leukemia—and the question is raised as to whether this is the result of faith or just a coincidence—Tomasz, his father, calls it luck, Olga, his mother, calls it more than this; he the rationalist but still a believer, she deeply religious. Indeed, the control over life or death does not appear to be entirely in human hands, but the undecidable status of the causes of recovery from illness and survival or death remains enigmatic. Recuperation through religious explanation is always possible, but both film series suggest that this is only one response to the infinitely complex occurrences of the experiences each film portrays. This is the locus of their ethical questioning, as opposed to an assertion of stable moral codes.

Ending affirmatively and on the side of life rather than death, both series conclude with a similar outburst of laughter, but one final difference remains to be brought out. The hapless brothers who inherit their father's priceless stamp collection in *Decalogue 10,* and who end up with nothing, conclude by each buying independently a set of stamps from the post office. When they compare and see that they have matching sets, they crease up with laughter. In contrast, Zanussi's series begins and ends with women, suggestive of a future that is not solely male-identified in the manner of the religions, the ethics, or the literary theories of influence that I have drawn on throughout this discussion. In *The Hidden Treasure,* Roza persuades Jola to give away what the latter's family had acquired by dubious means, but this still serves indirectly as a better inheritance for the young girl's future. As the women walk away into the distance in the final shot, we hear their laughter across the generation gap and across their very different histories. Informed by, but not limited to, the Catholic faith, Roza passes on her values to a new generation, compelling Jola to do as she suggests but not requiring her to adopt her belief system. In chronological terms, the laughter of women concludes this staged dialogue between these two directors. The brothers' experience in *Decalogue 10* is rather more tainted than Jola's, but in choosing to end on this note, both filmmakers are reunited in a positive gesture that suspends, even if only momentarily, the more agonizing times that inform the lives of those in each series. Kieślowski lives on through the laughter of Jola and Roza, as the ethical questioning of moral standards—whether these be dubious or reliable, sociopolitical or religious—suggests a future that need not repeat the past. It is here that Zanussi's debt to Kieślowski is arguably greatest.

Note

1. "Survivre" is the French title of the article, which was published originally in the volume *Parages.*

Works Cited

Andrew, J. Dudley. *The Major Film Theories: An Introduction.* Oxford: Oxford University Press, 1976.

Bloom, Harold. *The Anxiety of Influence: A Theory of Poetry.* New York: Oxford University Press, 1973.

Derrida, Jacques. "Living On: Borderlines." *Deconstruction and Criticism.* Ed. Geoffrey Hartman. London: Routledge and Kegan Paul, 1979. 75–176.

Garbowski, Christopher. *Krzysztof Kieślowski's Decalogue Series: The Problem of the Protagonists and Their Self-Transcendence.* East European Monographs, no. 452. Boulder: East European Monographs, 1996.

Iordanova, Dina. *Cinema of the Other Europe: The Industry and Artistry of East Central European Film.* London: Wallflower Press, 2003.

Kickasola, Joseph G. *The Films of Krzysztof Kieślowski: The Liminal Image.* New York: Continuum, 2004.

Labov, Jessie. "Kieślowski's *Dekalog,* Everyday Life, and the Art of Solidarity." *Screening the City.* Ed. Mark Shiel and Tony Fitzmaurice. London: Verso, 2003. 113–34.

Levinas, Emmanuel. *Totality and Infinity: An Essay on Exteriority.* Trans. Alphonso Lingis. Pittsburgh, PA: Duquesne University Press, 1969.

Michałek, Bolesław, and Frank Turaj. *The Modern Cinema of Poland.* Bloomington: Indiana University Press, 1988.

Privett, Ray. "Interview with Krzysztof Zanussi." *Facets Multimedia.* http://www.facets.org/asticat?function=web&catname=facets&web=features&path=/directors/zanussikrzysztof/interviewwithzanussi.

Schrader, Paul. *Transcendental Style in Film: Ozu, Bresson, Dreyer.* Berkeley: University of California Press, 1972.

Stok, Danusia, ed. *Kieślowski on Kieślowski.* London: Faber and Faber, 1993.

Woll, Josephine. "The Unacceptable Cost of Being Moral." *Kinoeye: New Perspectives on European Film.* http://www.kinoeye.org/01/04/woll04.php.

Žižek, Slavoj. *The Fright of Real Tears: Krzysztof Kieślowski between Theory and Post-Theory.* London: BFI, 2001.

3

Turning Director

Jerzy Stuhr Does Kieślowski

Renata Murawska

> One cannot see the world in any other way, but through one's own self. —Krzysztof Kieślowski, *Krzysztof Kieślowski: I'm So-So*

> He was building a tower. I'm building a little house. —Jerzy Stuhr, "Mam przemożna"

In mapping out the constellations of Krzysztof Kieślowski's legacy, Jerzy Stuhr holds a peculiar place. His career in film intersected with Kieślowski's over an eighteen-year period, and Kieślowski's influence on him has been such that critics have questioned Stuhr's authorship of the films he has himself directed. Kieślowski and Stuhr's cooperation and lifelong friendship started with a talented film director approaching a promising theater actor to appear in *The Scar* (*Blizna,* 1976), Kieślowski's third attempt at nondocumentary filmmaking and first at a full-length feature film.[1] Stuhr was asked to play a character only vaguely defined, with not one line of dialogue and, according to Kieślowski, utterly disposable. Stuhr's roles in this and Kieślowski's other early feature films made him one of the most recognized actors of the Cinema of Moral Concern and, after its expiration, of Polish cinema in general. At the same time, Stuhr's acute thespian sensibility assisted in Kieślowski's migration from the world of documentary to feature filmmaking in the mid- to late 1970s. When Stuhr decided to pursue directing after 1994, he drew on his experience of cowriting dialogue for *The Calm* (*Spokój,* 1976, released 1980) and *Camera Buff* (*Amator,* 1979), and his close observations of Kieślowski's directing method.

Even so, examining Stuhr-directed films for their Kieślowskian legacy, drawing on the professional connections between the two, is as much misleading as it is necessary. On the one hand, it highlights Kieślowski's influence on Stuhr's films. On the other, it forces a search for similarities between the cherished master and a relative newcomer to the directing scene, often followed by a critique of Stuhr's lack of originality, with each difference tempting an accusation of Stuhr's failure to achieve the heights of Kieślowskian vision. A more just approach to tracing the lines of influence between Kieślowski and Stuhr involves accepting Stuhr's authorial sovereignty, both as an actor and director, and examining the ways in which his association of sorts with Kieślowski informs and animates Stuhr's film work, while also giving some consideration to the ways in which Stuhr contributed to Kieślowski's directorial development.

Stuhr and Kieślowski: Actor and Director

The first intersection of Stuhr's and Kieślowski's film paths was (almost) haphazard. Both men knew of each other's early successes, but neither had seen the other's work (Stuhr Kieślowski's documentary films, and Kieślowski Stuhr's theater roles). Yet, prompted by his production manager, the documentary director approached the theater actor when making his first full-length feature film, *The Scar* (Zawiśliński 157–58). Stuhr soon impressed Kieślowski, who expanded his character, an assistant to the protagonist Bednarz (Franciszek Pieczka), from a set of insignificant appearances into the éminence grise of the story's structure. Still committed to realist documentary principles, Kieślowski found an ally in the young actor, whose sharpness of observation and ease in emulating real people allowed him to embrace unreservedly the challenges of the daily improvisations (Stuhr in Litka, "Najważniejszy" 22) that were the pillar of the directing method on *The Scar*. Based on his impression of Stuhr, Kieślowski "had to write a film for him, because he's so good" (Stok 106), and Stuhr became the lead of Kieślowski's next feature, for television, *The Calm*. That film tells the story of an ex-prisoner, Antek Gralak, and his impractical ambition for the "big calm," defined as a place to live, a family, an ordinary life. Not intended as a political commentary (Stok 108), it was refused screening in Poland for four years because it included strike scenes, which upset communist authorities. Although the shelving of a film was considered a compliment for a filmmaker at that time, and the public interest generated by the shelving often was a superior substitute for a commercially driven marketing campaign, another three years passed before Kieślowski completed his next feature film, although in the meantime he continued to make successful documentaries.

For both Stuhr and Kieślowski, their next film was a consolidation of the director-actor exchange they began in *The Scar*, and of their firm place within the echelon of the Cinema of Moral Concern, next to Andrzej Wajda, Krzysztof Zanussi, and others. For Kieślowski, the 1979 *Camera Buff* secured his position as a perceptive commentator on the ways in which social and familial contexts can trap an individual to the same degree as his or her personal predispositions. For Stuhr, already well-known to Polish audiences for his electrifying portrayal of the lead Danielak in Feliks Falk's *Top Dog* (*Wodzirej,* 1978),[2] *Camera Buff* reconfirmed his status as an outstanding actor able to convincingly convey the perplexities of the human condition. In Kieślowski's film, Stuhr is Filip Mosz, an amateur filmmaker who unwillingly sacrifices the calm of his familial existence for his filming passions only to discover that the latter are equally imbued with responsibilities to self and others. As was the case with *The Calm* before, Stuhr is recognized in the film's credits as a cowriter of the dialogue, a contribution that aids the realism of the character he portrays, and one that plays a part in Stuhr's description of *Camera Buff* as the pinnacle of his collaboration with Kieślowski (Stuhr "Dobry").

In the next ten years, their professional paths crossed only once, in Kieślowski's *Blind Chance* (*Przypadek,* 1981), where Stuhr has only an uncredited, episodic role. Between *Blind Chance* and the *Decalogue* (1988), Kieślowski made only one other feature film, *No End* (*Bez konca,* 1984), and only a handful of documentaries. As his interest in the specificity of the Polish social condition of the time was waning, largely owing to the imposition of martial law at the end of 1981, a stronger preoccupation with universal truths, rather than detailed verism, was taking hold of him. At the same time, Stuhr was diversifying his film acting career under the directing aegis of the master of Polish popular entertainment cinema, Juliusz Machulski.[3] For the large proportion of the Polish audience indifferent to the difficult questions posed by the Cinema of Moral Concern in the late 1970s and therefore unaware of Stuhr's position within it, the actor became synonymous with Maksio Paradys from Machulski's *Sexmission* (*Seksmisja,* 1984). After being cryogenically frozen, two males, Maksio Paradys and Albert Starski (Olgierd Łukaszewicz), are brought back to life in a world run by women in which men are extinct and perceived as an unfortunate aberration in the history of the female kind. This antifeminist cult comedy made known Stuhr's comic virtuosity, which he pursued in several other films of the 1980s, but which also limited the expectations of his audience to that particular acting range, which in turn has had a bearing on the discursive and commercial expectations of Stuhr's films.

When asked by Kieślowski to choose the character he would like to play in the *Decalogue,* Stuhr was originally intent on the part of Roman (Piotr Machalica), who learns he is impotent in *Decalogue 9.* Having finished filming seven of the ten parts of the *Decalogue,* Kieślowski asked Stuhr to abandon his original intent and instead become the older brother (Jerzy) in *Decalogue 10.* He wanted "the tenth part of *The Decalogue* to be more comical than the others," because the others were somber in tone, and "at least the last one" could be "different" (Stuhr in Mikos 132). From that followed a decision of pairing Stuhr with Zbigniew Zamachowski as the younger brother, Artur. After realizing that Stuhr and Zamachowski react similarly on the screen, Jacek Bławut, the cinematographer, was asked to keep the two brothers together in a shot, or in alternating close-ups (Stuhr in Mikos 132), an effect repeated to some extent in *Three Colors: White* (1994), in which Stuhr and Zamachowski again play brothers. *White* is also the last film in which Stuhr and Kieślowski worked in the actor-director configuration, yet it is not the last crossing point of their cinematic trajectories.

Stuhr and Kieślowski: Two Directors

Jerzy Stuhr debuted as a film director in 1995 with an adaptation of Jerzy Pilch's novel *List of Lovers.* Literary and theatrical, the film was generally well received, and apparently removed from the realm of Kieślowskian influences. That dissociation changed after Kieślowski's untimely death in 1996. Between 1995 and 2003 Stuhr directed four more films, each of which was dissected by Polish critics searching for Kieślowski's successors and suspicious of any actor's commitment to film directing.[4] Those critics saw two of Stuhr's five films as being particularly under Kieślowski's spell, that is, *Love Stories* (*Historie miłosne,* 1997), dedicated to Kieślowski and carrying signs of Kieślowski's preoccupations and style (but also clearly marked with Stuhr's own directing concerns), and *The Big Animal* (*Duże zwierzę,* 2000), produced by Polish television for cinematic release and based on Kieślowski's treatment from about 1973.[5] Another Stuhr film that at times attracts comparisons with Kieślowski's European work is *A Week in the Life of a Man* (*Tydzień z życia mężczyzny,* 1999). One particular set of scenes in the film has caused accusations of post-Kieślowskian derivation. A daily swimming ritual of the film's protagonist, Adam Borowski (Jerzy Stuhr), is apparently aesthetically cognate with the swimming pool scenes in *Three Colors: Blue* (1993). Originally, Borowski's swimming was scripted to be a morning shaving ritual taking place in a bathroom. The ritual migrated to a swimming pool only at the request for "greater breadth" by the film's cinematographer. At the interpretative level, Borowski's daily swimming rite signifies continuity that allows him to go on, rather than, as in the case of Julie Vignon (Juliette Binoche) in *Blue,* an expression of the need for separation by ablution. Yet, the ensuing perception of these scenes' affinity, despite their differing motivation and significance, only highlights problems inherent in tracing the legacy of one director in the work of another.

At the opposite spectrum of such comparisons is the exploration of the motivation and the underlying philosophy of a filmmaker. While readily admitting his indebtedness to Kieślowski, Stuhr refuses simply to fill the gap created by Kieślowski's death.[6] As in other interviews before, in 1999 he repeats,

"I have in common with Kieślowski technical issues, a way of leading an actor, a certain calmness of the narrative and photography, similar dialogues," but "the world of metaphysics is foreign to me" (Stuhr in Kuba 70). He also frequently reminds his interviewers of his linguistic, literary background,[7] and of his belief that literature is more important for a filmmaker than philosophy (Stuhr in Horton). From that follows his choice of the narrative forms he employs in his films, most notably the morality tale and the fable. Having already described his role as that of a social therapist in 1986 (Stuhr in Wysogląd 18), in the 1990s he is intent on telling stories of human weakness (Chyb 1997), yet he does not want to be perceived as a moralizer (Stuhr in Mikos 149).[8]

While both Stuhr's and Kieślowski's films are firmly based in the reality of human weakness that may define daily choices, Kieślowski is more averse to seeking answers based in morality or any clear divisions between right and wrong (Kieślowski in Janicka 4; Kieślowski in Ciment and Niogret 31). The shifts between the three phases of Kieślowski's filmmaking—that is, the documentaries, the sociopoliticized Polish features, and the metaphysical European ones—are motivated by his quest for the "ultimate reality" of human experience (Kickasola xii).[9] As Kieślowski puts it, "I am not looking for answers. Those who tell stories can be divided into those who know, and those who don't know. I belong to those who don't know. That's why I'm telling stories: because I want to find out, and that doesn't mean that I ever do" (Kieślowski in Lewin). One illustration of Kieślowski's aversion to finding answers is in the changes he introduced to *Decalogue 1* (1988), the final version of which depicts a boy drowning while skating on ice that, according to his father's computer calculations, should easily withstand his weight. Not wanting to offer any easy answers, Kieślowski deleted from the film the explanation of the disaster that was originally included in the script: a power station released hot water into the lake on which the boy was skating (Spula 112). No such explanation is given in the final version of the film, and the accident's cause remains a mystery. Yet it is a mystery that offers insight into Kieślowski's understanding of causality and randomness. The fear of an accidental change of one's fate (Stachówna, "Trzy Kolory" 107) prompted Kieślowski to adopt in his later films what Grabowski, following Horst Ruthrof, refers to as a narrative of a "liminal situation," in which a "person, narrator or hypothetical reader in an intuitive glimpse becomes aware of the full sense of existence" (44). A similar argument is woven by Joseph G. Kickasola, for whom immediacy, abstraction, and transcendence are the three main factors framing Kieślowski's filmmaking motivation (41–89).

Driven by different motivations—therapeutic and literary versus questing and philosophical—Stuhr's and Kieślowski's directing methods also vary. Yet both directors subscribe to the belief that the best dialogue is that in which two people on the screen are silent and the audience knows why (Stuhr and Piesiewicz 62), a lesson that Stuhr derived from cowriting dialogue with Kieślowski in *The Calm* and *Camera Buff* (Stuhr in Chyb 68; Stuhr in Maciejewski, "Piękno" 76–77; Stuhr in Zarębski, "Zapadlo"). Attention to the seemingly irrelevant detail, which would perplex and introduce ripples in the texture of his films, was another lesson Stuhr learned while working on *Camera Buff,* when its crew had to wait all day for a pigeon to be filmed by the film's hero, Filip Mosz (Jerzy Stuhr), despite Stuhr's objections. The reasons for Kieślowski's insistence on that detail became clear once Stuhr saw the scene in the final cut (Stuhr in Kot 22). Yet, while both appreciated the role of the script, for Stuhr, it constitutes the most important part of the filmmaking process, followed by acting and then editing, which he approaches as a means of improving the script (Stuhr in Mikos 160). For Kieślowski, on the other hand, editing is the most important part of making a film (Kieślowski and Takahashi 12), and only in the editing room, while making multiple and disparate versions of the same film, can he recover its "soul" (Kieślowski in Orzechowska 41). Despite these differences and Stuhr's authorial claim on his films, and not only because of the trajectories of film history that brought the two men together in 1975, Kieślowskian traces in Stuhr's *The Big Animal* and *Love Stories* are a marked presence.

Love Stories: Kieślowski by Osmosis

Love Stories stamps its connection to Krzysztof Kieślowski from the start, with a dedication to him written in white letters on a black screen at the beginning of the film. Kieślowski also played the (uncredited) role of cowriter of the script in the spirit of the cooperation that was part of the filmmaking process for Polish filmmakers active in the 1970s and 1980s. Stuhr approached Kieślowski first just with a concept for *Love Stories,* before he had anything committed to paper. Kieślowski got heavily involved in suggesting changes to the initial concept and then to the written script, some of which were accepted by Stuhr, others resisted. For instance, writing the protagonists' mothers into the script was dictated by Kieślowski's insistence that he needed to know more about the four heroes of *Love Stories.* The force of Kieślowski's suggestions was such that at some stage Stuhr decided not to seek his counsel on the script anymore. Kieślowski died before their next arranged meeting (Stuhr in Chyb). Afraid that Polish audiences familiar with his comic roles might not take him seriously, not only did Stuhr face the challenge of convincing the reluctant critics that he had "a right to say a few serious words" as a director and that his acting was not going to overshadow the main concept of the film (Michalak and Stec 4–6), but he also had to position himself in relation to the great director, his friend, and a major influence on his acting and directing career. However, the Kieślowskian legacy apparent in *Love Stories* takes place by osmosis rather than through Stuhr's conscious, premeditated effort to emulate Kieślowski's directorial stylistics or philosophy. Yet Kieślowski's ghost penetrates the film, at times against the director's will, but inescapably, to wink at the expectant viewer.

In *Love Stories,* Stuhr tells four stories of four characters, all played by Stuhr, who, one by one, arrive at an unassuming building that has the air of a public institution. A man dressed in a suit with no tie is followed by a Catholic priest, then a colonel in a uniform, and, finally, a handcuffed jeans-clad man delivered to the building by the police. The first man is an academic in a rush to arrive at an exam in time to collect his students' papers on literary composition. One of his students, Ewa Bielska (Dominika Ostałowska), hands in to him a clean sheet with "I love you" written on it, and outside the class she insists on the truth of her declarations. The academic finds her desirable, but he is unable to act on his feelings, which he believes could jeopardize his academic career despite his dean's reassurance that in a hypothetical similar situation, he should have no concerns about the security of his university position. In a brief instance of carnal weakness, the academic agrees to help Ewa during the oral examination by selecting the only exam question she knows an answer to. At the last moment, scared by the entry of a librarian who might have witnessed his indiscretion, he changes his mind while another examined student in the background discusses "beauty as a shape of love." Rejected, Ewa fails her exams and has to abandon her studies. The priest is confronted with an eleven-year-old girl, Magda (Karolina Ostrożna), who claims to be his daughter (conceived in a moment of weakness), orphaned by her mother's death six years ago. After much deliberation and against the advice of his superiors, parishioners, and mother, the priest decides to leave the church to devote himself to the daughter, who is helpless and thus deserves his sacrifice and love. The colonel, Jerzy Matałowski, receives a visit from his long-lost Russian love, Tamara (Irina Alfyorova), who finds him more than fifteen years after their love affair, and whom he rejects, after proclaiming his love for her, when he realizes that their relationship would jeopardize his military career. Finally, the drug smuggler, Zdzisiek, is repeatedly betrayed by his wife, Kryśka (Katarzyna Figura), who squanders his bail money while he serves his sentence, but he insists on loving and protecting her. At the end, she is also sentenced to two years in prison, to which Zdzisiek reacts by saying, "At least she can't give me the slip now," and then breaking into a big smile.

The four plots are delivered in intertwining sequences of two to four minutes, regardless of the differences in their stories' apparent duration, thus disregarding the linearity of time. Although it would be tempting to interpret this as a metaphor on the insignificance of time, Stuhr's decision on the film's setting and structure was dictated by the theatrical unity of place rather than some other, loftier concerns (Stuhr in Michalak and Stec 5). The concept underlying *Love Stories*' plot structure is quite Kieślowskian. Stuhr insists that all four characters are the same person placed in different situations, faced with permutations of the same choice in relation to love and its varying outcomes.

Unlike the case of *Blind Chance,* in which, as Paul Coates writes, "Kieślowski makes of one character three persons" (35), in *Love Stories* the four characters' (or one person's) choices are clearly valorized in the closing sequence of each plot to produce a set of morality tales. The colonel and the academic, who are unwilling to pursue their feelings, are driven in a lift to the lowest levels of the building, which—borrowing from Dante—can be interpreted as a limbo or hell, and then expelled from it through an empty, dark corridor with a light at its end, its impression slowly dwindling away while each man hesitates to take his next step. The priest's and convict's choices are rewarded with a dignified departure through the front door of the building.

Throughout the film, the characters' progress is diligently recorded by a mysterious Accountant (Jerzy Nowak), whose metaphysical propensity frustrated Stuhr especially strongly after the film's completion (Stuhr in Zarębski, "Zapadło" 52). The Accountant's assistant (Andrzej Hudziak) periodically summons each of the four characters into a spacious filing room, where the Accountant writes their answers to three questions on their particular condition of love on the pink pages of their files. After a time, his fountain pen malfunctions, and he is forced to let an ink drop out, a detail recorded in an aestheticizing close-up that is suggestive of Kieślowski's use of seemingly irrelevant details to punctuate his work. In general, however, Paweł Edelman's cinematography carries no particularly close resemblance to Kieślowskian stylistics, and it is mostly contained in the classical realist tradition.[10] The only plot that is clearly differentiated by the cinematography is that of the priest, who is mostly shown in a church with godly light seeping through the stained glass windows and contouring his silhouette, and an occasional shot in which the point of view is that of a god looking down on his priest while he makes his love and life choices. During conjugal visits, the convict entangled with his wife is also awash with the warm light absent from other scenes of the film.

One connection to Kieślowski's thought that is difficult to dismiss is the repeated reference to the calm, which, as Marek Haltof points out, "plays a seminal role in Kieślowski's films and in his artistic biography" (Haltof 39). The question of how daily choices among conflicting responsibilities to self and others relate to the stability of the individual's "calm" also permeates Stuhr's films. In *Love Stories,* when demonstrating his understanding of the situation, the priest announces that an inevitable loss of his calm, as well as of the church and of his parishioners, will be the consequence of his choice. In explanation of his reluctance to succumb to his desires for his student, the *Love Stories*' academic speaks to the Accountant of his anxiety that he might lose his calm. Another, more subtle connection between the four plots lies in a detail that is unlikely to have been inspired directly by Kieślowski's work but is reminiscent of Kieślowski's reliance on melancholic objects to convey the sentiments of his characters, for instance a lit cigarette left behind in *Three Colors: Red* (1994) to signify absence. In *Love Stories,* the strength of the love

Although Stuhr's *Love Stories* (1997) has structural connections to Kieślowski's *Blind Chance* (1981), such characters as the Accountant (Jerzy Nowak), who keeps a detailed record of the characters' decisions, mark Stuhr's film as a moral tale rather than a metaphysical investigation. (Photo by Piotr Muszyński, courtesy of Zebra Film Production, Poland)

link is expressed by objects that are that love's relics. In three cases, a photograph of the beloved person serves as a mummified instant of a love story. Little Magda holds on to the photograph of her father for years, until it is destroyed by a headmistress and is no longer needed because her father decides to put his claim on her. Ewa steals her professor's photograph and returns it to him in an envelope once he betrays her. Zdzisiek cannot separate himself from a photo of Kryśka in a bikini. Even when he tears it, angered by yet another of her betrayals, he promptly collects it from the rubbish bin on the way out of the court, causing a great deal of consternation to his guards. The only record of love that is not a photograph belongs to Tamara, who carries Colonel Matałowski's letters to her. To her disappointment, he has typed up hers to store them on an impersonal diskette. At the end, he steals hers and destroys them, perceiving them as a stumbling block to his progressing career. For Tamara, the disappearance of her lover's letters constitutes a definite end to their love story. Such memory prosthetics are a physical embodiment of the emotional and spiritual threads that connect the involved characters. Severing that liminal connection is only possible if there is a definite resolution to its realization in the nonliminal world, either by rejecting the type of love it brings, or accepting it and pursuing it in everyday physical closeness.

Coincidentally, the academic's heart condition connects him biographically with both Stuhr and Kieślowski, who died while undergoing treatment for his, and fictionally with Weronika/Véronique (Irène Jacob) in *The Double Life of Véronique* (1991). Perhaps the professor's choice is an analogue with that of Weronika/Véronique (to sing or to live) or of Kieślowski (to film or to live). He might be choosing between a barren life and an exciting love that could end his days prematurely. Stuhr's inclusion of the heart condition is Kieślowskian in that it only subtly suggests to the viewer that it is a factor in the professor's decision making. By contrast, the conclusion to the academic's story carries an unmistakably Stuhrian mark. It is obvious that in choosing his career, the academic is more likely to prolong his life, but his expulsion from the building reverberates with the words spoken by the Accountant's assistant to the departing colonel: "You'll live, but it's not much of a life." The difference in valuation of the same question by Kieślowski and Stuhr plays an even more prominent part in Stuhr's *The Big Animal.*

The Big Animal: Rationing Kieślowski

In 2000, at the time of *The Big Animal*'s release, Stuhr was in a position to do away with the anxieties that haunted him before and during the making of *Love Stories.* By then, he had made three films, so his commitment to film directing was proven. Polish critics appreciated the seriousness of his commentary on contemporary reality and Polish reality in particular, and film festival juries rewarded him for it. He managed to split his film acting between his roles in his own films and in the box office successes of *Killer* (*Kiler;* Machulski, 1997) and *2nd Killer* (*Kilerów 2-óch;* Machulski, 1999). Critical voices confining him tightly to a post-Kieślowskian discourse became less persistent, and his authorial claim on his films was less frequently questioned. It was the right moment for Stuhr to accept the challenge of a film based directly on one of Kieślowski's story ideas, rediscovered after his death.

At the beginning of 1973, Krzysztof Kieślowski signed a contract with the film unit TOR to direct *The Camel,* which was an adaptation of Kazimierz Orłoś's short story published a few months earlier in the Warsaw cultural magazine *Literatura.* In February of 1973, Orłoś's writings were banned in Poland, and consequently, so was any filming of his stories. Orłoś agreed to have his name removed from the credits; Kieślowski changed the title of the script to *The Big Animal* and tried unsuccessfully to make the film under that title in Poland and in West Germany (Stuhr, *Krzysztof Kieślowski* 99). The treatment lay dormant and forgotten until 1998, when Elizabeth Scotti found it in her files in Wiesbaden. She passed it on to Janusz Morgenstern, a Polish film director and producer, who asked Stuhr to direct it. What Stuhr received was a few pages with a sketch of a story that included two dialogues. He developed it into a seventy-minute film, giving writing credits only to Kieślowski and Orłoś.[11] In the process of realizing the film, Stuhr was motivated by two seemingly conflicting drives. On the one hand, he was mindful of the choices Kieślowski would be making in his situation (W. 66), and on the other, he discarded any Kieślowskian elements that would fall outside his own authorial sensibilities (Stuhr in Maciejewski, "Narodziny" 43). The result was praised by critics in Poland and abroad.[12]

The Big Animal opens with a circus leaving a camel behind. Mr. Sawicki (Jerzy Stuhr) and Mrs. Sawicka (Anna Dymna), a couple in their fifties, notice it while eating supper and looking out the window. They adopt the camel, which is at first welcomed by the people of the small town at the outskirts of which they live but then becomes a reason for their ostracization. Mr. Sawicki loses his position in a local orchestra, local mothers refuse to send their children to Mrs. Sawicka's for daycare, and Mr. Sawicki experiences tax problems, because a camel does not figure in a list of "taxable" animals, yet an animal must be taxed. The film ends with the camel's disappearance, to the relief of the townspeople and the distress of the Sawickis. Everything goes back to normal, and the Sawickis' longing for their lost camel is only partially satisfied by their nostalgic visit to a zoo at the end of the film.

The last zoo scene does not exist in Kieślowski's script. For both Kieślowski and Orłoś the story ends with the camel's death. Stuhr also changed the origins of the camel. In Orłoś's story, Mr. Mrówczyński (Mr. Sawicki's literary prototype) quite simply buys an old camel. In Kieślowski's treatment, the Sawickis notice a camel at the gate of their house while they are eating. For Stuhr, the camel is left behind by the departing circus. Just these two measures of altering the story's end and beginning place Stuhr's version closer to a form of no interest to Kieślowski but one favored by him, that is, a poetic fable, which protects its practitioners from the gruesomeness of seeing a loved animal dead. Even one of the two scenes for which Kieślowski wrote dialogue, although starting with the realist conventions employed in *The Scar,* is shifted by Stuhr to the register of the poetic fable when Mr. Sawicki walks out of his own trial, unnoticed.[13] The form is further accentuated by the black-and-white stock used in *The Big Animal,* which sets it apart from other contemporary television products and which connects it for some Polish critics to the "black series" of documentaries made in Poland in the 1950s on the bleak aspects of communist life (Kubisiowa 80).

Other narrative changes are influenced by Stuhr's understanding of Kieślowski's method, and the context of Stuhr's own authorial references. For instance, in Kieślowski's version (not in Orłoś's) Mr. Sawicki sings in a choir, but for Stuhr that concept had too obvious a connection with his own *A Week in the Life of a Man,* whose protagonist also sings in a choir (Stuhr, *Krzysztof Kieślowski* 11).[14] Instead, Mr. Sawicki is a clarinet player, and the scenes of his orchestra practice resemble *Sunday Musicians* (*Muzykanci*, 1960), made by Kieślowski's teacher, the renowned documentary maker Kazimierz Karabasz. Mindful of Kieślowski's usual desire to trace characters' development in a film, Stuhr expanded the role of Mrs. Sawicka. In the original script she was reduced to one descriptive comment—"Mrs Sawicka was not very fond of the camel"—after which she was to have no part in Mr. Sawicki's ordeals. Stuhr developed Mrs. Sawicka into a preschool teacher who, after initially mistrusting the big animal, succumbs to its charms, supports her husband's obsession, and is prepared to sacrifice the money saved for new furniture to build a shelter for the camel.

The script and plot development by Stuhr are in dialogue not only with Kieślowski's treatment but also with its timing. Around 1973, this would have been a politicized story of human intolerance aimed at criticizing the bureaucratic tendencies and excesses of the communist system, also captured by Kieślowski in his earlier documentary films. Orłoś's story was written within the Polish tradition of the absurd,[15] soon after the disappointment of the 1968 purges and the social unrest of 1970, so its surreal stylistics are expressive of the absurdities of the communist system. Orłoś's "The Camel" is narrated by an anonymous informer on the inappropriate appropriation of a camel by Mr. Mrówczyński, which is dangerous to the communist stabilization. Kieślowski's interests in 1973 focused still on recording the essence of Polish reality through individuals' placement within it. However, Stuhr's contemporaries would no longer be interested in that particular social reality, so Stuhr reworked his version of the story to make it an ahistorical and universalizing fable on freedom of choice by removing visual references to the time in which it was originally set.[16]

Another change between 1973 and 2000 is in the perception of Kieślowski and thus the code evoked by his name in association with any film work. In 1973, *The Big Animal* would have been the first feature film by an obsessive realist documentarist (Holland). In 2000, viewers and critics might watch it in the context either of Kieślowski's Polish feature-film phase or of his later more aestheticizing films, with their more pronounced quest for metaphysical truth. Indeed, a contemporary audience could draw on the whole varied range of Kieślowskian stylistics as reference points in Stuhr's film. A scene in a local tax office, for instance, echoes one of the first documentaries by Kieślowski, *The Office* (*Urząd,* 1966), which quickly gained cult status among his fellow students at Łódź Film School in the late 1960s. What in Kieślowski's *The Office* is a portrayal of human tragedy exacerbated by its juxtaposition with a dehumanized bureaucracy becomes, in *The Big Animal,* an exemplar of humorous absurdity. This type of recourse to the absurd is one aspect of the Polish intellectual and literary tradition that also informed Stuhr's acting style throughout his acting career. The film's black-and-whiteness may be seen not only in relation to Kieślowski's earlier films but also to his *Three Colors* trilogy. That comparison is best illustrated in an office scene after Mr. Sawicki returns from "walkies" with his camel outside the town. In response to Mr. Sawicki's poetic musings on the "yellows" and "golds" of the world outside the town, his younger female coworker says admiringly, "Mr. Sawicki, you have never spoken so beautifully before." The significance of this statement marks the stylistic difference in the treatment of color between the two directors. What in Kieślowski's *Three Colors* trilogy is a visual code and a source of phenomenological immediacy and ineffability (Kickasola), in Stuhr's filmic treatment resides in the domain of a literary, word-bound expressiveness. Interestingly, the possibility of shifts between referential codes also proves to be a source of confusion for some critics, when they are not certain whether to adopt a realist (early Kieślowski) interpretative code or a metaphorical/metaphysical (later Kieślowski) one.[17]

Conclusion

If we agree with Vincent Amiel's remark that for Kieślowski "le doute a fait son oeuvre" (31), the questioning of the extent of his legacy realized in direct or liminal references in Stuhr's films attests to that legacy's continuation. Even the motifs of Stuhr's films read by critics as derivative of Kieślowski should

For *The Big Animal* (2001), Stuhr uses black-and-white film to code his story as a poetic fable, even though his character, Mr. Sawicki (Jerzy Stuhr), comes to appreciate the color and beauty of the world as a result of his experiences with a camel. (Courtesy of Telewizja Polska)

not be approached without the possibility of doubting that connection (e.g., the pool scene in *A Week in the Life of a Man,* described earlier). When examining Stuhr's directorial work, glimpses of recognition are followed by rationalized doubt reminding us that a film director can look at the world, and then represent it, only through the prism of his own individual experience. In the case of Stuhr, he shares with Kieślowski his formative film-work experience, yet his *Love Stories, The Big Animal,* and to a lesser extent *A Week in the Life of a Man* are influenced by, but not derivative of, Kieślowski's work. Their elements, intentionally or not, are a tribute to a prominent director expressed by a colleague and a friend who has developed his own directorial approach of commentary on the condition of contemporary humanity, couched in the literary forms of the morality tale and the fable.

Whether discursive, structuralist, or commercially driven, the formulation of authorship also is subject to the forces pulling directors toward and away from one another. Nevertheless, there lies a point at the intersection of epistemological platforms that allows for authorial qualities, ill-defined and contested as they are, to persist. It is a point at which audience expectations and critics' perceptions intersect with filmmakers' stylistics and filmmaking philosophy to create a sense of identity across time and films. Regardless of what concept of authorship one employs to explore Krzysztof Kieślowski's work, its centripetal forces reassert its existence by drawing into it films like those of Jerzy Stuhr, Michał Rosa, Krzysztof Zanussi, and others discussed in this volume. Quite probably, all these authors have a similar authorial pedigree, qualified by their attraction to Kieślowski's vision.

Notes

1. The previous two are *Pedestrian Subway* (*Przejście podziemne,* 1973), a television drama of thirty minutes, and *Personnel* (*Personel,* 1975), a television feature film of seventy-two minutes. This tally does not count the unrealized *The Big Animal,* which was in the initial stages of preparation circa 1973.

2. Stuhr also appeared in Andrzej Wajda's *Rough Treatment* (*Bez znieczulenia,* 1978) and Agnieszka Holland's *Provincial Actors* (*Aktorzy prowincjonalni,* 1979) during that period, but it was *Top Dog* (1978) that defined his acting success and popularity before *Camera Buff.*

3. This essay focuses on Jerzy Stuhr's film acting, but parallel to it runs his strong theater career in Poland and in Italy. Juliusz Machulski plays the protagonist Romek in Kieślowski's *Personnel.*

4. Stuhr has complained of journalists and critics keeping a close count of the films he directs, as if mistrusting that an actor, and a comic actor for that matter, could possibly be serious about filmmaking (Stuhr in Mikos 166).

5. Interestingly, the Polish box office for *Love Stories* was higher than for any one part of the *Three Colors* trilogy. It sold 295,353 tickets with sixteen copies in circulation, while *Blue* sold 249,685 tickets with twelve copies, *White* sold 224,558 with

twenty-five copies, and *Red* 164,823 with fifteen copies. *The Big Animal* sold 70,503 tickets with twenty copies in circulation (Kucharski 348, 367).

6. For instance, in an interview with Małatyńska , Stuhr says, "I am not exaggerating when I say that [Kieślowski] taught me the truth, consequence and logic" (Małatyńska 10).

7. Before completing an acting degree at the prestigious State Theater School (PWST) in Kraków, he graduated with a master's degree in Polish from the Jagiellonian University.

8. Here, Stuhr also expresses his annoyance with the clearly morally stamped choices of the heroes of his *Love Stories.*

9. The "three-phase" distinction is employed only for the sake of simplicity, although it can be easily disputed by references to overlaps and borrowings between them. For instance, Janina Falkowska demonstrates how the distinction between the political values of Kieślowski's Polish feature films before *Decalogue* (1988) and the supposed lack thereof in his post-1989 productions can be questioned (Falkowska 136–159). In his book on Kieślowski's documentaries, Mikołaj Jazdon discusses how elements of the documentaries are used as building blocks in the feature fiction films to follow. Furthermore, Jessie Labov rightly argues that the "metaphysical" quality of Kieślowski's European coproductions is often used too liberally to differentiate between phases of his directing development because the "metaphysical" elements may also be traced to Kieślowski's earlier work (Labov 113–34, 115).

The "quest" for "ultimate reality" that Kieślowski speaks of is, coincidentally, the approach rejected by Peter Wollen as incompatible with the structuralist auteur theory (Wollen).

10. Paweł Edelman is known outside of Poland for his work on Roman Polanski's *The Pianist* (2002) and *Oliver Twist* (2005), and Taylor Hackford's *Ray* (2004). He is also the cinematographer for Stuhr's *The Big Animal.*

11. The motivation for this decision could be driven either by the recognition of the commercial viability of Kieślowski's name or Stuhr's authorial confidence in withholding his own name from the writing credits, or it could also be a compensation for not crediting Kieślowski in *Love Stories.*

12. For instance, two of the most important film critics in Poland praised *The Big Animal* for its authorial qualities (Lubelski) and for the absence of the influence of Kieślowski (Sobolewski). Similarly, in the *New York Times,* A. O. Scott referred to *The Big Animal* as a postmortem gift from Kieślowski.

13. The final version of the trial scene was not what Stuhr initially intended. After recording Kieślowski's original dialogue with its full cast and almost no cuts, Stuhr felt the realist effect of this scene was out of step with the rest of the film. Coincidentally, a large portion of the film of the Town Board scene was destroyed in the development process, so Stuhr had to do with a fragment of the recorded scene, which prompted his decision to change its register to the less realistic one.

14. Here, Stuhr also avoids making another obvious reference to Kieślowski, to *The Double Life of Véronique.*

15. Sławomir Mrożek is one of the main contemporary exemplars of that tradition. His writing may be compared to that of Eugéne Ionesco or Roland Topor.

16. In Tymbark, where *The Big Animal* was filmed, its people reacted to the camel as did those in the script: at first with curiosity and openness, and then annoyance and

displeasure (Stuhr in Mikos 147–49).

17. For instance, Artur Kłosiński argues that Stuhr's film is "stylistically chaotic" for its shifting between symbolism and realism (Kłosiński 43). Jan Olszewski sees *The Big Animal* as a belated example of the Cinema of Moral Concern, while Tadeusz Lubelski is able to differentiate clearly between the Kieślowskian referential properties of the film and Stuhr's authorial intentions.

Works Cited

Amiel, Vincent. *Kieślowski.* Paris: Editions Payot & Rivage, 1995.

Chyb, Manana. "Zrób to sam." *Film* 8 (1997): 68–70.

Ciment, Michel, and Hubert Niogret. "Pańskie filmy są rengenogramami duszy." *Film na świecie* 3–4 (1992): 26–35.

Coates, Paul. "Kieślowski and the Crisis of Documentary." *Lucid Dreams: The Films of Krzysztof Kieślowski.* Ed. Paul Coates. Trowbridge: Flicks Books, 1999. 32–53.

Falkowska, Janina. "*The Double Life of Véronique* and *Three Colours:* An Escape from Politics?" *Lucid Dreams: The Films of Krzysztof Kieślowski.* Ed. Paul Coates. Trowbridge: Flicks Books, 1999. 136–59.

Grabowski, Christopher. "Przestrzeń, czas i bohater." *Kwartalnik Filmowy* 24 (1998): 29–54.

Haltof, Marek. *The Cinema of Krzysztof Kieślowski: Variations on Destiny and Chance.* London: Wallflower Press, 2004.

Holland, Agnieszka. "Interview with Filmmaker Agnieszka Holland." *The Scar* (1976). DVD. Directed by Krzysztof Kieślowski. Artificial Eye, 2003.

Horton, Andrew James. "More than Education." *Kinoeye* 2.5 (4 March 2002). http://www.kinoeye.org/02/05/horton05.php.

Janicka, Bożena. "Beze mnie." *Film* 43 (1988): 3–5.

Jazdon, Mikołaj. *Dokumenty Kieślowskiego.* Poznań: Wydawnictwo Poznańskie, 2002.

Kickasola, Joseph G. *The Films of Krzysztof Kieślowski: The Liminal Image.* London: Continuum, 2004.

Kieślowski, Krzysztof, and Hiroshi Takahashi. "Piękne hasła i tajemnica." *Kino* 9 (1993): 11–12.

Kłosiński, Artur. "*Duże Zwierzę.*" *Cinema Polska* 8 (2000): 42–43.

Kot, Wiesław. "Szara strefa." *Wprost* 873 (22 August 1999): 22.

Kuba. "Sądne dni." *Film* 9 (1999): 69–70.

Kubisiowa, Katarzyna. "Bez morałów." *Film* 9 (1999): 80.

Kucharski, Krzysztof. *Kino Plus: Film i dystrybucja w Polsce 1990–2000.* Toruń: Oficyna Wydawnicza Kucharski, 2002.

Labov, Jessi. "Kieślowski's *Dekalog,* Everyday Life, and the Art of Solidarity." *Screening the City.* Ed. Mark Shiel and Tony Fitzmaurice. London: Verso, 2003. 113–34.

Lewin, Ludwik. "'Ja nie szukam odpowiedzi, ja stawiam pytania.'" *Tygodnik Powszechny* 6 (1993): 7.

Litka, Piotr. "Najważniejszy jest dialog." *Kino* 12 (1999): 22–24.

———. "Zrobiłem film, z którego jestedm dumny." *Jerzy Stuhr: Duże Zwierzę.* http://film.onet.pl/oficjalne/duze_zwierze/rozmowa.html.

Lubelski, Tadeusz. "Mieć wielbłąda." *Kino* 7–8 (2000): 38–39.

Maciejewski, Łukasz. "Narodziny nietolerancji." *Cinema Polska* 8 (2000): 43–44.
———. "Piękno, które czyni człowieka lepszym." *Cinema Polska* 9 (1999): 76–77.
Małatyńska, Maria. "Na razie jest cisza." *Przekrój* 7 (1993): 10–11.
Michalak, Bartosz, and Rafał Stec. "'Nie jestem Bergmannem.'" *Kino* 5 (1997): 4–7.
Mikos, Marek. *Jerzy Stuhr: Udawać naprawdę*. Kraków: Znak, 2000.
Olszewski, Jan. "Wielbłąd na biegunach." *Film* 9 (2000): 81.
Orzechowska, Joanna. "Widownia jest podobna do mnie." *Kino* 5 (1991): 40–41.
Scott. A. O. "A Ruminating Newcomer Stirs Things Up." *The New York Times*. 6 September 2004. http://www.polishculture-nyc.org/stuhr_reviews.htm.
Sobolewski, Tadeusz. "Bajka o szczęściu." *Gazeta Wyborcza* 198 (2000): 13.
Spula, Jarosław. "Kieślowski-konkret i metafizyka." *Film na świecie* 3–4 (1993): 111–12.
Stachówna, Grażyna. "Jerzy Stuhr—amator profesjonalista." *Autorzy kina polskiego*. Ed. Grażyna Stachówna and Joanna Wojnicka. Kraków: Rabid, 2004. 155–70.
———. "Trzy Kolory—nasze miejsce w Europie." *Dialog* 1 (1995): 104–7.
Stok, Danusia. *Kieślowski on Kieślowski*. London: Faber and Faber, 1995.
Stuhr, Jerzy. "Dobry człowiek Filip Mosz." *Film* 52 (1991): 28. Excerpt from Jerzy Stuhr, *Sercowa choroba*. Warsaw: Czytelnik, 2002.
———. *Krzysztof Kieślowski: Duże zwierzę*. Kraków: Znak, 2000.
———. "Mam przemożną chęć opowiedzenia o zmaganiu się mężczyzny z uczuciem." *Cinema Polska* 3 (1997): 65.
Stuhr, Jerzy, and Krzysztof Piesiewicz. "Goście Starego Teatru: Spotkanie dwudzieste drugie." *Teatr* 10–12 (1999): 60–65.
W., S. "Garbus." *Film* 8 (2000): 66.
Wollen, Peter. "The *auteur* theory (extract)." *Theories of Authorship*. Ed. John Caughie. London: Routledge & Kegan Paul, 1981. Originally published in Peter Wollen, *Signs and Meaning in the Cinema*. London: Secker & Warburg, 1967 and 1972.
Wysogląd, Monika. "Scenariusze dopiero powstają." *Film* 29 (1986): 18–19.
Zarębski, Konrad J. "*Przypadek*." *Filmowy Serwis Prasowy* 5 (1987): 16–18.
———. "Zapadło to we mnie." *Kino* 10 (2003): 52.
Zawiśliński, Stanislaw. *Kieślowski: Ważne, żeby iść*. Izabelin: Skorpion, 2005.

4

Form Is the Key, and Lessons in Kieślowski

An Interview with Jerzy Stuhr

Renata Murawska

This interview was conducted in person in a two-hour session on Friday, 17 February 2006, a sunny winter day, in Jerzy Stuhr's office at the State Theater School (PWST), which is next to Kraków's magnificent medieval old-town square, the biggest in Europe.

RM: How did you meet Krzysztof Kieślowski?

JS: It happened in spring 1975. I remember because my son was just about to be born. I was already a rising theater actor under the wings of Andrzej Wajda and Konrad Swinarski, and a student of Jerzy Jarocki. Those three dealt all the cards in one of the greatest eruptions of theatrical creativity. I was in love with the theater. It was my dream come true and my mission. At the time, I was playing in *Forefathers' Eve,*[1] Swinarski's famous production. I was Wojtek Pszoniak's[2] replacement in [Dostoyevsky's] *The Possessed,* directed by Wajda, and I was Jarocki's assistant. Everything was falling into place. I was in the best Polish theater. Wonderful atmosphere.

Then, one night after a performance of *Forefathers' Eve,* the concierge says, "Some Kieślowski is waiting for you downstairs." Kieślowski was already a popular documentarist, but documentaries did not inspire us young actors. So there he stands, a sad guy in spectacles, and he says, "I'm a documentary director and I'm making a feature-film debut. I want to give you a role in that film, except that role hasn't yet been written. It is just sketched out in a few scenes and if you don't accept it, I will delete it." So I say, "Mr. Kieślowski, this is not a very encouraging proposition; the role hasn't been written. I can't see it."

I went home, threw away that screenplay, but then started to think that it could be a chance to enter the unfamiliar film industry. On the one hand, it was not good that he was a novice, but on the other, we could get along because I also had no experience with film. I also had some kind of a complex that cinema was not interested in me. I worked a lot in television, gaining experience with the camera. Apart from that, I was in variety shows, and that was where Kieślowski spotted me first. Maybe he noticed me because of our common sense of humor. Not because of the theater. He wasn't interested in it that much.

I don't really know what made me decide to get involved with that man. Rationally, all was against it. I'm sure it was something irrational. One never knows. It proved to be the decision of my life. I left my wife with a one-week-old baby and went to the petrochemical works in Płock for a month, in summer. There, I spent a month with Kieślowski around grubby factories [shooting *The Scar* (1976)].

After a week I already knew I had next to me someone very familiar, who thought like me and could influence me. I didn't like anyone influencing me, that's why I never belonged to any parties, associations, unions. I had never wanted to have anyone [influence me], and he was the first person to do it. After two weeks on the set I felt some kind of relief. Those fetters of the theater, of words, of characters; you cannot change or add anything; you have to fit in, which is also beautiful, that your interpretation is so confined by a costume,

Stuhr's first appearance for Kieślowski was in a minor role in *The Scar* (1976), but Kieślowski immediately responded to Stuhr's improvisational ability, and Stuhr gloried in the freedom of film acting.

confined by everything that surrounds you, by the director's comments. And suddenly, all that freedom.

I remember that a great argument "for" [getting involved in the film] was that Franciszek Pieczka was the lead, because he was in the top echelon at the time, a splendid actor. I had seen him in the theater, and it was something to perform with him. However, on the set Pieczka could not come to an understanding with Kieślowski. They were two different generations. He detested improvisation. He was an actor who had to have all the tools given so he could sculpt with them. And there we had, "Let's improvise." Kieślowski would put real engineers in front of us. What was there to talk about with them? You couldn't find a topic at all, but there was something exciting in how he would tell me in points: "You will talk with that engineer about this, this, this and that . . ." I had to learn more about OHS [Organizational Health and Safety], etc.[3] The poor engineer didn't know I was manipulating that conversation.

After two weeks Krzysiek told me he would write me another role, and the next film we would make together. And he wrote *The Calm* (1976). That's how it started. He taught me film acting despite not being a teacher. He used to tell me a lot about what he likes. For instance, he showed me his documentaries for hours and would say, "This guy touches me." There, on the screen, some guy sat crushing a cigarette. I thought, "What's so touching about this?" The point was he had nothing to say because of the situation he was in. It was in *Curriculum Vitae* (1975), in which he was thrown out from the party. What was he to say? The party meant a job and much more. The guy was crushing his cigarette and that was touching.

RM: How did it happen that you ended up writing dialogue for* The Calm*?

JS: It was supposed to be set in Warsaw. It took place among workers, bricklayers. Kieślowski still used amateurs. I said, "Krzysiek, it's all fine, but if you throw me in among Warsaw bricklayers, I cannot talk like them, with that slang, that dialect, that Warsaw Volapük. We would have to write that I came from somewhere else. And in the script it is the other way around: that he comes back to the place where the prison is. I can't learn it [the dialect] in three days, even a week; I would always be linguistically different, and I know for you I would have to speak the way they speak. If you moved it to Kraków and we all started speaking the Krakówian way, I would know how, because I was born there." You can hear it in my voice, this sing-song accent. And he moved the action to Kraków so I could have that comfort. That's why we hired Jurek Trela and others who could speak our way. Linguistically, you could compare it to Ken Loach's films.

RM: You mentioned working with amateur actors. How did Kieślowski used to find participants for his early films?

JS: There were fewer amateur actors in his next films. In *The Calm* there were still real prisoners. They sat next to me in a cell. There were no casting agencies or castings at that time. I was his casting agent because I knew actors in southern Poland. I remember how he tormented me about Socha's character in *The Calm:* "He has to be like our set decorator Michał Szulkiewicz." There was no actor like him, so the set decorator had to do. We listened in on him. He had a funny saying: when he wanted a piece of bread or something, he used to say, "Sorry to cross your portion."[4] Kieślowski had that ear, a type of hearing, Karabasz's school.

RM: Working on* The Calm *and later* Camera Buff *(1979), did you notice any changes in Kieślowski's directing method?

JS: In *The Scar,* the first film, there were kilometers of improvising, kilometers of film, then editing. He started to tire of the documentary technique. He felt he needed different dramaturgy. For *Camera Buff* (1979) he told me: "We have to do something with it. We have to write it all first and then play it as if it was improvised." Dialogues for *Camera Buff* were different. They were written strictly. I remember that actor who played the manager, the late Mr. [Stefan] Czyżewski from Poznań, had a terrible problem. He learnt his role like an old-school actor, and we would rewrite the dialogue overnight to get it right. In the morning, Kieślowski was embarrassed to go and see him. I used to go and say, "Mr Funiu, this text is a bit different now," and he would say, "Jesus, but I've already memorized the previous one." I knew how much he suffered. Franek Pieczka was the same with Kieślowski, but us youngsters, we still had a good memory to join in the game.

***RM: How much creative freedom did you have working on the character of Filip Mosz in* Camera Buff?**

JS: I definitely had more freedom in *Top Dog* (Feliks Falk, 1978). I made up whole sequences, because that [compèring] used to be my previous profession. *Camera Buff* was more disciplined. However, I did have some input. Krzysiek was jealous of one scene at the end of the film, after Filip's wife left. He wakes up, empty house, and then a doorbell. Obviously, together with Filip, we all go, "Oh, the wife and the little daughter are back." He runs, opens the door, and there is a guy, "You forgot to put a milk bottle out." During communism they used to deliver milk to your door. I said to Krzysiek, "I walk to the kitchen and there is a full milk bottle. I grab it, click, pour the milk out, give the guy an empty bottle, and take a full one." Kieślowski went, "You pour the milk out because you don't need it, meaning no family. Why didn't I come up with this?"

RM: You said a few years ago* Camera Buff *was the peak of your cooperation with Kieślowski. Do you still see it the same way?

JS: Not necessarily. That was the film that threw Kieślowski into different, European waters. I keep hearing about it when I'm at international festivals. When Wolfgang Becker of *Good Bye Lenin!* (2003) met me in São Paulo, he said, "*Camera Buff!* I went to film school because of you. When I saw *Camera Buff* I was an engineer." It was the first role I got an acting award for, in Gdynia,[5] leaving the censored films for good. Nobody saw *The Calm*. That was a shame because I gave a great performance in it. I still think it was one of my best performances. It was important to me that the group called the Cinema of Moral Concern accepted me as their representative. It impressed me that it was me, Agnieszka Holland, then Kieślowski, and all of us under the aegis of Zanussi and Wajda. Suddenly *Camera Buff* became very important to me.

RM: You've echoed Kieślowski in different interviews that a perfect dialogue is when two people on the screen are silent, and a third one in the audience knows why.

JS: I repeat it in every directing class at the faculty named after Kieślowski in Katowice. Yet, you will never reach that ideal. Kieślowski meant by it that you should avoid like hell informative dialogue. You have to inform the viewer, but you have to weave this information in almost haphazardly. The best way is through behavior. It was the school of American actors, the Strasberg Studio, Kazan, through which I discovered that I could do it with behavior. Fillip Mosz wouldn't be the same without hiccups. As his film is shown at a festival, he's walking along the hallway hiccupping. In one of the most beautiful erotic scenes I've shot in my life, I'm hiccupping while being unfaithful to my wife. A beautiful woman approaches me, naked, and when I snuggle to her breasts, and everything is about to happen, and . . . bloody hell . . . hiccups.

RM: I don't recall that scene. What film was it in?

JS: In *Camera Buff*. Krzysztof threw it away. He said, "No, he shouldn't betray his wife."

The story of *Camera Buff*'s ending is also telling. It reflects Krzysiek's sense of ethics. *Camera Buff* was supposed to end with what is now the second-last scene. The hero finds out that his artistic activity may hurt somebody, so he runs to the post office and he recovers the material he has just posted. He tears into it, opens the tin with the negative, exposes it, and symbolically throws the roll away. That was to be the ending. I shaved my moustache, and

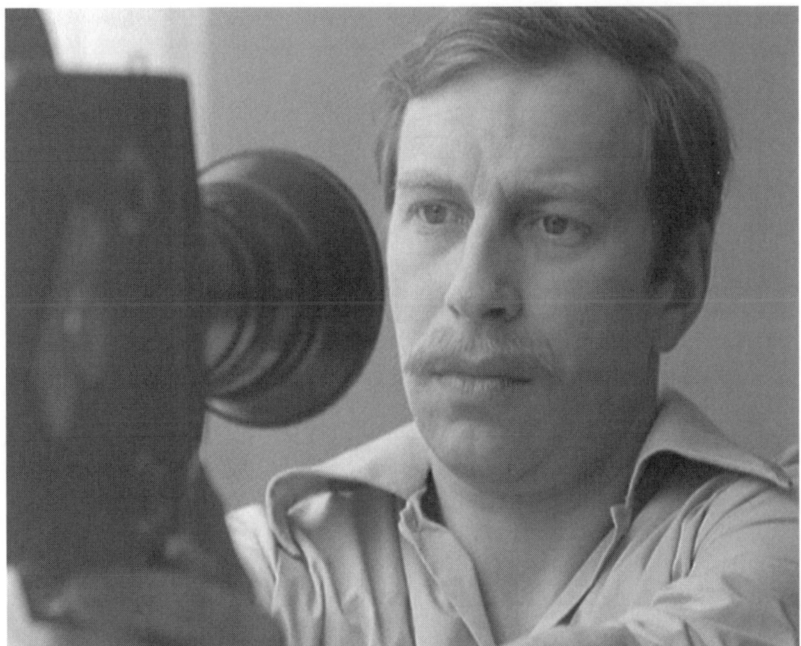

Kieślowski's decision to make a new ending for *Camera Buff* (1979) in which Filip Mosz (Jerzy Stuhr) turns his film camera on himself reflects what Stuhr has indeed done with his own films.

two weeks later I heard, "There is going to be a new ending." I said, "I have no moustache." He said, "Glue it on. Different ending." "Why, Krzysiu?" He said, "Because it's not true what we've shot. Are you going to stop making films? Am I? So what are we saying? [No,] we won't do it." You see the lesson? It's about the artist and his responsibility, and the agreement of what you say with your internal code of ethics. I arrived in Łódź, and he told me to take the camera and direct it at myself. He didn't write this dialogue. He told me to do it in my own words. I retold what I remembered from the beginning of the film. That scene went down in the history of world cinema. For me it was also a prophetic gesture. At some stage of my life I also directed the camera at myself and started telling people stories about me, because every film I've directed deals with my problems.

RM: One factor that motivated Kieślowski's work was fear, fear of an accident, unexpected changes in life, or fear of the future. And for you?

JS: No. Absolutely not. This is exactly what sets us apart. When my *A Week in the Life of a Man* (1999) was shown at the Venice Festival, the next day I bought newspapers with reviews. *La Republica* wrote: "Jerzy Stuhr, Kieślowski's successor." In *Corriere della Sera:* "Jerzy Stuhr, Kieślowski's epigone."

RM: How did you react?

JS: With laughter. They are serious newspapers: *Corriere* and *La Republica.* One somewhat to the right and the other to the left. I thought, "No, you don't know anything. I know exactly what I've got from him and what I will never get." Precisely that metaphysical stream, searching for god, darker matters, that tormented him all his life.

RM: Then, is fear foreign to you?

JS: Yes. I mean it is not my motivation. It's also somewhere there, but I'm motivated by curiosity. For example, in the film I'm writing now I'm curious why some people get together, then they leave each other and they find others. How does that work? The film will be called *Pageant.* That's how people seek others. It's not in the pejorative sense that they betray their partners, but they only search for one another in life. And what do they know about each other? How little they know. Yet that interests me, not scares, and this is the difference. Kieślowski used to ask me, "Why don't you have any problems?" "Because I have faith." "And that's it?" he asked. I said, "That's it."

RM: After so many hours, weeks, and months of working together, something of Kieślowski must have rubbed off on you and your films.

JS: Working methods. A film director is someone who can transfer what's in his head onto the crew so they think like him. Sometimes I look at these students of mine in Katowice, how they can't rig up an explication of their ideas to me. How will you explain what you want to cameramen, costumiers, make-up artists, if you can't stutter it out to me? One must be like a gendarme who can explain his film to the crew in the simplest possible way, and Krzysiek could do it splendidly. We all knew what he wanted. His irresolutions gave him nightmares, but in the morning he would say, "You must be able to answer all questions. You cannot say 'I don't know.'" That's when you energize the whole group. That's what I learnt from him. And how to talk with actors. Script. About 90 percent of film mistakes lie in the script, so that's where you have to focus most intensely to eliminate them. Write a third, fourth, and fifth version. These are his teachings. More generally, I'm interested in films about people. For example, I don't play in historical films. Recently, I refused a role in a Russian film where Daniel Olbrychski would be the lead. I said no to Wajda's *Pan Tadeusz* (1999) and *Revenge* (2002).[6] To Wajda! Do you know how hard it was? Kieślowski would sneer at me when I performed in the theater. He would phone me, "What dresses is the actor wearing today?" and I would say, "Krzysiu, don't sneer. It's a serious play, *Hamlet*."

RM: What exactly have you learnt from Kieślowski about scriptwriting?

JS: I didn't understand what Krzysiek was talking about then, "Scriptwriting and editing. The rest, what happens on the set, is a drudgery." I see it now. When you are writing, it's wonderful, you run a whole world. His other observation that I didn't understand was, "If you construct characters well, their relationships and their personalities, what they could do and what they would never do, starting at the twentieth page, the script writes itself." Only now, when writing *Pageant,* I can see it; the script writes itself and I just do a kind of a crossword. You just have to abide by its logic. "No, this girl wouldn't do it, wouldn't say that." "This boy would want to fib, but it's getting harder for him because he's already under the influence of that girl." So the girl says, "Listen, if you lie again I'm deleting you from my mobile." That means, "I'm erasing you completely." That's how they talk nowadays. It's writing itself. You're just like the puppeteer in *The Double Life of Véronique* (1991). You run it. You must be hellishly precise at the beginning defining the characters, and then you just throw them into different contexts. There is a great glee in throwing these people into more and more extreme circumstances. It's not about sitting on the beach. What circumstance is that? But if someone drowned there? So it's set in motion and it writes itself.

RM: You've spoken about working with actors, about scriptwriting. Was there anything you learnt from Kieślowski about editing?

JS: That's harder because I was never involved in that process. Ever. The actor's duty was over. You finished your material. That's why I would always tell my students, "Don't imagine you play a role in a film. Forget it. You just deliver some acting material. You make faces, do some talking, and then if someone creates a role out of it, lucky you; go get drunk and have a mass said for your joy. If not, collect your dough and get out." That's how it is, because I [as a director] can do anything: make a small role large, a large one small, cut something out, change the voice; I've done it all. In the theater, when the curtain is up, you are the king. And here? I modify it, a face from one scene, a close-up from another. I edit it. It's all in my hands.

RM: Kieślowski started with documentary, which was an attempt to describe the world and reality that surrounded him. Later he moved away from describing it, so he could . . .

JS: . . . express it.

RM: You started directing with* An Index of Lovers, *a theatrical and literary film with Brechtian overtones.

JS: Yes, formally it is Brechtian. There were comments like that. It was intentional. Each of my films has its roots in literature. *Tomorrow's Weather* (2003) is a diary. *The Big Animal* (2000) is a fable. *A Week in a Life of a Man* is diary notes from seven days. *Love Stories* (1997) is a morality tale. Everyman. Jederman. *An Index of Lovers* (1995) is a Brechtian grotesque. Form is the key. If you try, you could make up three subjects for important films that have to be made. But how? It's easy to say: about love, love stories. But how? When everyone has already said that 1,500 times, and we know it all. So all anguish is about form. These were my arguments with Kieślowski while making *Love Stories*. The film is dedicated to him because it was the last script he consulted on with me and tended to. He was bending me toward psychology a lot. I would say, "No, it's a fable, a morality tale." "What morality tale?" he would say. That's how he would try to psychologize me.

In my search for form, I rely on different genres. At the moment, mixing genres excites me most. Here, I turn to my great master Fellini, who could transform artificiality, which is the cinema's enemy, into film matter. That's why *Tomorrow's Weather* is a comedy-drama, which balances seriousness and humor. It is this balance, these ups and downs, that interest me. To cultivate this field you have to have thirty-something years of experience with audiences, and none of my director friends have that knowledge. Why has Andrzej Wajda been holding on to the theater? So he can listen to people. It is different in cinema. So when I'm writing a script, I think, "Ah! Here they should laugh. They have to laugh. I will tear them a bit. Now I can focus them." I work with them as if I were performing in front of them. While writing. Hardly anyone cultivates that field, and that could be my signature. Internationally, I'm now starting to be perceived as a representative of a certain type of cinema.

RM: How is it described?

JS: It's referred to as auteur cinema, or "psychological." In the explanation of the [Robert] Bresson award I received at the Venice Festival in 2005, it was referred to as a cinema in search of values. It's a cinema not afraid to speak of values.

When I was on Czech TV with Miloš Forman, he spoke of the difference between European and American films: "In an American film, bad guys fight good guys. They go on fighting. Eventually, the good guys win. In a European film, bad guys fight good guys, but after five minutes you see that the baddies are not that bad and the goodies are not that good. And the winner is nobody." Forman is right. I'm not interested anymore in such gadding about [characteristic of European cinema]. And that's why some Polish critics say, "the intolerable didacticism of Jerzy Stuhr's films again tells us what to do." Well, yes. I read such drivel and then meet the audience, where a woman or a man stands up and says, "Mr Jerzy, thank you that you have showed us the way; no one does it."

RM: In those accusations of didacticism there is also a note of comparison with Kieślowski. He asks questions, you give answers.

JS: No, in my opinion I give hope. Sometimes this hope is very slender, yet I would never end my film in a nihilistic way. That's why I find writing film endings most difficult; do I still give hope, or am I already a didactical professor who says, "Do it this way, not any other"? It's hard to write it so you could leave the cinema thinking, "Life can be better."

RM: Is it a coincidence that in* Love Stories *there are a priest and a scoundrel who make choices that lead to their salvation?

JS: No, it's not a coincidence. This is the symmetry of a morality tale. Everyman meets allegories of good and evil. Two [of the four protagonists] choose good and two don't. If you asked me who I felt for, sometimes I was more moved by those who didn't choose, because it's harder for them to be left behind in a dark hall. They are pushed away. Alienated. For the drug dealer, choosing love is not a civilized, intellectual choice, not even one motivated by an internal code of ethics or morality. It's a different choice. For me, the priest's choice was the hardest because he was prepared to sacrifice something. And the dealer just loves her, he can't help it, and she betrays, steals from him. The guy is in prison so the sympathy is already on his side, and she betrays, steals, swindles. It was a hard role, but Kasia Figura performed it beautifully. People had to like her, and they did. That's great acting.

RM: Following Kieślowski's suggestions, you added mothers of the main four characters to* Love Stories, *but one is missing.

JS: Yes, she didn't fit. It's about that declarativeness I was talking about. A great actress, Maria Kościałkowska from *Decalogue 8* (1988), played her, but then the editor said, "We already know that, what she says to you." So one sacrifices that structure to keep the story concise.

RM: While writing* Love Stories, *you thought of particular actors.

JS: That wasn't a good idea. Now I can see that Krzysiek was right.

RM: He used to write roles for particular people, also for you.

JS: But when I gave him the script with the cast for *Love Stories,* he said, "What for? Why should I already imagine Figura in this role? I don't want to." For me then, writing was easier that way. In my last film, however, I imagine the face, but it doesn't mean that I'll hire that person. I cannot get too attached, but that perfect face is somewhere there, inside me. I don't write female characters too precisely. I leave more freedom for women. Gosia [Dobrowolska] could say something about it. When she came [from Australia to Poland to shoot *A Week in the Life of a Man*], I told her what character I was after. I said, "Help me there; I don't know what a woman feels in this situation." For instance, she finds out she has no maternal instinct. She would write monologues, and I would say, "Too much. We've done this. We know that. This is great." I only guided her.

RM: As with your work with Kieślowski. How did your collaboration with him evolve over time?

JS: At the beginning he was learning too. The blind lead the lame. Later, when he already knew, he just pulled the strings. One must remember that the directing method does not depend on the director but on the type of a crew you're working with, the duration of shooting, technical resources and support at your disposal. Resources available to Krzysiek would change with time. His work conditions improved. He was surrounded by a growing production machine, big money.

He used to love my stories about villagers [from where I have a summer house in the Polish Highlands], but when I arrived on the set of *White* (1994) and started again about my Highlanders, he listened for a while and then pulled me aside and said, "Man, stop telling these jokes." I said, "C'mon, Krzysiu, relax." Him, "These Frenchies have no idea what you're talking about and they think we're wasting time."

RM: Are you suggesting there was a price for these changes in work conditions?

JS: His way to the feature film was already complicated and was an ethical choice. He started to feel the weight of interfering with the personal lives of others. When *Night Porter's Point of View* (1978) won the Short Film Festival in Kraków, I sat next to him at the winners' screening, when the whole audience roared with laughter after the porter said whom he was going to persecute. Krzysiek sat there with his head down. Afterward, Agnieszka Holland said, "What a character you've made." So it went on. In a feature film you can create a world without hurting anyone. At worst, some actor would fall into alcoholism because he expelled too much energy. But this is already on his private account.

RM: You spoke of Kieślowski's lessons in acting. What acting experience did you bring in with you to his films?

JS: I learned acting at acting school. Above all, you have to learn how you look on the screen, whether your usual expression looks credible on the screen, or maybe it is over the top. I watched myself for hours. It all started with a terrible shock when I first saw myself walking from behind. I said, "Damn, I thought I was walking like James Dean and here is some plumpy, flop-floppy guy walking. Clip-clop, clip-clop. Is this how I walk?" That was the first lesson. You have to learn your behavior, your face. Because it is not how you imagine it is. That's what Krzysiek always used to say, "No . . . act as if your hair was unwashed." It was his famous saying. And what it meant was that everyone washes their hair so it's nicer and fluffier, but that actually blurs your image.

You start with self-knowledge, and then you have to know what you act with. Do you act with your whole body or just the face? In the first scene of *Love Stories,* I use the whole frame. Once, Zanussi and I were on Italian television talking about Polish cinema, and they showed this fragment. I felt embarrassed that they showed my film, but Zanussi commented that this scene should be shown in film schools all around the world to demonstrate how an actor could use the awareness of a frame to construct a character, in this case, with walking. A colonel who spent his whole life in the army would walk in a particular way, differently than a guy clothed in jeans and sports shoes.

RM: You often speak in your films and interviews of the significance of our daily choices.

JS: These choices are the whole point. My characters very often have problems taking responsibility. Love in *Love Stories* is about taking responsibility for somebody else. That's love. Anything else is just fascination, infatuation, delusion.

I never did much loving in films in which I acted. I did sex, but not love. Maybe just in *Camera Buff,* where there was some kind of a relationship; I loved her and paid the price. That's the only intimate thread. So, I had to write love for myself, either pairing me up with four women, or a camel, or in a very close relationship with Gosia in *A Week in the Life of a Man,* or the unfortunate love of the unfortunate father in *Tomorrow's Weather.*

RM: When working on your films, do you ever invoke Kieślowski?

JS: Always. While shooting *Tomorrow's Weather* with Edek Kłosiński, every single day when there was something we didn't know, we would ask each other how Krzysiek would do it. Then, everything became clear: "Krzysiek would definitely scale it down." It's with me everyday. There is no other person I would keep referring to in this way. And, I still like watching his films. If I come across them somewhere at night, I always stay to watch. I know them by heart. I know what is going to be said next. Everything. But now I pay attention to different things: production and things that I might need today. It's kind of a lesson.

RM: Some critics compared the swimming pool scenes in* A Week in the Life of a Man *to those in Kieślowski's* Blue *(1993). But if I understand well, their motivation was different.

JS: This wasn't my idea but Edek's [Kłosiński]. In my script Borowski is shaving in front of the mirror, where he reviews the shreds of his daily arrangements. That's how it was in the script, but Edek said, "Am I supposed to show some guy shaving? Give me a swimming pool, some space." I liked the idea. I didn't think about *Blue* at all. I liked the swimming pool because it gave me a chance to return there in the last scene with those girls and lurid heterosexual encounters. I liked that at the end he could fall into this pool. For Ozon, a whole film happens at the swimming pool, so should it also be compared to Kieślowski? How many other films are there with someone swimming?

I was more afraid of the Accountant in *Love Stories.* I even panicked and wanted to delete the fountain pen and those little ink drops. I wanted to erase it because it was so metaphysical, that a drop fell and the guy lost. I couldn't because the Accountant's fingers were stained with ink, and if we cut that scene out, the viewer would ask, "And why are his fingers dirty?" I was afraid of *The Big Animal,* that it's a whole script. But strangely enough, I was compared least with Kieślowski in the case of *The Big Animal.* Paradoxically, it's his script and my film. Everything he wrote is in the film, and 70 percent comes from elsewhere; he didn't write it.

RM: How did you work on that script?

JS: This film was a present. Mr. Janusz Morgenstern phoned me to inform me about the recovered script. Once we started to make it, Krzysztof's widow also found some other version. Morgenstern said, "I'm sending you the script," and soon the script arrived at my hotel. I opened the envelope and there were five pages in it. I said, "Janusz, where, what script? This is a treatment, a short story." "Yes, but you will do it . . ." "I can't tell you now if I can do it. Give me a month to think about it." I took a month to think about the structure. Let me give you an example. In Krzysiek's script, there was one sentence written about Mrs. Sawicka: "Mrs Sawicka was not very fond of the camel." The end. I had to construct the whole character, make her a childcare worker, make her sew and knit for the camel. It wasn't there, but I knew how Krzysiek worked with actors and how he constructed characters in *The Calm*, *Camera Buff*, or even in *Decalogue 10* (1988). Later on, I lost touch with it, and was just executing tasks in *White* [rather than also contributing in other ways].

RM: In* The Big Animal *and your other films one can feel the Polish literary tradition of the absurd. Is it close to you?

JS: I'm its child. I'm a philologist by education. I was shaped by Witkacy, Gombrowicz, Mrozek, and the ethical and moral system underwriting them.[7] I understand it as a sense of our Polish provincialism and the ability to make fun of it. For instance, serious Polish historical events first amuse me and then enrage. Martial law, terror, tanks, arrests—I'm called in by the Security Office myself—dangerous issues, but my first instinct is to laugh. Furthermore, Andrzej Wajda held it against me in *An Index of Lovers*. In it, I'm telling a Swede that a student was killed in the gate where we are standing, and the Swede just shakes mud off his shoe. What does he care? Wajda told me, "Jurek, there are things you must not mock," as if he'd forgotten that he threw a hero on the rubbish heap [in *Ashes and Diamonds* (1958)]. These are weighty matters, but I continue to look for the absurd in them.

***RM: Do you also reach for it in the script of* Pageant?**

JS: In *Pageant* I deal with genres I have never cultivated before. From a thriller to a romantic comedy, and on the way a little bit of our reality, like a pinch of pepper. It's always with me, I want it to be in the background. Plus, this is going to be the first film I will not act in. Juliusz Machulski, who is that film's producer, told me, "At last you will prove yourself as director."

RM: What kind of a director would you like to be remembered as, and is there a master that guides you to achieve that memory?

JS: Konrad Swinarski was my great master. If you asked me if I have ever met a great artist, at once I would tell you: Konrad Swinarski, and then, later, I would say Krzysiek Kieślowski. It's not about creativity. It's about Swinarski's attitude toward life, that you have to lose yourself, burn away, that you will never ever have your private life as you imagined, that you have to live differently or stop doing it at all. Swinarski lost himself in what he did, he lost his health, burnt away. And I thought this was the only way to do it.

RM: Thank you very much.

Notes

1. *Forefathers' Eve* [*Dziady*] is a poetic drama written by Adam Mickiewicz

(1798–1855), considered the greatest Polish national poet, especially of the Romantic period.

2. Wojciech (diminutive Wojtek) Pszoniak (1942–), known for his film roles in Andrzej Wajda's *The Promised Land* (1975) and *Danton* (1983).

3. In the 1970s, the issues of Organizational Health and Safety (OHS) were a significant point of emphasis for plants' management.

4. Polish: "Przepraszam, że przez porcję."

5. Gdynia is the site of the annual Polish Feature Film Festival.

6. *Pan Tadeusz* (Wajda, 1999) is an adaptation of a Romantic epic by Adam Mickiewicz, written entirely in verses of thirteen-syllable lines. The film involved the upper echelons of the Polish acting world and was a great box-office success in Poland, selling over 6 million tickets. *Revenge* (Wajda, 2000) is a film adaptation of a popular theater comedy by Aleksander Fredro (1793–1876), a Polish Romantic playwright. Again, it was a tremendous box office success, with almost 2 million tickets sold, and star casting, including Roman Polanski.

7. Witkacy (Stanisław Witkiewicz) (1885–1939), Witold Gombrowicz (1904–1969), and Sławomir Mrożek (1940–) belong to the Polish literary tradition of the absurd characterized by surreal mockery of social realities and human foibles.

II. The European Legacy

5

After Kieślowski

Voyages in European Cinema

Emma Wilson

> Our psyches seem to be so constructed that we need and desire an imagined "other"—either a glimmering, craved, idealized other, or an other that is dark, savage, and threatening. —Eva Hoffman, *Exit into History*

This chapter explores Kieślowski's legacy in two senses. Specifically, I am concerned with his influence on two directors who worked as assistant directors on the set of films in the *Three Colors* trilogy. These directors, Emmanuel Finkiel and Julie Bertuccelli, have made their own mark in European cinema in the years following Kieślowski's early demise. Their particular achievement has been to develop the potential imminent in Kieślowski's work—both Polish and transnational—for the exploration of bilingual and diasporic identity. More broadly, beyond Kieślowski's personal influence on these particular directors, I set out to question here the ways in which contemporary film in French, taking its cue from Kieślowski, has moved on to explore the experience of the exile and the immigrant within a new historical frame—that of the late 1990s and early part of the new century—yet with a melancholy and commitment familiar from Kieślowski's work. Generational influence, filiation, and departure are themes in films by Bertuccelli, Finkiel, and others who allude to Kieślowski yet claim their material boldly, with new independence.

Emmanuel Finkiel, a former student at the Femis film school, worked first as an assistant director on a film by Jean-Louis Bertuccelli about a family reunion (*Aujourd'hui peut-être . . .* [1991]). He then went on to work as assistant director with Kieślowski on *Three Colors: Blue* (1993), *Three Colors: White* (1994), and *Three Colors: Red* (1994), before making his own debut films, the short *Madame Jacques on the Croisette* (*Madame Jacques sur la Croisette,* 1997) and the feature *Voyages* (1999), which won the youth award at Cannes in 1999 and two César awards, including the one for best first film. Jean-Louis Bertuccelli's daughter, Julie, studied philosophy before going on to make documentary films. She also worked as apprentice assistant director and apprentice editor on her father's *Aujourd'hui peut-être . . .*, as assistant director on *Blue,* and as assistant to Kieślowski on *White.* She worked as assistant director to Finkiel on *Madame Jacques on the Croisette* and made her own debut feature, *Since Otar Left* (*Depuis qu'Otar est parti*) in 2003 (she thanks both Jean-Louis Bertuccelli and Emmanuel Finkiel). *Since Otar Left,* which will receive most attention in the discussion that follows, won the Grand Prize at Cannes in 2003 and was nominated for three César awards.

Finkiel and Bertuccelli have been recognized as part of a new generation of young French and Francophone filmmakers emerging in the 1990s. Both feature in Freddy Buache's recent *Vingt-cinq ans de cinéma français,* which also treats *The Double Life of Véronique* (1991) and the *Three Colors* trilogy. René Prédal, writing in *Le Jeune cinéma français* in 2002, the year before *Since Otar Left,* counters the popular notion that contemporary French cinema focuses too exclusively on the individual and on subjectivity: he argues instead that it looks outward to reveal "a striking picture of a France which is in ruins, in economic, human and moral terms" (125).[1] One of the notable features of this political landscape, Prédal argues, is the memory of the Shoah (as evidenced very richly in Finkiel's *Voyages*). *Since Otar Left* explores another part of this terrain: the experience of the immigrant worker in contemporary Paris. As these two films draw attention to the Shoah, and to immigration, they also draw force and resonance from their status as transnational and diasporic films. I argue that they follow on from Kieślowski in this enterprise, yet extend the ethos and aesthetic of his films.

In *The Double Life of Véronique* and *White* Kieślowski manifestly explores possibilities of bilingual and transnational filmmaking, even if immigration itself is only a minor concern in his work. Writing previously about *The Double Life of Véronique,* I argued: "in a film about France and Poland, if such this is, virtual France and virtual Poland resemble each other, and cinematic and artistic representations of each other, more properly than they resemble either of their actual referents" (Wilson, *Memory* 28–29). I concluded: "Kieślowski's success is in creating scenes in another country, in another language, which are nevertheless always already familiar to viewers of his films" (29). My point was that Kieślowski's filmmaking was first and foremost self-reflexive and an achingly beautiful reflection on cinematic art. In those manifold moments where he did look outward to capture human experience and sensation, his concern primarily—as demonstrated in the overarching themes of the *Three Colors* trilogy and his reprise of many motifs and gestures in both his Polish and French filmmaking—was to point toward universality and common aims, despite the atomized state of contemporary existence. Indeed, Kieślowski's Polish and French protagonists are, ironically, linked precisely by their introspection and by their closed subjective worlds, by the hesitance and pathos of their attempts to relate to others. This is not to say that Kieślowski's work is apolitical or ungrounded in material history—far from it—but that his films encourage the viewer to look at continuities in human behavior, beyond national difference.

In *The Double Life of Véronique,* Kieślowski does still use one point of material contact, in the town square in Cracow, to differentiate between France and Poland, between Véronique and Weronika (both Irène Jacob). This is the source in the plot of the uncanny encounter, witnessed by Weronika but missed by her French double; yet it says much too about the type of interface Kieślowski envisages between the two countries at that moment, just after the fall of communism. Véronique is a tourist in Poland who captures only photographic images of this country. As the demonstration in the town square becomes violent, she, with the others in her group, is herded back into a tour bus. After being momentarily at large in this alien space, she finds herself taking refuge behind plate glass. This window, this sheet of glass, protects the

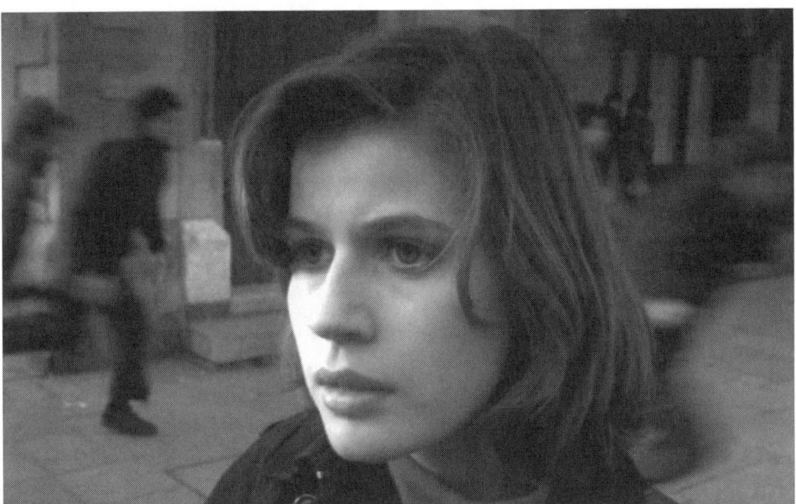

In *The Double Life of Véronique* (1991), Polish and French realities echo each other, even while the two cultures maintain a voyeuristic distance. Here, the Polish Weronika catches a brief glimpse of her French double, Véronique, who unwittingly photographs Weronika from her tour bus.

two spaces and two cultures from each other. In one reading, it represents the consumerist culture of the capitalist West and its sterile, hard-edged distance from the open politics of postcommunist Poland. Véronique views Poland through a frame, through plate glass, as if the turbulence and actuality of this country were resumed in a series of televisual images. Véronique has no knowledge of the encounter with her double here, and only comes to appreciate the moment of (visual) contact and recognition later in a hotel room in Paris as she stares at the contact sheet showing her photographs from Poland. A bilingual film, *The Double Life of Véronique* is notably reticent about cultural interchange; it establishes the connection between its Polish and French protagonists as primarily psychic and mystical, rather than material.

White arguably moves one stage on from *The Double Life of Véronique,* with renewed reflections on the possibilities of bilingual and diasporic filmmaking. Yet, while the film begins with an immigrant worker in Paris, Karol Karol (Zbigniew Zamachowski), it rapidly transports him back to his homeland of Poland. Kieślowski pays acute attention to the visceral and psychological pain of Karol's immigrant experience—embodied specifically in his affective rejection by his French wife Dominique (Julie Delpy), and the physical knocks of his journey home. We witness too Karol's subtle disenfranchisement in the French court where he needs to speak through a Polish translator; we see his rejection by the French system symbolized in the failure of his card in a cash machine. After his divorce from Dominique he is at large on the streets of Paris and in its metro tunnels, playing a Polish tune on his comb. The drift of the film is subtly regressive, or at least it gives way to a type of restorative nostalgia: after his painful migrant experience, Karol returns to his motherland; reinstalled on his home territory, Karol creates his own empire and finds the means to engineer the incarceration of his newly loving ex-wife. The viewer is offered a strong sense of the emergent economy in Poland and the deals and exchanges it requires; congress between East and West is viewed here satirically and with black humour, but, in a film about equality, there is little sense of reciprocity.

There is some sense, throughout Kieślowski's filmmaking, that the other, elsewhere, is a threat to the self, that it opens the self to a risk that is threatening, even if salutary. *Blind Chance* (1981, released 1987), for example, ends with the crash of the plane supposed to take the protagonist, Witek, away from Poland to a medical symposium in the West. This is the end of the third strand of the narrative, that in which Witek is successful professionally in his private career as a doctor; his demise seems particularly ironic. Žižek suggests that "it is only the third version that is 'real': just before dying, Witek runs through the two alternative life-histories in which he does not die . . . but they both end up in a deadlock which pushed him on to the next story" (*Fright* 80). A first reading might see the West associated with threat, risk, and death, with the scream that initiates the virtual backward glances of the film as a whole: elsewhere is threatening. Yet, following Žižek's argument, it may also be seen that the first and second narrative strands of the film also end in deadlock, if not in death. There is also a possible argument that, where virtual Poland and France resemble one another in *The Double Life of Véronique,* so, for Kieślowski, lives in isolation from the West or in communication with a capitalist elsewhere are eventually virtually similar. One might conclude that the self is threatened in Kieślowski, life is interrupted and unsettled, whether those interruptions come from within or without.

This sense of alienation and disruption, allied with tropes found in Kieślowski's bilingual and other films—travel, hotels, the tour bus, the airport, the suitcase—come to align his late work with what Hamid Naficy describes, importantly, as "accented cinema." Glossing his chosen term, Naficy writes: "The accent emanates not so much from the accented speech of the diegetic characters as from the displacement of the filmmakers and their artisanal production modes" (4). This does not quite apply to Kieślowski: his displacement—moving to France to make his late films—was temporary; his auteur filmmaking is largely removed from the artisanal modes Naficy highlights. Yet the space, technologies, and emotions represented, from *Blind Chance* through *The Double Life of Véronique* and the *Three Colors* trilogy, do foreshadow Naficy's concerns. Indeed, a director's displacement and modes of production are only one means of identifying "accented" cinema; Naficy comments further on the prevalence of specific tropes recurring in "accented" films: "transitional and transnational places and spaces, such as borders, tunnels, seaports, airports, and hotels and vehicles of mobility, such as trains, buses, and suitcases" (5). These spaces and places are familiar in Kieślowski; indeed, thinking the epistolarity of accented cinema, Naficy himself refers extensively to the representation of telephone communication at the start of *Red.*

While tracing the tropes and networks favored in "accented" cinema, including Kieślowski's, Naficy offers further a rich and comprehensive checklist of the themes and more properly the affect of such works, listing components as follows: "fragmented, multilingual, epistolary, self-reflexive, and critically juxtaposed narrative structure; amphibolic, doubled, crossed, and lost characters; subject matter and themes that involve journeying, historicity, identity, and displacement; dysphoric, euphoric, nostalgic, synaesthetic, liminal, and politicized structures of feeling; interstitial and collective modes of production; and inscription of the biographical, social, and cinematic (dis)location of the filmmakers" (4). While these components can be found in Kieślowski's films—in his emphasis on temporal fragmentation, flashforwards, and flashbacks, in his close attention to the senses, in his focus on spatial navigation, both in the cities he films (Warsaw, Kraców, Paris, Geneva) and in the interiors where his protagonists are variously inhabitants and intruders—it is rare that they are connected literally to the theme of exile or immigration. In this,

Kieślowski differs from the generation of filmmakers who follow in his wake.

Finkiel and Bertuccelli are not themselves (unwillingly) dislocated or migrant filmmakers; yet in their filmmaking, continuing the lines of Kieślowski's investigations with renewed commitment, they have linked Kieślowski's interest in connection and communication, fantasy and projection, literally to experiences of migration in Europe. They have brought the accents of diasporic Europe all the more fully into contemporary French filmmaking. (The different contribution of Michael Haneke to this mix is explored further by Georgina Evans in chapter 6). While *The Double Life of Véronique* and *White* are bilingual films but offer only limited attention to transit between France and Poland, *Voyages* and *Since Otar Left* make the voyage itself, both physical and fantasmatic, the material of their narrative. I offer an overview of *Voyages* before going on to more extended analysis of *Since Otar Left.*

Voyages is a film in three parts, each focused on an elderly woman. It is more literally an "accented" film than some Naficy mentions; as Buache writes about the protagonists, "their strong accents or mother tongue [Yiddish] reveal that they represent the survivors of the unimaginable massacre of the Jews in the Second World War" (314–15).[2] In the first strand of the film, Rivka (Shulamit Adar), an elderly Jewish woman, travels with a French party to Auschwitz. In the second strand, Regine (Liliane Rovère) is contacted in Paris by a Lithuanian man who may be her father who was deported to the camps. In the third strand, Vera (Esther Gorintin), a Russian immigrant, seeks connections to family and strangers in Israel. Through the film we hear dialogue variously in French, Polish, Russian, and Yiddish. In the first and third part, travel itself is literally a trope of the film. The first strand depends for its trajectory on the tour bus whose windows reveal the Polish landscape. When it breaks down on a deserted road, the travellers are left to contemplate the snowy landscape and spectral images of other travellers through the windows of another bus that passes. In the third strand, Vera attempts to cross Tel Aviv first in a taxi, then on foot and on a bus. The last images of the film show her, dispossessed in this new homeland, waiting at a bus stop in the night. An Israeli woman, a fellow Yiddish speaker, watches Vera as she sits on, letting the buses pass by; she watches too the empty space left by Vera after she has finally departed.

Prédal finds in Finkiel's work "a minimal feature style which is very close to documentary" (128).[3] The documentary ethos aligns Finkiel with Kieślowski, of course, as it aligns him with Bertuccelli, whose early work was in documentary. *Voyages* bears comparison with more recent films such as Natacha Samuel's *Pola à 27 ans* (2003), a documentary in the form of a personal diary about a grandmother's return to Auschwitz, or *La Petite Prairie aux bouleaux* (2003), Marceline Loridan Ivens's loosely fictionalized account of her own experience of return to the camps. (Kieślowski has made the personal and ethical heritage of the Holocaust his subject too, notably in *Deca-*

logue 8 [1988], but this is just one of the strands of concern in his braided image of 1980s Poland).

If Finkiel makes postwar Jewish heritage—commemoration and the sensibilities of the Jewish community in Paris and Tel Aviv—his dominant concern in *Voyages,* he also threads into the film questions about family, identity, and loss that link him back to Kieślowski, and to broader trends in Eastern European filmmaking (and also look forward to the central drama of *Since Otar Left*). Alluding to the second strand of *Voyages,* Buache writes: "Fathers, mothers, sisters, brothers, friends have disappeared, leaving no trace, but sometimes the hope of a return through some chance miracle in the disordered aftermath of conflict" (315).[4] Regine, in *Voyages,* is faced with the question of the identity of the very elderly Lithuanian man who claims he is her father. She examines his responses to her questions and compares his identity photographs with the faded remaining image she has of a young man from her childhood. (Throughout the film, photographs and personal documents, relics and evidence, are filmed with the same minute, tactile attention, and abundant pathos, found earlier in Kieślowski's work.) When the father's false identity is proved and he packs to leave, she has a change of heart and invites him instead, as a type of revenant, to find his place in her family. They play along together with the fiction that he is indeed her father returned.

This questioning of identity, and eventual disregard for a distinction between truth and fiction, echoes *Decalogue 4* and the *Three Colors* trilogy (for example, the question of whether Julie, rather than her husband, was all along the composer of the Concerto in *Blue;* or the question of whether Auguste embodies a younger avatar of the Judge in *Red*). More substantially, *Voyages* recalls the repeated disavowals of identity in Holland's *Europa Europa* (1990) and *Olivier, Olivier* (1992). In the latter film, a missing child appears to return home; when the truth of the child Olivier's murder is discovered, the returning boy is allowed still to remain within the family and act as a binding agent among them.

In *Since Otar Left,* the issue of the missing relative and doubts about his demise or survival are transposed from the context of the Shoah, as found in *Voyages* or a film such as *Europa Europa,* to the issue of the immigrant worker lost in a foreign country. This film, more than *Voyages,* I see as important in implicitly acknowledging debts to Kieślowski yet as transitional in shifting focus to the fantasies of migrant families and the politics of immigration. As such, it might be compared to other prescient films about Europe and immigration that also bear Kieślowski's imprint, such as Pawel Pawlikowski's *Last Resort* (2000) or Lukas Moodysson's *Lilja 4-ever* (2002) (on the influence of Kieślowski in the latter film see Wilson, "Children").

Bertuccelli recounts: "*Since Otar Left* is based on a true story that I was told. It was true but it seemed so unlikely that it made me want to appropriate it. And in any case, it was a story that could not be told as a documentary—it was much too intimate" (Zeitgeist). Her words here are reminiscent of Žižek's more elaborate discussion of Kieślowski's move from documentary to feature film; for Žižek, "It was precisely a fidelity to the Real that compelled Kieślowski to abandon documentary realism—at some point, one encounters something more Real than reality itself" (*Fright* 71). In Žižek's terms, a move away from documentary comes in response to an event or actuality that is more disturbing, more intense, more skewed, than reality. Bertuccelli's motivation may equally belie a preference for creating a fiction of events over attempting to capture their brute reality. Žižek also explains the sense of disjunction between reality and the Real experienced by Kieślowski in historical and political terms: "Kieślowski's starting point was the same as that of all cineastes in the socialist countries: the conspicuous gap between the drab social reality and the optimistic, bright image which pervaded the heavily censored official media" (*Fright* 71). This climate of disjuncture inspired Kieślowski's move into fiction, a space and medium in which he could approach the Real with more veracity, more verisimilitude. *Since Otar Left* was made more than a decade after the fall of communism in the Eastern block, yet arguably the film still exploits the gap between reality and representations, though here those representations are largely more subjective and fantasmatic.

Where *Voyages* explores the literal journeys made possible after communism—tourist development of Auschwitz, a bid by a Lithuanian man to be reclaimed as survivor of the Shoah, a Russian immigrant's move to Israel—*Since Otar Left* looks more closely at subjective journeys, at fantasies of France and Georgia.

Since Otar Left shows three generations of women: Eka (Esther Gorintin, offering a further link to *Voyages*), her daughter Marina (Nino Khomassouridze), who sells antiques and bric-a-brac, and her granddaughter Ada (Dinara Droukarova), a student of French literature. Eka speaks French at home to Ada; the language becomes the conduit of their loving relationship to each other. French volumes decorate the walls of the family's Georgian apartment (its mise-en-scène as precise as that of Kieślowski's interiors in *The Double Life of Véronique* or *Red*); we learn that the books were ordered from France by Ada's great grandfather. Bertuccelli explains in an interview: "Georgia is a land which has a long tradition of links with France, though they are not well known. Many French people have travelled there and many indeed have settled there. There has been a constant process of exchange. Georgians are fascinated by French culture" (Zeitgeist). For Buache, the family's borrowed cultural heritage, their investment in France and French literature, offers them virtual rather than actual journeys (315). Bertuccelli continues in the Zeitgeist interview: "I am not interested in talking about France so much as in talking about how one comes to fall in love with a foreign land one knows from one's imagination, with all the potential for disillusionment that that contains."

In a film such as Michale Boganim's *Odessa . . . Odessa!* (2005), about Jewish emigration from the Ukraine, we see a miniature shrine to Odessa that one woman has created in her apartment in Israel. Svetlana Boym offers a chapter of *The Future of Nostalgia* on immigrant souvenirs in which she challenges the typical understanding of their function, arguing that "rooms filled with diasporic souvenirs are not altars to . . . unhappiness, but rather places for communication and conversation" (336). Rather than look at memories and constructions of Georgia from an exile in France, Bertuccelli shifts again, looking at projected fantasies of France garnered in Tblisi. The "Making of" documentary on the French DVD of *Since Otar Left* shows the careful construction of the set, with the faded flea-market images of Paris that decorate Ada's corner in the apartment; reproductions of paintings by Chardin and Renoir are also glimpsed within the film. Continuing this collage aesthetic, the film shows close-up shots of Ada reading from Apollinaire's *Calligrammes* by candlelight. Bertuccelli reveals three women dreaming not of Moscow but of Paris (though this fantasy is shared less wholeheartedly by Marina than the others). Echoing Kieślowski's presentation of the Judge and Auguste in *Red*, Bertuccelli has said that the three women might be the same woman at three different stages in her life. More politically, they might show three different generations in the aftermath of communism. Bertuccelli relates: "The idea was to show a triple relationship between three women caught in a changing world, sometimes changing for the better, sometimes for the worse" (Zeitgeist). One of the specific changes Bertuccelli explores is the new possibility of travel to the fantasy space of Paris.

Connections are made in the film between the family fantasy of Paris and the literal journey made by Otar, Eka's son, who has himself moved to Paris as an illegal immigrant. Otar is absent from the film in actuality, but his photographs are found on the walls of the apartment (such that the space around the women becomes a screen for their fantasies). In the early part of the film, letters arrive from Paris, and Ada reads Otar's French words to her grandmother. His letters allow the idea of Paris to circulate in the film as a literary fantasy; he has found a place to live near the foot of "la butte Montmartre"; he tells his mother that from his window he can see the streets where she dreamed of walking with his father. Reading his letters to Eka, Ada makes France and Otar spectrally present in the garden in Tblisi.

Although he was a physician in Georgia, as an illegal immigrant in Paris, Otar can only work initially on a building site. The fantasy of Paris, of French culture, does not quite conceal the reality of immigrant experience. Bertuccelli's strategies are different from those, say, of Luc and Jean-Pierre Dardenne in *La Promesse* (1996) or Nicolas Klotz in *La Blessure* (2004), where the living hell, the transactions and betrayals, of immigrant life are made viscerally evident. Otar's actuality, withheld in his letters, is carefully suggested but not represented within the film.

In *Since Otar Left* (2003), three generations of Georgian women—perhaps one woman at different stages of her life—share the imagining of another country.

This dissimulation continues even after Otar's demise in an accident, which Marina and Ada learn about while Eka is away at the family dacha. In this brute knowledge, mother and daughter come closer to one another—their faces shot together resembling two portraits by Ingres. Together they learn that Otar fell from scaffolding on the fifth floor of a building and that he was buried in a pauper's grave (in the Thiais cemetery). In following shots, we see Marina sitting with her sometime boyfriend Tenguiz in the open space of a partially constructed building in Tblisi. Looking out at the evening city, she seems to call up images of Otar and his precarious work, imagining him from Georgia. The accident of Eka's absence at the time of the call allows the two younger women to embark on a strategy of deception, born out of the impossibility of imparting the potentially devastating news to Eka. (Throughout the film Eka's strongest attachment is to Otar, her missing son.)

Kieślowski offered prescient and harrowing representations of a father losing his son in *Decalogue 1* and a mother losing her daughter in *Blue*. Bertuccelli looks more tangentially at a mother's loss of her adult son, in another country. The grief over the loss of an adult son—anticipated though barely actualized in the film—is shown to be as intense as that for a child, but mediated through the other losses that adult departures bring with them (Otar has already in some senses left his mother, to live his life in France). The title, *Since Otar Left,* is usefully ambiguous here. His departure for France seems itself a rehearsal for his more complete disappearance in death. Notably, death too, whether actual or staged, is used as motif in the mediation between France and Poland in both *The Double Life of Véronique* and *White;* the move between two countries creates an unbridgeable before and after, as in death.

Where Otar's letters in French and his phone calls from France have allowed the family to deny his absence from them and feel the presence of his words in their company, after his death, the ritual of the letter writing is still maintained. Ada and Marina appear at first to succeed in their deception. The women conjure up the dead Otar in the space of their home, resuscitating him as they invent his virtual life. In one fake letter Otar compares himself to a character in a film they have seen; in retouched photographs he appears in front of the Moulin Rouge. Ada's imagination makes use of the tourist images of Paris already found in the film and, in more muted forms, in Otar's previous real correspondence. That there should be such close resemblance between Otar's actual letters and her fake constructions points subtly to the ways in which Otar too was constructing a life for his mother's distraction. His death, and Ada's perpetuation of his voice in writing, only confirm the poignant delusions on which his relation to his family and theirs to France depended.

The tension of the film in its latter stages derives from uncertainty about how far Eka realizes that she is being deluded. At first there seems no intimation that she knows that her daughter and granddaughter are hiding a truth from her. Her demeanour is stoic and unreadable. There is, however, a stray scene at dinner where Marina speaks about Ada's father, who was a soldier in Afghanistan. Though she wrote to him every week, he only called her twice; she consulted a clairvoyant, who continued telling her details about his life even when he had been dead for three weeks. As the film continues, however, the deception seems to continue, too: Ada manages to forestall the arrival in the apartment of Niko, Otar's friend from Paris who is returning Otar's belongings; she encourages him to collude with them in deceiving Eka, making him receive gifts of food that he will take back to a fantasy Otar. The tone of the film is delicate and fairly melancholy throughout, but in such scenes it bears comparison with more comic explorations of delusion and disavowal such as *Good Bye Lenin* (Wolfgang Becker, 2003).

While the community of the women, the tight if sometimes irascible bond between them, has been the focus of early parts of the film, as it continues, a sense emerges that each woman also functions as an individual; each is, like the characters in *Voyages,* on a separate journey. This is manifested in particular in plans Eka develops to visit Otar. She writes her own letter to him and sells the French books from the apartment to fund the trip. She reassures an anxious Marina and Ada that she understands that Otar may be lying to her about his quality of life, but that she wants to see her son. Her motivation and the extent of her understanding are still left unclear; perhaps her determination to visit Otar, to decrease the distance between them, suggests that she too has been infected by doubts about his survival.

Once in Paris, the film confirms Otar's demise as Marina and Ada make a trip to visit his grave. The dismal scene, with tower blocks in the background, is far from the tourist images of Paris found in Tblisi. The same is true of the streets around Barbès and the aerial metro (line 2) where we find Eka wandering on her own. Her search for Otar takes her into the courtyards and staircases of dilapidated apartment buildings. She speaks to a neighbor behind a closed door; her determination and ritual actions recall the single-mindedness of a mother animal. When she finds the apartment where Otar used to live, she learns what we have known all along: that he died a few months before. Compounding the tragedy of this news, the gentle neighbor hands her back one of her own letters to Otar. The return of the letter underlines the delusion with which she has lived. The fetish of letter writing that she and the others have, unwittingly or not, used to maintain the illusion that Otar is alive as an addressee (and that France is a utopia) is suddenly stripped of its power of denial. While this is perhaps the most intense scene of the film, it is also curious in excluding the viewer and refusing us full knowledge of Eka's state of mind. It is only on a physical level that we see her response to the confirmation that Otar is gone; Gorintin conveys this beautifully in her huddled and frightened posture. This part of the film makes fine use of scale and perspective, showing Eka from different levels as we try to gauge her disorientation. The film follows her as she walks under the aerial metro and sits in a city square. There are expressive shots of her from above, from the metro line itself. The film creates a space around her as, in this foreign yet beloved city, she reckons with a loss that she has perhaps already known; we see her react, but we are left still to wonder what she feels and knows.

When she returns from this excursion into the Real of immigrant life in Paris—its transience and material dilapidation—the play with dissimulation continues as she entertains her daughter and granddaughter with a new fantasy. Rather than pass on knowledge of Otar's death, she tells them that Otar was hiding something from them in turn. Tired of waiting for his papers in France, he has left without warning for America. One day or another he will write to them. By her new fantasy construction, Eka strangely reasserts her power in the family. She has the power now to contest the brute reality, the Real, with which they are faced. She now seems to manipulate Marina and Ada, who must in turn fall in line and corroborate her fantasy.

Bertuccelli has said: "As a concept, lying is fascinating. It's a great place to set a film because it is a twin force, both destructive and creative" (Zeitgeist). She invests lies with this dual power in the film, entertaining very fully their creative possibilities. Buoyed by her new lie about Otar, by the new solidarity it creates between the women, Eka can open a space of beauty and relief. Whether the lie is to comfort herself, to protect her relatives, or simply to delay knowledge of Otar's death once more, it is convenient in allowing pleasure as well as mourning on this exceptional trip to Paris. With the reassurance that Otar will write eventually, Eka can continue: "and now, I want to see Paris."

The film presents a collage of shots of the city. We see the three women with their arms linked as they cross the road. The beauty of the shots of Paris is gleaned through the filter of these women's collective investment in fantasy. Bertuccelli stitches together locations as we see the places they visit: the Champs Elysées with the Arc de Triomphe glimpsed in the shot, the Boulevard St Germain where we see the lighted windows of the legendary bookshop "La Hune," and elsewhere the pastry shop Ladurée with a confection of stacked, decorated madeleine cakes. The Paris visited is a space of monuments, spectacle, culture, and luxury. We see the three women in a taxi; Ada looks out at the Boulevard Haussmann seeing Christmas lights and the shop fronts of Printemps and C&A. There is stylization in Bertuccelli's Paris, as there was in Kieślowski's (with its images of café interiors, arcades, the Ile de la Cité, Pigalle, and architectural echoes of *Last Tango in Paris* [1972]). By the end of Bertuccelli's film, the image of the city is constructed from a glorious blaze of lights. Yet by showing real locations and shop signs, Bertuccelli also points more subtly to the fact that there are material referents for the dreams of these three women. Their love of Paris depends on the disavowal of an immigrant reality—evidenced in the lies they tell about Otar—but the objects and locations they love are no less real for that.

As between Kieślowski's Poland and France in *The Double Life of Véronique,* there are uncanny resemblances between Bertuccelli's Tblisi and Paris. The film opens with shots in a cake shop in Tblisi, foreshadowing the culinary pleasures of Ladurée in Paris. In one of the extras on the DVD, Bertuccelli presents a collection of her personal snapshots of Tblisi—the cake shop is among them—and in the beauty of the images, and the words Bertuccelli uses to describe them, we gain a sense that the film incorporates also her (French) tourist's vision of Georgia, her outsider's view of and love for this former Soviet state. (Bertuccelli had worked for six months in Georgia previously with the filmmaker Otar Iosseliani.) She has said that the plot of *Since Otar Left* gave her a pretext to film in Georgia: "I wanted to make a film a long way from home and use the distance to say something about myself, in other people's eyes" (Zeitgeist). (Of the choice of location, Bertuccelli has said: "my heart led me to an old-fashioned apartment, despite the fact that I was a little afraid of making things seem too beautiful.")

Buache argues that the three women find hope and lies in equal measure in Paris as in Tblisi (315). While this is manifestly true, on another level the trip to Paris allows the relationship between the three to shift gears. The final scenes of the film take place at the airport. Eka has witnessed Ada's love of Paris on this trip, her radiance in this new space. Ada's French would allow her new mobility here (as it has when she has taken temporary work as an interpreter in Tblisi and been handed a business card by a French entrepreneur). At the airport Eka consciously facilitates Ada's move to distance herself from the trio. Ada hangs back to buy magazines in the departures hall; Eka insists that she and Marina go through to the gate. By this gesture, Eka allows her granddaughter to stay in France, opening the infinitely moving possibility that she has known about Otar all along and brought them to Paris to allow Ada's departure. This departure is delayed and drawn out: we see Ada looking at the shelves of French magazines in the airport shop as she finds herself in a hiatus between her past and future. Marina is unaware until she finds herself watching her daughter waving goodbye through a glass security partition (recalling still Kieślowski's sense of the separation of East and West). As Ada waves, her image also momentarily recalls that of Dominique waving to Karol at the end of *White*. Eerily recalling Otar, too, Ada gestures that she will telephone them. She then turns away with her suitcase and disappears into the underground.

The meanings of this ending are complex. As I have suggested, Eka's connivance with Ada raises the specter that the trip to France has never really been a trip to find Otar; it may always already have been a trip to set Ada free in the city of her fantasies. Marina here is the victim of Eka's act, but a disregard for her daughter's feelings has characterized Eka's attitude throughout the film. Yet it seems puzzling that Ada should be delivered by Eka to the country that has removed Otar, her most precious child. Despite Otar's failure and death, we may wonder whether the fantasy persists that a new life is possible in Paris. Ada may even be sacrificed to this myth. Or maybe the film is more realistic and less clear-cut; with her language skills and understanding of French culture, Ada may yet have a better life in this country than she could know in contemporary Georgia. While refusing a facile hierarchizing of West and East, and reminding us at times of the constants between the two, Bertuccelli also buys in enough to immigrant fantasy to show that the dream of Paris is not entirely insubstantial.

Bertuccelli has said in an interview: "Transmission is indeed one of the themes in the screenplay" (Zeitgeist). Her inheritance from Kieślowski, and the Polish director's influence on French filming of immigrant lives more broadly, has been one of the themes of this chapter. Like a dead relative's, Kieślowski's influence is felt in *Since Otar Left* (as in *Voyages*), yet Bertuccelli's aim, like Ada's, may be to find her own path, somewhere between resemblance and originality. Discussing Kieślowski, Žižek writes:

> There is an unexpected formal homology between the two central instalments (5 and 6) of Kieślowski's *Decalogue, A Short Film on Killing* and *A Short Film on Love* [all 1988]: in both cases we are dealing with a failed metaphoric reversal-substitution. The sec-

> ond act, instead of accomplishing a successful "sublation" [*Aufhebung*] of the first act (by way of compensating for its damage and re-establishing the lost balance), actually makes things worse by ending up as a *repetition* of the first act. ("There Is" 238)

If the hanging of Jacek in *A Short Film about Killing* certainly makes things worse, rather than offering any compensation for his murder of the taxi driver, we may perhaps come to a different conclusion about *Since Otar Left*. Ada's departure at the end of the film surely seems a repetition of Otar's leaving, yet Bertuccelli's focus on different paths taken by different characters, on individual voyages through Europe and through European cinema, may suggest too that Ada's fate is not necessarily predetermined. She may yet know a different outcome from her uncle. So Bertuccelli, repeating Kieślowski's focus on East and West in Europe, shows yet their different imbrication; already, in a decade, lives and filmmaking have moved on.

Writing about nostalgia and immigrant experience, Svetlana Boym counsels: "The ethics of reflective longing recognizes the cultural memory of another person as well as his or her human singularity and vulnerability. The other is not merely a representative of another culture, but also a singular individual with a right to long for—but not necessarily belong to—his place of birth" (337). Coming closer than Kieślowski to the divisions and realities, the Real, of immigrant experience, Bertuccelli (and Finkiel) make their immigrants individuals, with separate paths through a heterogeneous and diasporic Europe. Kieślowski has said in discussion of *The Double Life of Véronique*, "The realm of superstitions, fortune-telling, presentiments, intuition, dreams, all this is the inner life of a human being, and all this is the hardest thing to film" (Stok 194). Bertuccelli and Finkiel take up his challenge, testing the capabilities of film to capture and reveal the dreams and fantasies fostered in a yet-divided Europe.

Notes

All translations from the French are my own.

1. "le tableau 'politique' saisissant d'une France délabrée économiquement, humainement et moralement."

2. "elles annoncent par leurs accents très forts ou par leur langue maternelle, qu'elles représentent les rescapés de l'inimaginable massacre antisémite de la Deuxième Guerre mondiale."

3. "un style de fiction minimale très proche du documentaire."

4. "Des pères, des mères, des soeurs, des frères, des amis ont disparu, ne laissant aucune trace, mais quelquefois l'espoir d'un retour au gré d'un miraculeux hasard dans le désordre des lendemains du conflit."

Works Cited

Boym, Svetlana. *The Future of Nostalgia.* New York: Basic Books, 2001.

Buache, Freddy. *Vingt-cinq ans de cinéma français.* Lausanne: Editions L'Age d'homme, 2005.

Hoffman, Eva. *Exit into History: A Journey through the New Eastern Europe.* New York: Penguin, 1993.

Insdorf, Annette. *Double Lives, Second Chances.* New York: Miramax Books, 1999.

"Le Making Of." *Depuis qu'Otar est parti.* DVD. Directed by Julie Bertucelli. Paris: Editions Montparnasse, 2004.

Marks, Laura U. *The Skin of the Film: Intercultural Cinema, Embodiment, and the Senses.* Durham: Duke University Press, 2000.

Naficy, Hamid. *An Accented Cinema: Exilic and Diasporic Filmmaking.* Princeton: Princeton University Press, 2001.

Prédal, René. *Le Jeune cinéma français.* Paris: Nathan, 2002.

Stok, Danusia, ed. *Kieślowski on Kieślowski.* London: Faber, 1993.

Wilson, Emma. "Children, Emotion and Viewing in Contemporary European Film." *Screen* 46.3 (2005): 329–40.

———. *Memory and Survival: The French Cinema of Krzysztof Kieślowski.* Oxford: Legenda, 2000.

Zeitgeist Films Pressbook to *Since Otar Left.* 2003.

Žižek, Slavoj. *The Fright of Real Tears: Krzysztof Kieślowski between Theory and Post-Theory.* London: BFI Publishing, 2001.

———. "There Is No Sexual Relationship." *Gaze and Voice as Love Objects.* Ed. Renata Salecl and Slavoj Žižek. Durham: Duke University Press, 1996.

6

Social Sense

Krzysztof Kieślowski and Michael Haneke

Georgina Evans

The deeply aestheticized humanity of Kieślowski's last, French films may seem to share little with the hostile world portrayed by Michael Haneke. But the two directors have much in common, not merely in the paths they took from home-grown television projects to feature films in France, but in their thematic concerns and their considered approach to their art. Their work invites the spectator to contemplate the predicament of the individual in an increasingly atomized European society and at the same time questions the ability of cinema to represent this fragmentation. In this piece, I shall focus largely on Kieślowski's *Three Colors: Red* (1994) and set this against Haneke's *Code Unknown* (*Code Inconnu,* 2000). I do not seek to make any claim for direct influence. Rather, my aim is to explore the threads that run through both men's careers and through these works in particular. I believe that the social critique offered in *Red* takes it closer to Haneke's social vision than might generally be acknowledged. At the same time, I propose that beneath the more obvious themes of immigration and social upheaval, *Code Unknown* offers an interesting consideration of human and filmic perception that connects it with *Red.* Ultimately, both films step back from their subjects to accept the realization that perfect knowledge is beyond the reach of directors, protagonists, and spectators alike.

Given the context in which this essay appears, and the extensive existing writings on Kieślowski, it seems less necessary to provide basic details of biography and synopsis for him than for Haneke. Despite a long and distinguished career, Haneke has emerged to a comparable level of worldwide notice only gradually over the last decade. Born in Munich in 1942, less than a year after Kieślowski, Haneke identifies himself as Austrian, having grown up there and studied philosophy, psychology, and theater in Vienna. Like Kieślowski, he made many films for television, beginning his career in German television before becoming an independent writer and director of films for cinema and television, as well as working as a theater director. His first feature film, *The Seventh Continent* (*Der Siebente Kontinent),* appeared in 1989, followed by *Benny's Video* (1992), *71 Fragments of a Chronology of Chance* (*71 Fragmente einer Chronologie des Zufalls,* 1994), and *Funny Games* (1997). All these films confront unfathomable violence striking at the heart of apparently ordinary family lives and situations (with the possible exception of *71 Fragments*). His first French-language film, *Code Unknown,* was followed by an adaptation of Elfriede Jelinek's 1983 novel *Die Klavierspielerin,* entitled *The Piano Teacher* (*La Pianiste,* 2001), the dystopian *The Time of the Wolf* (*Le Temps du Loup,* 2003), and most recently, *Hidden* (*Caché,* 2005). Again, the theme of the family connects all these pieces, reflecting Haneke's belief that this is the "germinating cell for all conflicts" (Haneke, "The World" 31). *Code Unknown* is the least typical in this respect, in that although families are represented, the film is more concerned with a larger picture of interaction among those who are ignorant of their connection to each other.

Kieślowski and Haneke shared the same two points of contact with the French cinema industry. The first of these was the actress Juliette Binoche, who in both cases sought out her casting directly and brought with her a kind of emblematic national spirit. Kieślowski had to be convinced by Binoche that she was mature enough to play the widowed Julie in *Three Colors: Blue* but ultimately said that she lent the production "that which does not exist in me: France" (Kieślowski, "La liberté" 125). Haneke remarked similarly that "it was she who, because she had seen *The Seventh Continent,* called me one day. It was she who, with *Code Unknown,* opened the doors of French cinema to me" (Grassin 86). Haneke, of course, had to deal with the imprint of Kieślowski on Binoche's screen presence: *Blue* was one of the films that set her iconic status. As Ginette Vincendeau has argued, it established her as a model of minimalist close-up acting, with all the fetishization of her coolly sculptured features that this implies. Haneke addressed this by casting Binoche as an actress in *Code Unknown,* thus tempering the conspicuousness of her fame and beauty. Indeed, the sequences of "film within film" that occur in *Code Unknown* recall *Blue* in some respects, first by offering us close-ups (something Haneke does not use in "his own" parts of the film), and more specifically in taking place in a shimmering turquoise swimming pool that recalls one of the leitmotifs of *Blue.* This might be interpreted as a distancing move that establishes such approaches to her as belonging to another world and a different type of cinema. A similar need to defuse the mesmeric aspects of Binoche's presence may lie behind the fact that in the opening dialogue with Daniel Auteuil in *Hidden,* Haneke does not show her face at all in the first minute of their screen time.

The second figure linking Haneke, Kieślowski, the *Three Colors* trilogy, and Haneke's first two French films (*Code Unknown* and *The Piano Teacher*) is the producer Marin Karmitz. If Binoche brought France to both projects,

Karmitz embodies the overarching notion of a diasporic Europe expressed by them. The child of immigrants "chased out of Romania by communists" (Karmitz, *Profession* 22), Karmitz has lived in Paris since the age of thirteen. A lifetime of involvement in film lies behind his present status as a producer, distributor, and founder and president of the MK2 cinema chain, and his work in all these roles is characterized by an intense personal engagement with every aspect of cinema. The first meeting with Kieślowski was, for Karmitz, "something like a thunderbolt" (Karmitz, *Profession* 135) in which the two men found an intellectual compatibility beyond their mutual involvement in film. Specifically, Kieślowski's description of the concept behind the trilogy drew Karmitz's interest immediately: "In two hours we had gone to the heart of everything I had been dreaming about for ten years. I told him of my interest in the subject, explaining how it affected me personally as a Romanian émigré, as a Jew saved by France" (Karmitz, "Three Colours" 31). Karmitz describes at length the intellectual background to Kieślowski's project and his own understanding of the issues it addresses. Of particular note is the fact that he sees *Code Unknown* as a natural continuation of this work:

> Kieślowski had the idea of making European films. Does European cinema exist? Can one make it exist? The answer to the first question is no. European cinema does not exist. Europe, yes. What is its cultural meaning? The theme liberty-equality-fraternity or Three Colours was a European theme in so far as these notions have permitted the emergence of democracies, in particular those of the eastern countries. I have always thought that those who could best express the idea of Europe were the people of Central Europe, between Warsaw and Vienna. Whence my call later to Michael Haneke to commission a film considering Europe, *Code Unknown*. (*Profession* 138)

Kieślowski in his turn was happy with the interventions of Karmitz, possibly because this collaborative approach recalled the Polish production climate of cooperative coauthorship that he so valued (Stok 199). He found stimulation and support in his producer's contributions: "Karmitz . . . is far more experienced than my previous producer and therefore has far more pronounced opinions. Yet he's always ready to talk, discuss, and find a way which will suit us both. He's helped me resolve a good many artistic problems" (Stok 227).

After Kieślowski's death, Karmitz admitted that without this director whom he saw as his "double," his state of mourning left him no desire to continue producing at all (*Profession* 149). His claim that his desire to commission *Code Unknown* sprang from the same interest behind his enthusiasm for the trilogy suggests that it was precisely this comparison that prompted him to make the investment, having previously turned down Haneke's *The*

Time of the Wolf and *Funny Games*. *Code Unknown* may have convinced him that such thoughtful approaches to Europe were still possible and that the work he did with Kieślowski might to some degree find a continuation. Again, Karmitz's personal background was brought to bear, this time on Haneke's film: "he came to Paris to investigate African immigration, and I pushed him to go and look also at the area of Romanian beggars" (*Profession* 110). Unfortunately, though, this relationship was not to develop into the harmonious partnership that flourished between Karmitz and Kieślowski. Karmitz seems to have found Haneke too concertedly auteurist in his approach, writing that, even with Juliette Binoche as the star, there were problems securing funding for *Code Unknown* because "the authoritarianism, the inflexibility and the demands of the director turned conversations into never-ending and unequal shows of force" (*Profession* 110). Despite this, the lack of formal recognition for *Code Unknown* at the Cannes Film Festival in 2000 seems to have engendered a defensive sympathy in Karmitz, who had been similarly dismayed by the favoring of *Pulp Fiction* (1994) over *Red* at Cannes in 1994, a decision that left him, and apparently Kieślowski, "shocked and wounded" (*Profession* 148). It is perhaps for this reason that he agreed to their next collaboration, *The Piano Teacher*, a film Karmitz found in its first edit to be too long and pointlessly provocative (*Profession* 111). When it eventually received the Grand Prix at Cannes in 2001, in spite of Karmitz's reluctance to send it there at all, he declared, "I would not have wished to drop Haneke after the failure of *Code Unknown*, but I am very happy to leave him after the success of *The Piano Teacher*" (*Profession* 112).

The "European" films *Code Unknown* and the *Three Colors* trilogy, therefore, represent the point of nearest contact between Kieślowski and Haneke, at which they share most both in their thematic concerns and in their production circumstances. This correlation was noted in the British newspaper the *Daily Telegraph* on 17 May 2001; S. F. Said wrote, "*Code Unknown* . . . feels like an urgent state-of-the-world address. It may be to this decade what Krzysztof Kieślowski's *Three Colours* trilogy was to the Nineties: the most serious, searching interrogation of its times that cinema has to offer. Like those films, it is set in the contemporary age of globalisation, and shows individuals caught up in wider currents, increasingly isolated as misunderstanding grows."

Sheila Johnson remarks less favorably on the parallel careers of Haneke and Kieślowski, suggesting in a Cannes report on *Code Unknown* that "the director's followers may see this as a muting of his vision (much as happened to Kieślowski with *Blue*, his Paris-based collaboration with Binoche and Karmitz)" (20). In both cases, the move to France attracted a critical spotlight that sought to reveal some shift in focus or quality as well as in location. Julia Dobson demonstrates the way the *Cahiers du Cinéma* critics in particular imputed, in their reception of *Blue*, a dereliction of Kieślowski's "true nature . . .

through their reception of *Blanc* as a welcome return to form" (236). Haneke in turn said of the French reaction to *Code Unknown* that "I'm really very irked by the reaction because in the past it was always the same people who were for or against my films. This time, those who were for my other films [i.e., the French left] were against *Code Unknown* and vice versa. I just don't understand" ("Code" 8). In fact, the problem in both cases may be that they did not so much cross the bounds of national cinema but stretch them to such a point that it is very difficult to situate the resulting works. Kieślowski made his last three and a half films in a language he did not really speak. Haneke, a competent French speaker, made *The Piano Teacher* entirely in French while maintaining its Vienna setting and making no allusion to the linguistic shift from the German of the novel. It is surely most useful to respond in the mood in which these pieces were made, to view both the trilogy and *Code Unknown* as belonging to the "European film" category described by Karmitz and to examine them as social critiques probing deliberately universal Western themes.

Red is characterized by a tight focus on a very small number of characters, of whom the central pairing of a model and a judge, played by Irène Jacob and Jean-Louis Trintignant, are by far the most significant. Others enter the stage largely to reflect or illuminate their unlikely friendship and its place in a cycle of personal histories. Aside from its very first seconds, the film is firmly anchored in Geneva until the final scenes of a ferry accident, which close and define the trilogy. *Code Unknown,* on the other hand, announces itself in its subtitle as an "incomplete story of several journeys." After a title sequence showing deaf children playing a kind of lexical charades in which the actions of the little girl interpreting a word are met with incomprehension by her classmates, the film then moves to a complex opening sequence on the streets of Paris, which plays out in a single eight-minute shot. Anne, an actress, played by Juliette Binoche, emerges from her apartment building to encounter her lover's teenage brother. Pressed for time, she gives him her keys and buys him something to eat before rushing away to an audition. The young man, Jean (Alexandre Hamidi), unthinkingly throws the food wrapper into the lap of a woman begging in the street. When challenged by a black passerby, Amadou Traore (Ona Lu Yenke), he refuses to apologize, and the scene escalates into a violent microcosm of the ills of contemporary Europe, encompassing racial prejudice, illegal immigration, rural disaffection, and police brutality. Henceforth we are shown fragments of the story of each individual concerned in the encounter, punctuated by blackness and two sequences of still photographs taken by Anne's news-photographer lover, Jean's brother Georges (Thierry Neuvic). These journeys lead us to rural France, where Jean and Georges' father is a struggling farmer; to Mali, where Amadou's family originated; and to Romania, the homeland of the beggar woman Maria (Luminita Gheorghiu). They also include glimpses of Anne working as a film actress, first addressing the camera directly in a screen test, later on set, and ultimately in a highly edited sequence from the final cut. These excerpts from another filmic world are signalled as such only in an unnervingly gradual fashion. The final sequence of Haneke's film returns us to the location where it all began, showing Maria back in France and once again looking for a place to beg, Anne back in her apartment, and Georges trying unsuccessfully to gain entry to the building. Her failure to alert him to the new door code may be a sign that their difficult relationship is at an end. Alternatively, we may simply deduce that their long separations have disconnected their emotional bond from the practicalities of day-to-day life.

The unconventional pairing of these films might, as I have argued, be justified on biographical and circumstantial grounds alone. However, there are more subtle parallels worth exploring. Just as Haneke's film begins with a scene of failed communication, *Red* establishes a world of disconnection from the unsuccessful telephone call of the titles onward. This background to the narrative of *Red* should not be overlooked in our fascination with its later weaving of social links. Whatever we may think of the Judge's eavesdropping on his neighbors, it seems clear that there was no "community of Pinchat" until they are called as such to testify against the Judge in court. Valentine and her very near neighbor Auguste (Jean-Pierre Lorit) are able to pass each other in the street and stand next to each other in a record shop with no flicker of recognition whatsoever. The strangeness of the Judge's behavior perhaps distracts from the idiosyncrasies of Valentine's life, but she too leads what seems on film to be a strangely detached existence. Irène Jacob has noted that Valentine's mother and boyfriend are never seen, observing that "we get the feeling

Even when people do come face to face in *Code Unknown* (2000), even when they speak the same language, they can only regard each other with incomprehension, suspicion, and anger.

that her life is almost dreamed." Despite her nominal status as a student, she seems to have no associates who ever share her physical space; when the photographer who takes her picture for an enormous advertising billboard asks if people will recognize her, she can only ask, "Who?" In both these visions of a populous Europe, society is shattered into autonomous splinters that come into contact only in moments of violence, such as the fight at the start of *Code Unknown,* the ferry accident in the case of the trilogy, and the moment when Valentine hits the Judge's dog with her car in *Red.*

Haneke's film exposes not the underlying connections between people but the fact that there may be none, and that the investment we make as spectators in one moment of visual connectedness is not bound to be repaid by the filmmaker's narrative. This investment is of course repaid in *Red,* which moves ultimately to fulfil our sense of the rectitude of relationships that have their filmic germ in the shared frame. In the simplest summary, both Kieślowski's trilogy and Haneke's film draw the individual threads of their stories from one such climactic incident, albeit in different chronological directions—Haneke's film working forward from one moment, Kieślowski's powered relentlessly forward toward one by Zbigniew Preisner's bolero soundtrack. The narrative of *Code Unknown* proceeds by picking out individual threads from this core and unravelling them so the spaces between the characters grow wider and wider, until even those who already knew each other are alienated (Amadou's father bound for Mali, Anne and Georges' relationship in trouble, Jean having left home, Maria returning to a life of solitary scavenging rather than remaining with her family). Personal meetings seem driven by duty or fraught with difficulty. In contrast, *Red* is a film of convergence, with its archly prescient progress toward the grand finale as particles of Kieślowski's Europe drift into larger and larger clusters. Arguably, though, this does not represent destiny of the sort Haneke denies so much as narration with hindsight, a mood in which *Red* reveals the whole trilogy to be set. (It is, in fact, easy to envisage a similar structure for *Code Unknown,* whereby the grand clash with which it opens might represent a satisfying climax to the hitherto disjointed interweavings of its cast.) What both films suggest is that a human story of apparently remarkable coincidence might be excavated in retrospect, probably from almost any busy populace (here, too, these stories resemble the *Decalogue* [1988], with its central housing estate).

Each of these films represents, then, a very particular social vision, requiring and produced by a very particular cinematic expression. Given the near-complete absence of conscious connection between the people inhabiting the same city, their shared physical world is thrust into significance by the need for an organizing principle. Both films therefore insist initially on the everyday topography common to their characters. This is not to say that they are interested in the geographical or cultural specificities of those places; they eschew the landmarks of Geneva and Paris. Instead, there is a desire to establish the simple physical coherence of a neighborhood, without even the mild disruption of the cuts required to create virtual geographies in the edit suite. The significance of this urban terrain is emphasized by the long mapping sequence shots used in both opening scenes. In *Code Unknown,* the location was selected to permit the camera to move unhindered between places of significance, in this case Anne's front door, the metro, and the ends of the side streets that host the scenes with the beggar. Haneke is extremely suspicious of continuity editing, and his work is characterized in general by long takes using a single camera setup. Even within his oeuvre, however, the eight-minute shot that establishes the central location of *Code Unknown* is exceptional. Kieślowski did not generally share such suspicions, and yet in this case we find his motives surprisingly similar to Haneke's. He was uncharacteristically insistent on the absence of cuts in these introductory moments, to the point of requesting a large sum from the production budget to avoid using an apartment that might require this: "We could have cut and made links in the editing, but this would have been much less credible. . . . I am talking about this detail to show the kind of decisions you have to take to produce one shot which gives the film a certain credibility. The intersections you are talking about [between Valentine and Auguste] would not otherwise exist" (Kieślowski, "Entretien" 30). The resulting crane shot takes us directly through the air from one interior to the other, generating an expectation of connection between Valentine and Auguste. The need for visual, topographical cohesiveness in these works testifies to the absolute absence of any other bond between their protagonists that might impart this quality in more conventional narratives. The coherence of these communities exists on two levels only: that of geographical proximity and the concomitant possibility of simultaneous visual representation.

The lack of intradiegetic consciousness of the stories we are offered is reflected in both films by the fact that the lens is not subjectively entangled with any character. *Red* is rather peculiar in Kieślowski's oeuvre in its heavy stress on the mechanical nature of the camera, which is communicated most notably through such conspicuously complex shots as the early crane shot. The cinematography expresses an overtly dehumanized point of view from the very first, following Valentine's phone call under the English Channel, and then later as it chases a bowling ball down its lane. In a vertiginous dive, it mimics the fall of a book from a theater balcony decades before, adopting a point of view identified with an inanimate object in a different time rather than that of either participant in the dialogue. This refusal to confuse the eye of the camera with the subjective worlds of characters is enacted most definitively when we follow Valentine into the Judge's house for the first time, looking left and right to take in the scene, as we might think she is also doing. Convention requires us to identify this point of view with her own, until the moment she steps into the frame from the side, and Kieślowski neatly warns us off assuming that human perception can be identified precisely with the lens. As I shall go on to demonstrate, one of the aims of *Red* is arguably to demonstrate the varied perceptual worlds that are implied by the figures on the screen but rarely successfully suggested. Haneke also is concerned by the relationship between camera and perception, but he rejects Kieślowski's creative use of cinematography on grounds of realism. Asked whether he would accept a comparison between *Benny's Video* and Kieślowski's *A Short Film about Killing* (1988), he answered: "Yes, all this comes from the same direction. What bothers me in Kieślowski is the aestheticisation, the use of colour filters—the story would not have had that. But the basic attitude is similar" (Haneke, "Das Gegenteil" 39)[1]. Instead, he claims that the long takes and narrative ellipsis which characterize *Code Unknown* represent "an artistic technique which is aimed at showing that our perception is fragmentary" (Haneke, "Code" 8). This tallies with his long-standing complaint that conventional cinema offers an omniscient vision that is outdated, inconsistent with his idea of art, and bears little resemblance to human knowledge: "If film wants to be an art form then it has the duty to deal with reality and in life you don't know everything and the reasons for everything. . . . In nineteenth century novels you have the one narrator that knows every thing [*sic*] but nobody dares to still do that in literature; only the genre of cinema still lives in this style of story telling and my films protest against that" (Haneke, "Breaking" 23). His personal mode of realism perhaps owes something to his theatrical background. Within individual scenes, he adheres to a unity of time as part of his attempt to achieve a kind of verisimilitude. As he has described it, "it's the closest you can get to the feeling of reality . . . doing one take and having the action happening in real time" (Haneke, "Breaking" 22). Certainly, his paring down of the narrative makes us work harder at the processes of assumption, deduction, and extrapolation we employ less consciously in watching most films. By not thrusting his story at us with suggestive cuts and emotive soundtracks, he delineates and hands over the processes of selective attention involved in extracting significance from a broad scene, although arguably the net result is hardly less artificial for that. It is true, though, that he achieves an effect akin to that of Kieślowski's manifestly mechanized camera by asserting his distance through editing. The brief windows into the world of *Code Unknown* display, as much as they do their contents, the unknowability of characters' lives and the uncharted space stretching around any framed image.

Yet however much Haneke might strive to avoid the conspicuously cinematic, his fragmentary style does not really mimic the limitations of human perception. For the individual subject, perception is not fragmentary and confused but controlled by the processes of selective attention that help produce a comfortable gestalt. Fractures lie not within the individual but between the different interpretations people form of a superficially shared world. The limitations of our understanding lie in the need to eliminate stimuli from the huge breadth presented simultaneously, not in interruptions on the plane of time. Haneke keeps his camera at human height, in "hearing" distance of any conversation, with no extradiegetic music or insights into the "other" side of telephone conversations, yet his film is not an image of human perception. None of his protagonists, and presumably nobody in this city, is able to engage with their immediate context fully enough to register half of what has been selected for the very different mode of consumption of the film spectator. The diversity of individual lines of attention within the same environment is illustrated eloquently in the opening scene, where a street musician draws Jean off his course, but others seem entirely oblivious to the sound. Within the bustle of Amadou's family home, coherently contained by one space, people are engaged in two different overlaid conversations, one in speech and one in sign language. A more unusual suggestion of these disparate perceptual worlds is given in sequential form, in a series of monochrome still photographs ostensibly taken on the metro by Georges.[2] Each shows one person and is positioned in the center of the frame, surrounded by black. Given the subjects' ignorance of the fact that they are being photographed and the general aversion to looking at people on public transport, they are all casting their eyes in any direction but our own, apparently out into the void (which does in fact mirror the blackness of the pointless "view" of the tunnels beyond the windows). The result is a relentless parade of starkly drawn diverging eyelines that will never meet either each other or our own. Whatever the nature of our point of view, it is not shared by any of the residents of Haneke's Paris, nor do these people perceive it in the same ways as each other. Here Haneke's film draws close to some of the subtler concerns of *Red,* in which we see Auguste so absorbed by the sight of Valentine's poster that he is deaf to the cars hooting around him, in contrast to Valentine herself, who was earlier so absorbed by her radio that she was blind to the road ahead. We see people standing next to each other in a music shop, lost in the separate aural worlds conveyed through their different sets of headphones. The changes of music as the camera sweeps over them offer one of the few instances of subjective sound in *Red,* illustrating that although these people are united on the visual plane of the frame, they are absorbed in a very different process. Even those who are listening to the same thing do so in individual bubbles, without sharing the experience, with the exception of Auguste and his girlfriend, who are listening together. Both Haneke and Kieślowski illustrate a place in which people are isolated in their perceptual worlds, attending to such wildly different combinations of stimuli that they can barely be said to be experiencing a shared space.

In asserting the power of sound to peel his protagonists' attention away from their physical, visible settings, Kieślowski points both to the artificial visuality of cinema and to the lack of synthesis between sight and sound that obtains in life as much as in art. In this respect, then, his use of a grand musical soundtrack may not be as antirealist as Haneke would consider it but instead exposes the synthetic quality of focussed narrative and mimics the

In *Three Colors: Red* (1994), Valentine (Irène Jacob) and her neighbor August (Jean-Pierre Lorit) and his girlfriend Karin (Frédérique Freder) stand right next to each other in a music shop but remain mutually unaware, separated in their own aural worlds, demonstrating what Derrida has termed the "private sociality" of our contemporary, technologically mediated existence.

splitting of the visual and the aural that is endemic to a technologically advanced society. Asked whether "cars, immigration and the telephone" were the cause of his characters' unhappiness in *Red,* Kieślowski answered: "I feel that this technology is responsible for a great many ills. Technology is developing greatly, but what we call culture is not following. . . . To tell the truth, we are not really conscious of the danger it represents, and there lies the problem of contemporary culture" (Kieślowski, "Entretien" 27). This invisible web of communication has been identified by Jacques Derrida as "private sociality, far beyond the territory of measurable-surveyable space" (57), describing the way the telephone in particular accords to the individual the ability to be ever more selective in social encounters, physically close to hundreds of others but emotionally connected to those far away. This is perfectly encapsulated by the dazzling opening of *Red,* in which we track every inch of the long telephone wires between Valentine and her boyfriend Michel before the long crane shot moving from Auguste's to Valentine's apartment establishes their close association in space in spite of their mutual ignorance of each other. In a similar vein, we see Anne in *Code Unknown* reach first for the telephone to consult Georges upon receiving a note from one of her immediate neighbors, and Amadou's taxi-driver father entirely preoccupied by a call on his mobile phone to the extent that he drives extremely dangerously and eventually deposits his passenger early (who remains unseen, in a visual translation of the insignificance of his presence). The inevitable conclusion of the visually prioritizing spectator is that these aural connections are setting people further apart from a full sense of their physical context and diminishing the possibilities for the kind of redemptive shared experience proposed by the frame.

Contact may not ultimately involve sensation of the other so much as sensation shared with the other. Here we see a parallel with the shared vision of the heavens identified by Georg Simmel as a key component of all religions, offering an "identity of impression" with a powerful "communalizing sociological effect": "This fact must foster, on the one hand, that transcendence from the narrowness and particularity of the human subject which every religion contains and, on the other, support or favour the element of a union of the faithful, which every religion likewise contains" (Simmel 116). Clearly, neither of these films proposes any cohesion on such a grand scale, but *Red* certainly employs the idea that a coincidence of perceptual worlds fosters a particular bond between people in spite of themselves. This starts with Valentine's reluctant but beautiful moments of shared focus with the Judge when they both concentrate on the voices emanating from his eavesdropping equipment, and then on the "beautiful light" that breaks into the room. Auguste and Karine's shared listening experience in the record shop signifies their early apparent closeness (and the fact that Valentine is listening to the same music implants our notion that she and Auguste are living on parallel lines that require a chance turn to become one). Valentine is thrust into a romantic scenario with her photographer by their shared contemplation of the transparencies glowing on the light box, and the similarities between Auguste's and the Judge's attentive choices are established by their mutual absorption in Valentine's poster. Haneke's film does not provide much in the way of mutual visions. The grim parallel walk of Julie and her elderly neighbor from a little girl's funeral speaks of two separate worlds of self-absorption. The shiny droplet hanging from the older woman's nose that so distracts us on the screen is apparently remarked by neither of them. Yet, perhaps surprisingly, it is *Code Unknown* that offers us a single extraordinarily tender moment of contact. Amadou's family may be splintering, but his evident happiness in his work and his budding relationship with a young white colleague promise an alternative connection, not unlike that suggested by Valentine and Auguste's final frame. As they sit in a café together, she removes her watch because he does not like it. He kisses the newly vulnerable spot on her wrist and she withdraws her hand, yet continues to stroke the place herself in exploratory imitation of the original gesture. For Robin Wood, this is a rejection indicating the racial barrier between them (46), but I see only a rather nervous occasion infused with tentative promise. Her action shows us the strange duality of touch, which allows us to sense from both inside and out, to half leave our own bodies for an instant and find them as others do. In this moment, she senses what he senses and quits the perceptual bubble surrounding so many of these city-dwellers to move between both their worlds.

A review of *Code Unknown* in the popular French weekly *Télérama* declared that "as Krzysztof Kieślowski did for *Blue* (1993), Michael Haneke has left his country, Austria, to come and make a film in France with Juliette Binoche, produced by Marin Karmitz. The parallel ends there" (Strauss 65). The preceding discussion has, I hope, demonstrated that the two share far more than circumstantial connections; indeed, there are far more links that might be explored, in particular the play between still images, film images, and film images within film images, which lends a significant accent to both these works. Both *Red* and *Code Unknown* present us with fragmented societies, and at the same time move to illustrate the fragmented perceptions of the individuals who compose that society. In so doing, both directors face up to the conundrum that now confronts anyone now wishing to make a serious film on this subject. As real-life sociality becomes ever more disconnected from spatial proximity, it becomes ever less cinematic. Haneke chooses to adhere rigidly to a human perspective on the physical, visual locations of the action, refusing to bend the nature of the society he records to make it appear more conventionally "cinematic" and thus inevitably revealing a confusion of cracks and layers. Kieślowski instead uses cinematographic wizardry and the aural espionage of the Judge to manifest the invisible networks of private sociality and set these against the alternatives he presents by populating the frame with suggestive pairs. He can then move to his meticulously orchestrated conclusion without any suggestion that he is unaware of the limitations and demands of his medium or of his subject. *Red* is a vision of humanity and cinema that is optimistic in spite of its manifest awareness of the problems inhering in both. Haneke's piece, made ten years later in an era when Europe's promise seems perhaps less real, is clearly more urgent and no source of succor. It is, however, imbued with the same delicate consciousness of the world it describes, leading us to find our own sense of the paths that lead through it.

Notes

1. I am indebted to the generosity of Mattias Frey of Harvard University for this quotation.

2. These photographs, and the war photographs also included in *Code Unknown,* are actually the work of Luc Delahaye.

Works Cited

Where references indicate a source in a language other than English, all translations are my own.

Derrida, Jacques. *Of Hospitality: Anne Dufourmantelle Invites Jacques Derrida to Respond.* Trans. Rachel Bowlby. Stanford: Stanford University Press, 2000.

Dobson, Julia. "Nationality, Authenticity, Reflexivity: Kieślowski's *Trois Couleurs: Bleu* (1993), *Blanc* (1993), *Rouge* (1994)." *French Cinema in the 1990s: Continuity and Difference.* Ed. P. Powrie. Oxford: Oxford University Press, 1999. 239–45.

Grassin, Sophie. "Binoche cachée." *Première* 344 (October 2005): 85–86.

Haneke, Michael. "Breaking the Code." Interview by Paul Farren. *Film Ireland* 80 (April/May 2001): 22–23.

———. "Code Uncracked." Interview by Nick James. *Sight and Sound* 11.6 (June 2001): 8.

———. "Das Gegenteil von Hollywood." Interview by Wolf Donner. *Tip* 12 (1993): 35–39.

———. "The World That Is Known: An Interview with Michael Haneke." Interview by Christopher Sharrett. *Cineaste* 20.3 (Summer 2003): 28–31.

Jacob, Irène. "Irène Jacob Talks about *Red.*" Interview by S. Toubiana and P. Truffault. *Three Colours: Red.* DVD. Directed by Krzysztof Kieślowski. Artificial Eye, 2001.

Johnson, Sheila. "*Code Unknown* (*Code Inconnu*)." *Screen International* 1262 (9 June 2000): 20.

Karmitz, Marin. *Profession producteur: conversations avec Stéphane Paoli.* Paris: Hachette Littératures, 2003.

———. "Three Colours Blue, White and Red: Krzysztof Kieślowski and Friends." Interviews by Serge Mensonge. *Cinema Papers* 99 (June 1994): 26–32.

Kieślowski, Krzysztof. "Entretien avec Krzysztof Kieślowski: [La fraternité existe dès que l'on est prêt à écouter l'autre]." Interview by Vincent Amiel and Michel Ciment. *Positif* 403 (September 1994): 26–32.

———. "La liberté est impossible: entretien avec Krzysztof Kieślowski" Interview by Michel Ciment and Hubert Niogret. *Krzysztof Kieślowski.* Ed. Vincent Amiel. Paris: Jean-Michel Place, Positif, 1997. 124–34.

Said, S. F. "Are We Waving or Drowning?" *Daily Telegraph,* 17 May 2001: 24

Simmel, G. "The Sociology of the Senses." *Simmel on Culture.* Ed. D. Frisby and M. Featherstone. London: Sage, 1997. 109–20.

Stok, Danusia, ed. *Kieślowski on Kieślowski.* London: Faber and Faber, 1993.

Strauss, Frédéric. *Télérama* 2653 (15 November 2000): 65–66.

Vincendeau, Ginette. "Juliette Binoche: From Gamine to Femme Fatale." *Sight and Sound* 3.12 (December 1993): 22–25.

Wood, Robin. "In Search of the Code Inconnu." *Cineaction* 62 (2003): 41–49.

7

Just Gaming?

Kieślowski's *Blind Chance,* Tykwer's *Run Lola Run,* and a Note on *Heaven*

Paul Coates

Debates on the interrelationship of art and games sometimes pose the question of the degree of possible homology and conflict between those two time-based and visually oriented forms, the film and the video game. For instance, in his work on the nature of video games' intertextual relations with such narrative forms as those of genre film, Henry Jenkins has meditated on, and sought to mediate in, the dispute between the adherents of ludology and those of narratology. The last decade has seen the emergence of films whose structures clearly resemble the ludic ones of video games, allowing their protagonists a number of "lives" wherewith to negotiate a certain scenario, suspending both expected outcomes and the notion of narrative teleology itself. In an essay on one such film, *Run Lola Run* (1998), Margit Grieb likens Tom Tykwer's filmic Lola to the Lara Croft of the eponymous video game. And given the clear connection between *Run Lola Run* and Kieślowski's *Blind Chance* (1981, released 1987), one may be tempted to read the Polish director's film as a primitive anticipation of video-game structure. Among other things, this essay will debate the validity of such a reading.

I would like to begin, however, by arguing that the categories of "art" and "game" are opposed in most cases. Whereas the video game offers a fantasy of control and safety in endless resurrection, a snakes-and-ladders facility of endless restart with the final fantasy—if there is one—being escape from death, the filmic fantasy is one of safe surrender, for even though protagonists may die, they are not oneself; identification is not identity. If the former is organized around a blatant identification of protagonist and player, with the body of the one the mirror of the other (so that the player's real hand may even be echoed within the game in virtual form), in the latter, identification is usually more diffuse, fusing recognition and misrecognition, and could arguably be described more accurately as identification with a world, its presuppositions, and its rhythm of growth and unfolding than with a character engaged in a near-paranoid battle with the world. And of course, no individual game or film ever actualizes either fantasy completely, as the control offered by the game occurs within parameters set by another person, while the filmgoer is only likely to surrender to certain genres and/or films reviewed favorably by certain preferred critics—and even such promising foreplay may end in a refusal. The tendency to deem video games possibly compatible with film, meanwhile, may well be a misunderstanding generated by—among other things—the prevalence of individualistically focused action scenarios both in video games and in the U.S. cinema, which dominates world markets; by the fashion consciousness of filmmakers, spectators, or theorists anxious only to be seen with the latest technological thing; by a confusion of fiction-making with modelling; by the video game's growing adeptness at mimicking the surfaces of everyday life; by the intersection of philosophy, physics, and science fiction around the question of possible worlds; and by the desire to have the best of these worlds. Game-playing, meanwhile, may display some similarities to the process whereby an artist produces a work, shuffling and reshuffling the deck of possibilities, but the customary final selection of one configuration freezes a potentially infinite play, and the receiver has no idea how many shufflings may have preceded the combination actually inserted into the public sphere.

If the distinctions between film and video game are indeed quite robust, one may ask whether film can ever be said to "just game." Is its generic play, a play with and against preexisting scenarios, ever just play? In words that reflect a key preoccupation of post-Schillerian art theory, "Ist die Kunst heiter?" (Is art light-hearted?)—to which one might add, "*Nur* heiter"? (*Only* light-hearted?). Such questions become particularly acute in the case of films that explicitly entertain alternative scenarios and so seem to offer spectators the opportunity to follow in the footsteps of a filmmaker who declares the material of character and narrative endlessly subject to revision, to enjoy a video-game-like "eternal return." Is this attitude necessarily playful—which may mean "postmodern"—or could it also be adumbrated in modernism, as part of its reaction to the evaporation of authority; or is it even perennial, logico-philosophical? The following paper will pose this question to two interrelated texts, each one preoccupied with alternatives. This is particularly justified inasmuch as these texts may themselves be seen as alternative versions of one another: Krzysztof Kieślowski's *Blind Chance* and Tom Tykwer's *Run Lola Run*. Among other things, I will consider whether Kieślowski's film proposes an outdated modernism desperately in need of Tykwer's (postmodern?) techno-revision, or whether the relationship between these texts is more complex than that.

Comparisons between *Blind Chance* and *Run Lola Run* are inevitable. For Slavoj Žižek, one of the first to make such a comparison, it comes out in favor of Tykwer. Having asserted that "the formal matrix is the same: in both cases one can interpret the film as if only the third story is the 'real' one, the other two staging the fantasmatic price the subject has to pay for the 'real' outcome," he concludes that "it is *Blind Chance* which ultimately appears clumsy and artificial, as if the film is trying to tell its story in an inadequate form, while *Lola*'s form perfectly fits its narrative content" (81, 82). Žižek does not say just why Kieślowski's work should be seen as inadequate, though one may guess that this is because it only dimly anticipates and so offers only partial allegiance to the new, hypertextual life experience of alternative worlds hailed by Žižek himself a few pages earlier (78–79). (The absence of any suggestion that such textual multiplicity might be linked to hyperconsumerism is somewhat surprising in a Marxist *Kulturkritiker.*) Žižek seems to suggest that the video-game format available to Tykwer's generation might be the proper objective correlative of this experience, something Kieślowski ostensibly could not achieve, be it because of the Pole's existentialist and political seriousness, because of the fabled technological backwardness of the East ("fabled," because—among other things—Poland had produced Stanisław Lem, the Soviet Union spawned the Tetris game, and Kieślowski had a great interest in computers)—or simply because of the technological limits of his own lifetime. And yet, of course, even though Tykwer draws on some of the procedures of video games, his work too unfolds in "the old cinematic medium that promotes linear narrative" (Žižek 79) and so can hardly be fundamentally different. Žižek gives no clear reason for preferring *Run Lola Run,* being too busy pursuing various associative thought-slides to do so. His critical move may recall T. S. Eliot's ranking of the formally more achieved *Coriolanus* above the messier, more haunting *Hamlet,* though one is loath to ascribe such provocative aestheticism to him.

Žižek's evaluation of the two texts is interesting, but it begs several questions, the most fundamental of which concerns whether Kieślowski and Tykwer really are doing the same thing, and whether *Blind Chance* can be seen as history's clumsy first draft of a preferable revision known as *Run Lola Run.* One may also wonder whether the third section really can be called "the most real" in each case. It is arguable that this is true only of Kieślowski's work, while Tykwer's grows closer to fantasy—in the Freudian sense of daydreamed success—with every re-run. However, even *Blind Chance* issues conflicting signals regarding the relative degrees of reality of the three sections: the final one may link up with the beginning by explaining Witek's screamed "No!" and so seem to offer the real context of the others, but the decreasing length of the stories appears to obey a law of diminishing returns, as if each were in fact a reconjugation of the longer prototype that is the first story, which thus can *feel* "the most real." (This effect is even more pronounced in the posthumously published treatment, in which story one is twenty-seven pages long, story two is six, and story three only three-and-a-half pages [Kieślowski 141–77]). If it comes to the paying of a price, Tykwer spells one out only in his first two sections. Although Kieślowski does so explicitly only in his third, Witek's opening scream reverberates across the work with an intimation that any price may well be the highest one: death. Moreover, a two-way comparison may not be enough: after all, Tykwer's film could be seen as having a double Kieślowskian prototype, its other progenitor being *The Double Life of Véronique* (1991), whose female protagonist, dependence on music, momentary elimination of the protagonist near the thirty-minute mark, and game-like experience of one incarnation learning from another it could be described as adopting, albeit inflecting them differently. To take only the final example: just as *Véronique* expresses the theme of one life learning from another through the French protagonist's abandonment of the singing that prompted her Polish namesake's heart attack, Tykwer's film shows the second story's Lola removing the safety catch from her gun—something Manni had to instruct her to do in the first story—while Lola 3 now knows to jump over the threatening dog and to let herself into the ambulance rather than make the mistake of requesting a ride. If *The Double Life of Véronique* is arguably as much a prototype as *Blind Chance,* could the new "life-experience" to which Žižek alludes as likely be the New Age belief in reincarnation of which his materialism would disapprove as the passion for video games that renders philosophers hip?

Nor are the works formally "the same." If *Run Lola Run* and *Véronique* show death as survivable even by the person who dies, *Blind Chance* pursues two possible alternatives to it (though leaving it simply a suspensefully unidentified horror at the time), only to find it again at an end that is indeed the Eliotic beginning invoked by Tykwer, to which one returns in order to know the place for the first time: a death scream that is another form of the film's birth in a scream (it is no surprise that a bloody traumatic birth—amidst the Poznań riots of 1956—should follow this scream, as if that scream were indeed Witek's birth cry). The first story apparently dismisses the trauma echoing through that opening scream, though spectators may speculate whether this is simply the temporary stay of execution known as the flashback, which so often rebounds from an initial arresting catastrophe. Once the film has unfolded completely, however, the first version seems less like a flashback than an alternative life itinerary followed by another alternative, and the extreme polarization of the life lines pursued in the first two versions by Witek suggests the presence of fantasy: the fantasy of a self that thinks it might have escaped had it been sufficiently different; a fantasy whose actual incapacity to overrule the reality that generates it generates its own destruction and replacement by an opposite fantasy unfolding as it were in the mind of a Proteus seeking to elude the grasp of Menelaus. What then follows as the third story would be classifiable as a postponed flashback. The film's structure can thus be read as having four parts: the initial scream that is reality; a fantasy alternative to it; another fantasy alternative to that; and then the reality that concludes in the scream and the death of its protagonist. Its shape may even be comparable to that of Christopher Nolan's *Memento* (2000), which is structured in reverse, taking one step after another backward through time down to the twist of its ending, in which the apparent victim—unlike Witek—is allowed to choose his fate.

Although the idea of the game is more obviously and blatantly relevant to Tykwer's film, inasmuch as games and chance are related—with each configuration of game-events being unpredictable—comparison with Kieślowski is also warranted: all the more so because chance not only furnishes his film with its title but is also a leitmotif of the Polish director's interviews. But although chance is a recurrent theme in Kieślowski's work, by beginning *Blind Chance* with Witek's scream and by deploying opposite scenarios that logically require a middle one to complete and close them, he gives it a structure that preserves it from succumbing entirely to the dictates of the random. As Rudolf Arnheim notes in a passage whose use of a plane's flight as an example uncannily anticipates this film:

> Suppose you watch a straight line growing—a vapor trail in the sky or a black mark in an animated film or on the pad of an artist. In a world of pure chance, the probability of the line continuing in the same direction is minimal. It is reciprocal to the infinite number of directions the line may take. In a structured world, there is some probability that the straight line will continue to be straight. A person concerned with structure can attempt to derive this probability from his understanding of the structure. How likely is the airplane suddenly to change its course? . . . The information theorist, who persists in ignoring structure, can handle this situation only by deriving from earlier events a measure of how long the straightness is likely to continue. . . . Being a gambler, he takes a blind chance on the future, on the basis of what happened in the past. (16)

Despite its title, the world of Kieślowski's film is structured in terms of logical oppositions and hence not according to simple chance (the Polish *Przypadek* has none of the connotations of the English *blind*). Witold's scream is the logical terminus—as well as the point of departure—of Arnheim's "line."

A concern with chance and alternative scenarios is of course not unexpected in the Kieślowski whose filmmaking passion was largely centered on the possibilities of editing. Different juxtapositions of images generate different scenarios in the case of the bodies of footage that generated *Decalogue 5* and *A Short Film about Killing*, or *Decalogue 6* and *A Short Film about Love* (all 1988), for instance (Coates 46). As described by the Polish literary critic and theorist Artur Sandauer, the modernist pursuit of chance combines two

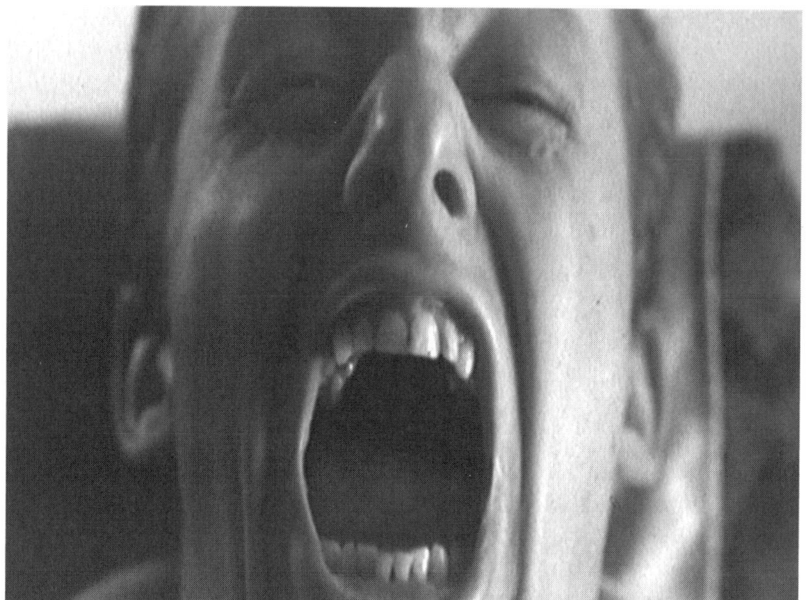

Witek's (Boguslaw Linda) scream in *Blind Chance* (1981) is both the terminus and the point of departure for a narrative line that is not "blind" at all, but entirely logical.

impulses: "it is a matter of 1. shaping the work in accordance with the objective conditioning factors within the material and 2. of, along with this, probing one's own psyche" (Sandauer 131). Sandauer argues also that the widespread nature of such human practices as the casting of lots "indicates how natural a state of indecision is to us" (131). The two impulses enumerated by Sandauer suggest a minihistory of Kieślowski's work avant la lettre, with the attention to "the objective conditioning factors within the material" characterizing the documentarist and the desire to probe the psyche, the later works. The link between these phases becomes the element of chance, which begins by determining so much of the documentarist's material and then becomes an explicit theme of Kieślowski's feature films. Its foregrounding in the title of this particular work suggests that it represents the fulcrum of Kieślowski's career. Meanwhile, Sandauer's correlation of indecision and superstitious practices suggests that the formal indeterminacy of the body of footage, as perceived by Kieślowski, and the themes of superstition, are the recto and verso of a single phenomenon, arguably converging in the variety of foresight known as the flashforward, which Kieślowski was far more prone to use than he was flashbacks. (Whether Kieślowski himself might be comparable to Arnheim's "gambler," whose life unfolds under the sign of chance and superstitious ritual, would of course be a dubious assertion, though the arguments of those critics who attribute New Age beliefs to him—and they include Žižek [121]—might well head in this direction.)

Where Kieślowski's work—that of a former documentarist—is unsurprisingly governed by the reality (or, if one likes, "sobriety" [Nichols 3–4]) principle often associated with the form, plunging toward a death from which any respite is only temporary, Tykwer's flees it under the pressure of a pleasure principle whose probable eventual victory is strongly signalled in story two, when the SWAT-team member bundling bank-robber Lola to safety, away from the bank, asks her if she has a death wish, rendering Freud's principle of Thanatos a joke. *Run Lola Run* in fact reverses the structure of the earlier film in a manner that could be attacked as subordinating art cinema inventiveness to the fatally commodifying laws of the happy ending, though one might also defend it as simply recasting the scenario in the comic mode. (Inevitably, since parody requires a prototype, and first comes tragedy, then farce?) In other words, the ending is not the only thing that is happy, and the comic mode is evident from the very start, for which the cartoon is the primary intertext. Lola's intermittent zapping into cartoon form is highly appropriate, as her punk hairdo is a nonnaturalistic, cartoonish dramatization of the human form and the laws of animation are the pleasurable ones of plasticity, serialization, and endless reanimation. Because these laws prevail, the death that ends Tykwer's first section takes one's breath away only for a moment (a reaction recalling spectatorial ones to the death of the Polish Weronika) as one wonders what could possibly follow it. The various corrections occurring between stories one and two suggest that even Manni's death at the end of story two will undergo revision. If Tykwer's exhilarating work has a flaw, it is that the first death makes a gesture suggestive of an ambition ultimately alien to it: for this brief moment, one might say, the spirit of Kieślowski—the gravitas of real mortality, the unbearable weight of falling being—invades it. Subsequent developments lead one to realize, however, that this death is to be categorized as inconsequential, merely one move in the game of a smart system whose feedback permits corrections until the narrative arrives at the solution known as a happy ending (the best of all possible worlds emerges by trial and error); at which point, of course, the game can stop, the jackpot literally having been won: Lola retains the bag of cash won at the casino. Of the two works, it is Tykwer's that is more obviously "game-like." In Kieślowski's *Red*, by way of contrast, the absence of the best of all possible worlds is signalled by the melancholy demonstration, when Valentine wins on a one-armed bandit, that good fortune of this kind precludes luck in love. In terms of the comments on gambling made earlier, it suggests Kieślowski's opinion of this often superstition-riddled activity—which is of course Lola's solution to her problem. However great the differences between Tykwer and Kieślowski, they resemble one another in their refusal clearly to identify the source of the replay facility. Tykwer's opening reference to the playing of a ninety-minute game signposts only the possibility of game-like procedures, not how the protagonist is able to access them for a revision of her life, despite strong suggestions that her triumph is a possibly alarmingly stereotypically "Germanic romantic" one "of the will": Lola simply refuses to leave, or to let Manni go. "Just one more game," she replies to the casino attendant seeking to escort her out as inappropriately dressed. Kieślowski's mechanism, however, is far more enigmatic: the hypothesis that each of the first two scenarios represents Witek's fantasy reaction to death is worth entertaining, but the work itself does not clearly code the scenarios as his fantasies.

The opening of *Run Lola Run* is both aggressive and supercilious in its playfulness: "after the game is before the game," an epigraph tells us, implying that the game is never-ending. The initial accompanying quotation from T. S. Eliot toys with a seriousness undercut by the deadpan Zen of that "after the game is before the game," and the mock-serious effect is reinforced by the opening voiceover's reflections on mystery and the relationship of question to answer, which are suspiciously akin to parodies of key themes of Kieślowski's late interviews. (The high-low fusion leans, of course, toward the postmodernity often characterized as essentially playful.) Kieślowski references will soon spurt forth in a rush, but not before the work has played yet again with the idea of the game by placing in the mouth of a doltish security guard the platitude that the game lasts ninety minutes—the game in question being of course the so-called beautiful game (art as a game of beauty?); he then kicks upward the soccer ball that lands as the camera does in Lola's apartment, starting this film's game. The implication is that although games may model experience for a Wittgenstein or a Lyotard, they should not be taken too seriously. The possibility that a high philosophy might be an appropriate accompaniment to game-playing is parodied by the platitudinously low one of the proverbially inarticulate soccer fan; whatever goes up is bound to come down. Tykwer extends his game with temporality into self-parody, as his own film—less than the ninety minutes the football reference would cause one to expect—recalls Kieślowski's "short films" (*A Short Film about Killing* or *A Short Film about Love*), which approximate that length, and yet—possibly ironically—is even shorter than either. Should the game-within-the-game need a title, it could be "Love Can Do Anything," which Manni derisively declares is Lola's credo as he grows ever more hysterical at the thought of the consequences of the loss of the money.

The next set of allusions mostly cross-reference Kieślowski. After the credit-sequence disappearance of the camera into the mouth of the monster, which echoes the opening of *Blind Chance,* a key element of that film will recur when the underground guards prevent Manni from entering the train—just as the station guard wrestles with Witek 2. In between these two moments comes a recollection of the opening of *Red* (the forward zoom between telephones); and naturally, Lola's phone is red. The importance of speed

Run Lola Run (1998) begins with a doltish security guard kicking the soccer ball up into the air, parodying the notion that high philosophy is an appropriate accompaniment to the "game" that follows.

for the film is signalled also in the opening use of the spiral, recalling *Vertigo* (1958). It pulls the swirling Lola in, though Tykwer's spiral is the sucking force of a suspense narrative that runs on speed and makes things spin increasingly rapidly as it draws elements into it, like water about to go down a drain: Tykwer's spiral is both that of the opening credits of *Vertigo* and the shower drain of *Psycho* (1960). It also appears behind Manni as he waits in the phone booth. If it is the imagistic form of the circular epigraph identifying the game's "before" with its "after," could its recurrence also be a gesture toward Siegfried Kracauer's description of the spiral as a leitmotif of Weimar cinema? Its significance both for Hitchcock and, say, Fritz Lang's *M.* (1931) may underline the internationalism of Tykwer's film, with its virtuoso MTV rhythm and magpie style, but it also displays a self-conscious, albeit implicit, allegiance to and awareness of German film history, of which the name *Lola* itself is a key metonym. (Lola's glass-shattering scream has also been described as recalling Oskar's in Volker Schlöndorff's *The Tin Drum* [1979].) Echoing the terms of that history, in story 1 the spiral becomes Fate as the camera describes a 360-degree turn around Lola and Manni once police have blocked both ends of the street where they stand.

The story Tykwer retells again and again can indeed be defined as game-like in that it poses a problem in need of a solution, then tries out a variety of them. Remembering my earlier discussion of "becoming another person," one is tempted to say that the rule that defines a game as such is that the game-player chooses to enter each new scenario as the same person, not to become another one. Any variables involve plot, not character. Lola and Manni always play the same roles; only the outcomes differ. Manni is not a dealer in one scenario and a solid citizen in another (punished or rewarded according to square or hip norms). Despite the vatic, Zen-like opening quotations, the self-correction is not karmic. Are matters any different in *Blind Chance,* where Witek both is and is not the same person? His choice of strongly contrasted career paths would seem to make each Witek potentially a different person, but in each case he is fundamentally decent (becoming a communist, for instance, does not make him the blackguard of Solidarity stereotype), and his reactions to analogous situations are the same. How significant is the similarity between Witek 1, 2, and 3, though? Does each alternative version itself solicit or permit opposed readings, as the plot mechanism stresses difference while the characterization foregrounds similarity? Could the work's paradoxes be described as the result of combining temporality (narrative) with an ambiguous spatial image ("Witek as both same and different"), such as the one psychologists use that can be seen as both a vase and two profiles *simultaneously*? Imagining alternative versions at one and the same time issues in a "whole-field" effect of mutual suspension and vertigo akin to that of the viewer of the innumerable balls held in the air by the two jugglers in the final story. In the alternative version of *this* scenario of virtuosity, the one that affects Witek 3, all narratives collapse at once: as he attempts to juggle, his apples fall when he adds the third that is possibly an image of himself. The jugglers' balls would then be mise-en-abyme images of *Blind Chance* as a whole, not of the story of Witek 3 within which they appear. Thus, it may well be the *nearness to the end* of the third story that permits the suggestion of totalization embodied in their appearance.

Blind Chance may be described as moving from a simple binarism to fissiparousness, ending as one binary begins to fork into further ones in a paradoxical manner that both upholds and destroys either/or logic. Thus, the binary of "catch or miss the train" has superimposed on it, in the third story, another one: "miss the train with a positive outcome" or "miss the train with a negative outcome." This corresponds to a new binary situation: "catch or miss the plane." Symmetry dictates that if the catching or missing of the train is the decisive event in Witek's life, the catching or missing of the plane determines his death. As he succeeds in catching the plane the third time, he dies—enabling the story to end. The story becomes an unfolding of the moment that creates three Witeks and ends when one of them ceases to be. Beginning when freedom from either/or (political) logic appears a possibility and ending when that logic reasserts itself, it is poised between the overlapping but separate systems of train and plane, located in the interference of the ripples they generate: the train is caught by Witek 1 but missed by Witek 2 and 3, while the plane is missed by Witek 1 and 2 but caught by Witek 3. The elegance of this construction needs to be noticed. It indicates that the logic of *Blind Chance* is not just that of either/or and the intermediacy that is repressed by it under the supposed law of *tertium non datur* (literally, "there is no third") (having missed the train, failed to reach Warsaw, and failed to attach himself to the moving forces of Polish history, Witek 3 ought to be too marginal to the system to be in danger); it is also one of fissiparously ramifying binaries. Its effect may be likened to the dark logic of Miroslaw Kijowicz's short animation *Droga* (*The Road*, 1971). Here two halves of a self go separate ways at a fork in the road. They keep taking new forks but in the end move back in the right direction to reunify. However, although they then fuse—after all, they belong together—they have grown apart in the meantime: the right and left sides are no longer symmetrical, and the new whole is misshapen. Whether one can extrapolate this logic into a description of Witek 3 as in a sense "misshapen," and hence possibly "inviting" abortion, is doubtful, but his eventual nonexistence may well correlate with the mutual cancellation of the two scenarios that precede his arrival, their reciprocal nullification rendering him "always already" a nullity. *Tertium non datur* indeed. However, the story of Witek 3 may simply be that of the happiness that has no history, or at least none in the People's Republic of Poland, and whose incipient actualization prompts the envious revenge of invisible gods.

Each of these two films dramatizes the interrelationship of fantasy and repetition. For Gilles Deleuze, in a triple repetition of this kind, the third repetition would mark the onset of a Nietzschean eternal return (93–94). Deleuze's formula for triple repetition might seem to fit Tykwer's endlessly renewable circularity, for it does indeed recall a game, and games can by definition be played ad infinitum, but since it is a film, it does in fact end. However, the formula is far less applicable to Kieślowski's exploration of what can be seen as an individual's vain, last-ditch effort at survival. Each work represents a concretion of the logical diagram of the three main permutations of a situational set. One could say that the eventual rhetorical effect of having thereby seemingly exhausted possibilities enables each work to end convincingly and so banish the possible sense of entrapment in a bad eternity, granting the aesthetic satisfaction of form. It could be, though, that the exhaustion of temporal possibilities takes one up to the edge of time and so generates a sense of eternity by negation. Dialectically, fantasy simulates realism as it inspects the key logical possibilities of a situation to generate a sense of reality by creating one of totality, *totality* being a defining characteristic—and near-synonym—of *reality*. As we will see at the end of this piece, however, realism may require more than any one work can deliver.

Although the theory of repetition might seem centrally relevant to *Blind Chance* and *Run Lola Run,* as each permutates the elements of what seems to be a single narrative matrix, the extensive divergences between retellings indicate that what is required is a theory of the interrelationship of repetition and difference. Indeed, if one views Tykwer's film as Richard Falcon does, arguing that "none [of the stories] is more real than any other" (52), it may even be impossible to speak of a single narrative matrix, as one is confronted with variations without a theme. It is possible, though, that as a result of this *askesis,* the first telling of the story functions or is read—or recoded retrospectively, "art cinema" style—as a presentation of the theme. A recollection of the work's opening sequence—or just of the program notes' statement of the work's length—marks the first ending as false, a premature entry into a blind alley, as the game has to last ninety minutes. In any case, the form of storytelling both Kieślowski and Tykwer employ results in a thoroughgoing digitization of their works, their Zeno-like splintering into a potentially infinite array of atomized, substitutable elements. One could also speak of a punctualization, an endless openness to editorial punctuation and temporal shifting. The work becomes a series of points digitally marked as ones or zeroes depending on whether or not a new element comes into play (if one likes, score one in the game for each new element, and zero—in the sense of "no new information"—for each repetition). It is of course a truism that a combination of difference and repetition animates all storytelling, and all conceptualizations of eventfulness per se. Works reshuffle elements of existing genres, remake past stories, and pursue a plethora of mostly implicit negotiations with a past whose fixity they partly problematize, whose externality they partly ingest. What is unusual about the form Kieślowski and Tykwer employ is that, after the first telling, each subsequent reworking oscillates continually, visibly, and explicitly between a present moment (the story currently running) and outcrops of the past jutting up into it. Previous stories are not the usual phantom (lost-yet-here, i.e., *remembered*) presence beyond the door—which sometimes knocks surprisingly hard for a phantom—but rather latent fists coming through it at points, propelling traumatic splinters into the surface story-space. The Kieślowski/Tykwer narrative mode responds powerfully and modernistically to an evacuation of authority, the lack verbally thematized in Witek's father's statement that "you don't have to do anything." The narrative's only authority may well be its own first incarnation, whose setting of parameters it can never escape entirely. It has another authority, though, antecedent even to that first telling: the moment at which it theorizes its own procedures, be it in what one may call the pre-story of *Blind Chance,* when the father makes this remark—a section that is not repeated at all—or in the epigraphs and vatic pseudophilosophical meditations that begin *Run Lola Run.* This habit of self-reference is the persistence of modernism in these works, though Tykwer's may be seen as balanced precariously on the point at which modernism tips over completely into postmodernism. Kieślowski and Tykwer kill their own stories to turn them into the ghosts that can haunt their works. In Tykwer's case, though, matters are more complicated, as this modernist self-reference is overlaid with multiple allusions to someone who becomes the hidden authority of his work: Kieślowski. Kieślowski becomes the father figure whose presence—however ghostly—not only permits but surely even requires Tykwer to be the child, his work infantilized (in a word, perhaps, postmodern?). Kieślowski's lack of any such external point of reference renders his work far more deeply subversive of authority: there is no daddy—however impotent—as a first port of call in a time of trouble. (Is this difference between the works also gendered as that between the traditionally more self-sufficient male protagonist and the traditionally more dependent female one?)

In this context, it is worth adding a few words about Tykwer's later adaptation of the Kieślowski/Piesiewicz scenario for *Heaven* (2002), where the fact of death is again buffered, albeit in a different manner. That buffering, however, is justified by Kieślowski's own melting of death into an endless heavenward helicopter ascent that may be likened to the even less plausible, but also mythical, defiance of gravity by the car at the end of *Thelma and Louise* (1991), two endings that are further linked by the motif of flight from the police. A keyword of Kieślowski's interviews—and the title of one of his early films—was *peace,* and Tykwer's version of the *Heaven* script could be retitled *Peace* also: providing a real form of the peace denied in Kieślowski's own, earlier ironic use of that title. As Tykwer's film proceeds, moving beyond the suspense of Philippa's attempted murder of the drug dealer and her subsequent escape with Filippo, heaven begins to infuse earth through three formal strategies in particular: symmetry, the slow piano score of Arvo Pärt, and overhead shots. All three distance events, and it is significant that the quotient of symmetry in particular rises markedly near the work's end, as the punk hairdo Philippa adopts serves not only for disguise but also permits images of the two escapees' heads to balance one another on either side of the frame, male and female becoming as nearly one as their names already are: thus, they peer together over the windowsill into the house of Philippa's friend, or bookend the image in profile. Sometimes these strategies will appear together, as when the camera rises to an overhead shot with a tree on either side as the two run away into the distance. In the end, peace has so enveloped the work that the soundtrack is virtually silent as the two appropriate the helicopter, its reality looping back to fuse with the silent virtual reality of the helicopter flight simulation with which the film began. Peace can be seen as having been adumbrated earlier in the overhead shots of the city, muting distant noise, or of Filippo asleep alone or opposite Philippa in the attic, but only after their escape does it become pervasive, its advent facilitated by the unearthly quiet of the sealed train whose still slide shuts out the passing world. The light at the end of the tunnel, toward which it is heading, can be seen as a horizontal version of the point in the sky into which the helicopter disappears. As this happens, the artificial and the mythical fuse. The artificial had been present at the outset in the images of the helicopter flight simulation. It becomes mythical as Philippa and Filippo stand opposite one another against the sunset beneath an Edenic tree: having become generic images of humanity, a new Adam and Eve, through their reduction to silhouettes by the setting sun, they then reverse the Fall by rising. Confessing to Filippo in the church, Philippa had said she wanted death to come quickly, a statement one senses—and fears—may have been a disguised first-person one from Kieślowski himself. As puppet master, he grants his puppets that deliverance, pulling them rapidly up to the sky and from the scene. Trapped on earth—and *trap* was another Kieślowski keyword—they have nowhere to go but up, into a sky that becomes heaven imperceptibly. Since in many languages (including Polish) a single word designates both sky and heaven, perhaps their fusion—the fusion of the real and the artificial under the sign of myth—is more than just a puppeteer's legerdemain. Is it perhaps the *fourth* version of Witek's story in *Blind Chance*—the one logically required by the semiotic square of A. J. Greimas—in which he *escapes* (which would mean that, like Lola, he escapes death—making Tykwer's filming of this script ironically appropriate)? If *Heaven* and *Blind Chance* may be combined to form one realistic entity, one's conclusion may be that no work can achieve the totalization realism requires.

Works Cited

Arnheim, Rudolf. *Entropy: An Essay on Disorder and Order.* Berkeley: University of California Press, 1971.

Coates, Paul. "Kieślowski and the Crisis of Documentary." *Lucid Dreams: The Films of Krzysztof Kieślowski.* Ed. Paul Coates. Trowbridge: Flicks Books, 1999. 32–53.

Deleuze, Gilles. *Difference and Repetition.* New York: Columbia University Press, 1994.

Falcon, Richard. "Run Lola Run/Lola rennt." *Sight and Sound* 9 (November 1999): 52.

Grieb, Margit. "Run Lara Run." *ScreenPlay: cinema/videogames/interfaces.* Ed. Geoff King and Tanya Krzywinska. London: Wallflower, 2002. 157–70.

Jenkins, Henry. "Game Design as Narrative Architecture." http://web.mit.edu/cms/People/henry3/games&narrative.html.

Kieślowski, Krzysztof. *Przypadek i inne teksty.* Ed. Hanna Krall. Kraków: Znak, 1998. 141–77.

Nichols, Bill. *Representing Reality: Issues and Concepts in Documentary.* Bloomington: Indiana University Press, 1991.

Sandauer, Artur. *Matecznik literacki.* Wydawnictwo literackie: Kraków, 1972.

Žižek, Slavoj. *The Fright of Real Tears: Krzysztof Kieślowski between Theory and Post-Theory.* British Film Institute: London, 2001.

8

The Picture of Marriage

Godard's *Contempt* and Kieślowski's *White*

Steven Woodward

> I very much like and admire Godard's early films and would gladly pay them some kind of homage. —Krzysztof Kieślowski, qtd. in Paul Coates, "'The inner life is the only thing that interests me': A Conversation with Krzysztof Kieślowski"

> I imagined one could make a film about what remained of this hope afterwards. About the people who look into the sky. —Kieślowski, qtd. in Paul Coates, *Cinema, Religion, and the Romantic Legacy*

Polish critics who decry Kieślowski's late non-Polish features on the basis of their elision of the material world, their exclusion of politics, and their aesthetic framing of suffering ignore how these films effectively engage with the larger European filmmaking tradition, with that tradition's discourses and aesthetics. As Emma Wilson notes, "Kieślowski's French cinema is in part a cinema of artistic exile and of visual self-consciousness. Kieślowski takes his place in French filmmaking through a series of internal references, homages, debts which filter his vision" (xvi). Furthermore, as Wilson has so astutely argued, Kieślowski's displacement, his estrangement from his own language and filmmaking community, are essential components of his metaphysical explorations. The Polish critic Tadeusz Lubelski has defended Kieślowski in similar terms, arguing that Kieślowski was the preeminent Polish practitioner of the "strategy of a tale-maker," largely ignoring the strategies of psychotherapist or of witness more typical of Polish cinema. For Lubelski, too, Kieślowski pursues a consistent line, both before and after 1989, with his last films constituting "his crowning cinematic achievement" (34). Kieślowski's move to international coproductions was undoubtedly necessary in the face of post-1989 economic and cultural conditions in Poland, but the move enabled the natural progression or extension of his own work, even if the resulting films were less recognizably Polish. The challenging circumstances of production—with the French-based Romanian-Jewish Marin Karmitz acting as producer and the monolingual Kieślowski directing a largely French cast and crew—were not a liability but an opportunity for a filmmaker perennially concerned with the foundation of ethics, with relation of self to other.

In this essay, I consider how the whole of the *Three Colors* trilogy (1993–94)—from its coding in blues, whites, and reds, through its focus on the struggle for connection between self and other and for a related transcendence, to its self-reflexive concerns with the process of filmmaking in a transnational context—can be interpreted as Kieślowski's extension of his own work *through* his response to one particular European filmmaker, Jean-Luc Godard, and even to one particular Godard film, *Contempt* (*Le Mépris,* 1963). In this reading, *Three Colors: White* (1994) is the central link between Kieślowski and Godard, not only because it includes a direct diegetic reference to *Contempt,* but because it is focused on the subject of equality, the genuine mutual regard of one subject and another, the opposite in fact of contempt. Furthermore, I argue that Kieślowski's response to Godard's film continues, even beyond his own death, in *Heaven* (2002), a detailed treatment for which Kieślowski and his longstanding writing partner Krysztof Piesiewicz had completed before Kieślowski's death and that was ultimately made by Tom Tykwer.

What is the point of the allusion to Jean-Luc Godard's *Contempt* that Kieślowski placed in *White,* the middle film of the trilogy that was his last completed project? In *White,* the Polish hairdresser Karol Karol (Zbigniew Zamachowski) is down and out in Paris after being divorced by his French wife, Dominique (played by an icy Julie Delpy), on the grounds that he never consummated their marriage. Meeting a fellow Pole, Mikolaj (Janusz Gajos), in the metro, Karol explains that he is essentially trapped in Paris. Without money or passport, he cannot return to Poland, where he might be able to capitalize on his skills as a hairdresser. But Karol is not just a man without a country; he is also trapped in a liminal mental space, unable to renounce the woman who has treated him with contempt. He speaks to Mikolaj in awed tones of the beauty of his ex-wife, then leads him aboveground to point her out to Mikolaj. Her apartment, it turns out, is just above the entrance to the metro station where Karol has been languishing. Mikolaj misreads Karol's gesticulating arm, noticing not the window of Karol's ex-wife's apartment but a larger-than-life image of Brigitte Bardot on a movie poster for *Contempt.*

Kieślowski himself explained this allusion in entirely pragmatic terms, and some critics have accepted that explanation with only minor qualifications. In the published screenplay (the fourth version, according to the translator Danusia Stok), the movie poster is simply described as of "an actress laughing" (122), though the dialogue indicates that the actress would be Michelle Pfeiffer. When asked by Paul Coates why Pfeiffer had become the Bardot of *Contempt* in the film, Kieślowski shrugged off its implications:

> I had absolutely no intention of putting up a poster from Godard or *Contempt* or anything that would make an allusion. I wanted to put up a contemporary poster with an actress considered beautiful and sexy—someone like Kim Basinger—and it was a matter of complete indifference to me who it was. But that turned out to be tremendously expensive. So the producer [Marin Karmitz] suggested putting up one of his own posters, and since he'd distributed *Contempt* it didn't cost a thing. So we used that. The reasons were purely financial and had nothing to do with homage or love, and absolutely nothing to do with any distaste for anything either. (Qtd. in Coates, "The inner life" 161)

In his 2004 book on Kieślowski, Marek Haltof accepts the casualness of the allusion, arguing that Polish filmmakers in general did not have a positive view of Godard because of his procommunist views: "In Poland . . . no artist or intellectual was taken seriously if he expressed explicitly pro-communist sympathies" (140). Consequently, Haltof sees the poster as being a very limited point of reference, simply "a comment on the state of affairs between Karol and Dominique" (140).

Certainly, as Haltof implies, there is a connection between the scenarios of the two films. Godard's film, based on Alberto Moravia's novel *Il Disprezzo* or *A Ghost at Noon* (1954), concerns a French playwright, Paul Javal (Michel Piccoli), and his beautiful but uneducated wife, Camille (Bardot), who are living in Italy. Javal is hired by the American film producer Jerry Prokosch (Jack Palance) to rework the screenplay for an adaptation of Homer's *Odyssey.* In fact, the film is already in production, but Prokosch is furious at what the director—none other than Fritz Lang, playing himself—is doing with the story. Instead of creating a spectacle of adventure and eroticism, Lang has chosen to create a heavily stylized representation of the action and of the obscure forces of the gods whose conflicting powers could be envisioned as determining that action.

In direct parallel with this conflict over the making of the film is a more intimate conflict between Paul and Camille. Immediately after passively submitting to Prokosch's offer to work on the film, Paul introduces Camille to Prokosch and then allows the wolfish American to cart off his wife to his villa in his red sports car. By the time Paul arrives at the villa by taxi, just a half-hour after them, his wife's adoration of him has evaporated, to be replaced by an increasingly contemptuous mistrust. Lang's film production moves to the island of Capri and, indeed, to Prokosch's house there, none other than the Casa Malaparte (that architectural anomaly built by the fascist sympathizer Curzio Malaparte). Here, as Paul works with Prokosch and Lang on the film, he endeavors to unmask the reasons for his wife's contempt, but they remain as impenetrable as the stony stares of the Greek gods.[1] At the film's conclusion, Camille finally abandons her husband, driving off with Prokosch only to be killed with him when his convertible wedges itself under a truck. At the moment of their death, Paul Javal stands on the flat roof of the Casa Malaparte watching the filming of the *Odyssey.* Lang's camera crew tracks past Odysseus as he supposedly catches sight of his island home after his long wanderings, closing their shot and Godard's film with a vista of a conspicuously empty sea and sky almost melded into one tone of blue, accompanied by a shout of "Silencio" from Lang's assistant director, played by Godard himself.[2]

The obvious connection between the failed marriages in Godard's and Kieślowski's films poses a challenge to Kieślowski's pragmatic explanation of his allusion to *Contempt* and qualifies Haltof's labeling of it as "a very limited point of reference." Both films begin with the estrangement of a husband and wife formerly bound by deep passion as the wife develops a powerful aversion for her husband even while the husband remains enraptured with his wife and is tormented by her distance.[3] If we move beyond this similarity of scenario to consider the aesthetics of Godard's film, the discourses with which it is engaged, and the circumstances of its production, we discover a provocative array of connections not just with *White* but with the whole of the *Three Colors* trilogy.

Godard and Kieślowski make conspicuous use of red, white, and blue lighting and an array of objects coded in those colors in their films.[4] This conspicuous use of stylized color derives from the circumstances of coproduction in each case. Godard was working with American, Italian, and French money and producers, and the coloration reflects the national colors of two of the countries of coproduction (as well as reflecting the opposition between Athena and Poseidon in the film-within-the-film, Lang's *Odyssey*). Similarly, Kieślowski claimed that the use of the colors blue, white, and red both in the titles and in the coloration of the films was solely a result of the French dominance in the coproduction arrangement and the *producer's* liking for a title "that falls under a particular Godardian tradition" (qtd. in Coates, "The inner life" 170).[5]

Furthermore, both Godard and Kieślowski reflect the circumstances of production in the scenarios of their films. In making the *Three Colors* trilogy, Kieślowski was embarking on a complex and ultimately exhausting international coproduction, working on a far larger scale than he had ever done before and with a cast and crew whose language he did not understand. *White* is the part of the trilogy that most self-reflexively addresses this situation, figuring it in the union of the Polish husband with the French wife (though the idea was prefigured in the doubled protagonist of Kieślowski's first postcommunist project, *The Double Life of Véronique* [1991]). Godard found himself in a similar situation in the making of *Contempt,* an American-French-Italian coproduction. And like Kieślowski, Godard reflected the context of production within the content, using a swaggering Jack Palance to represent a smug, self-righteous, monolingual American movie producer who is enraged by Fritz Lang's rendition of the *Odyssey* in philosophical rather than sexual terms. Indeed, Godard had clashed with the producers of *Contempt,* Carlo Ponti and Joseph E. Levine, for identical reasons: they wanted a nude scene to capitalize on the most costly element in the production, Brigitte Bardot, and Godard obliged with the post-title scene. In this, a naked Camille quizzes Paul about the most attractive parts of her body as the camera tracks across her prostrate form.

Finally, two of the three main actresses in Kieślowski's *Three Colors* had been earlier "discovered" by Godard. Juliette Binoche had appeared in *Hail Mary* (1985) and Julie Delpy in *Detective* (1985). Given this extraordinary degree of coincidence between the films, I am tempted to enter into Kieślowski's own thematic territory in calling the constrained choice that producer Marin Karmitz supposedly placed before Kieślowski—"choose a poster, any poster"—a remarkable contingency that reeks of the fateful. (Indeed, the fact that Mikolaj is drawn to the poster for *Contempt* suggests that Kieślowski was bound to take into account the French cinematic tradition in his French coproductions).[6]

Beyond these congruities of narrative, symbolism, and style, one other point of coincidence between the two films is even more engaging and richly meaningful, for the subject of marriage is linked in both cases with more-or-less subtle self-reflexive commentary on the cinema. Both films are concerned with cinematic representation and voyeurism: the degree to which the cinematic image can become ontologically identical with its object, as André Bazin insisted it could; and the extent to which the camera eye can enable or disable genuine recognition of and interconnectedness between self and other.[7] Marriage in both *Contempt* and *White* is therefore a complex figure, applying as much to film's regard for the world it represents as to the romantic union of man and woman.

In *Contempt,* the failure of Paul and Camille's marriage becomes complete only at the end of the film, when Camille's death cuts off any possibility of redemption. However, the failure of the cinematic image to apprehend the world is figured from the very beginning, when the naked Camille, in a kind of reverse blazon, catalogs the parts of her own body—"Which do you like better, my breasts or my nipples?"—objectifying herself as an assemblage of fetishized parts both for the viewer and for her husband, Paul. However, although this scene was foisted on Godard by the producers, he was able to turn it to his own purpose, as he explained in one interview: "Under other conditions I would have refused this scene; but here, I shot it in a certain way, using certain colors—I used a red lighting, and then a blue lighting so that Bardot would become something else, so that she would become something more unreal, more profound and more serious than simply Brigitte Bardot on a bed. I wanted to transfigure her, because the cinema can and must transfigure reality" (Godard, "Shipwrecked" 38). The unmotivated and jarring switch between different lighting—along with Camille's bizarre self-objectification in her catalog of parts—disrupts the viewer's voyeuristic reverie, reminding us that we are seeing a cinematic image. Even so—or perhaps *precisely because of* this self-consciousness—the scene simultaneously maintains a kind of reverence for the way the camera can apprehend the world: as Godard puts it, Bardot becomes "unreal" but "more profound." Perhaps this tension between voyeuristic objectification and reverence for existence explains why, at the end of Camille's cataloging, Paul defies her reductionism, insisting that he loves her "totally, tenderly, tragically." He may indeed, at this moment, love her as a totality, but his slide of terms prefigures the failure of such love. Indeed, Paul himself precipitates the fulfillment of the tragic part of his own grand proclamation when he accepts a check from Prokosch to rewrite Lang's *Odyssey* and immediately thereafter delivers Camille up to Prokosch. The prostitution of his art and his wife go hand in hand.

The increasing alienation of husband and wife and of camera and reality is signaled most forcefully when Paul and Camille return from Prokosch's villa to their costly, new, but unfinished apartment. In a thirty-minute-long scene, as they move around the apartment and speak to each other from different rooms, the camera tracks and pans through its space, but out of sync with the characters, so that its view is often mismatched with the source of aural interest. Even when Paul and Camille do have a face-to-face conversation, the camera, holding a close shot, tracks backward and forward between them, but again completely out of rhythm with their exchanges of dialogue (and this pattern continues in the following audition scene at the cinema). Paradoxically, then, the increasing alienation of the couple within the film is more and more effectively expressed not by the camera's relentless gaze at its subject but by its dislocated wanderings.[8]

Godard's obsession in *Contempt* with this question of the status of film's regard for the world—as empty cliché and simulacrum or as indexical truth—is fruitfully explored in Nicholas Paige's careful analysis of the film. Paige considers whether *Contempt* is in fact an anomaly in Godard's career or a film that can tell us about the difficulties of defining the postmodern in the monolithic way that characterizes Fredric Jameson's theories and so much criticism derived from them. Although evoking the sense of the "classical" and "timeless" that we might expect of an art film, *Contempt* is in fact about "the position of the artist vis-à-vis both socioeconomic realities and the Western artistic canon" at the time of its production (3). As Paige claims, "Godard's films can be said to propose a hygiene of the gaze, one that enables us to restore specificity to the images we see" (9). His analysis of *Contempt* ultimately finds that the film conforms to this larger project. He reveals just how dialectical the film is, alternating between a postmodern detachment from the fiction of the image and reverence for its documentary truth. Thus, Brigitte Bardot is both a star persona who does not disappear into her character, Camille, and the actress Brigitte Bardot (14). Only by avoiding immersing the viewer in a fictional world and eschewing a psychological presentation of character can Godard maintain the ontological weight of the film image.

Paul and Camille's marriage, I have been arguing, is a narrative figure for the same ontological possibility. In using marriage in this way, Godard is drawing on a long-established notion of romantic love, especially as this is elaborated in the European artistic tradition and the Christian theology of marriage. The theologian Derrick Sherwin Bailey notes that the early Christian church failed to understand the ontological import of sexuality in marriage and saw marriage only in institutional terms (45). Only with the emergence of the notion of romantic love in the eleventh century, as expressed in the work of the troubadour poets, does the possibility of understanding the sexual aspects of marriage in ontological rather than institutional terms emerge (5). Bailey draws on Martin Buber's notion of the I-Thou relationship in marriage, whereby one member alternately relates to the other as subject (Thou) and experiences the other as object (She/He/It), to elaborate on what that theo-ontological significance is, concluding that "there can be no love without the experience of meeting in personal relation, and that is impossible where the other is merely an object, part of the world of *It,* and is allowed to remain so. And with the loss of true personal relation goes all participation in the *Thou* of eternity" (13). In love, one subject apprehends the other as an equally valid subject and both thereby escape the solipsism that limits our existence and apprehend something beyond our mortal condition. While Christian theologians have increasingly drawn on this logic to defend human sexuality and to insist on the sacramental quality of marriage, it is by no means limited to Christian thinking on the subject. As the religion scholar Elaine Pagels notes, "throughout history, mystics of many traditions have chosen sexual metaphors to describe their experiences" (18).[9]

In *Real Presences* (1989), a polemic against the then-current orthodoxies of academic discourse such as deconstruction, George Steiner projects the theo-ontological weight given to marriage onto our encounter with film and the other arts: "The wager on the meaning of meaning, on the potential of insight and response when one human voice addresses another, when we come face to face with the text and work of art or music, which is to say when we encounter the *other* in its condition of freedom of existence, is a wager on transcendence" (4). For Steiner, art does deliver us to a sense of presence, allowing us to *re-cognize* the world. He thereby endows the experience of a work of art with the sacramental quality theologians like Bailey ascribe to marriage. We should hardly consider it coincidental, then, that the stylistic twists and turns of Godard's oeuvre, necessary to his "hygiene of the gaze," are accompanied by narratives that remain focused on the relationship of a couple, practically a laboratory for the exploration of otherness. This combination supports a point Geoffrey Nowell-Smith has recently argued, that the mysteries of the human person were central to Godard's early filmmaking, at least until *Wind from the East* (1969) (21).

As a filmmaker working for much of his career in a communist-controlled industry, Kieślowski was inevitably deeply concerned with the moral dimensions of the camera's representation of the world, and his narrative films, too, often relate this issue to the possibility of the communion of subjects in romantic relationships or marriage. Thus, in *Camera Buff* (1979), Filip Mosz (Jerzy Stuhr) destroys his marriage when he allows his aspirations as a filmmaker to be misdirected by the communist authorities. In *Decalogue 6/A Short Film about Love* (1988), the young postal clerk Tomek (Olaf Lubaszenko) monitors the daily routines and sexual trysts of an older woman in an apartment opposite his, Magda (Grazyna Szapolowska), through a telescope that he has stolen from a school. Kieślowski claimed, "I probably changed *A Short Film about Love* in the cutting-room more than any other film I've ever made" (Stok 166), and the net result of those changes was to limit severely the point of view: "We watch from the point of view of the person who is loving and not the person who is loved. The loved one is merely in shreds, an object" (Stok 169). When Tomek slits his wrists and is taken to hospital, the formerly cynical Magda begins to believe in Tomek's love and the film switches to her perspective, but now he is conspicuously absent. Thus, while the film clearly comments on the ethical dimensions of the cinematic gaze, it does so by carefully controlling rather than disrupting conventional cinematic language, a fact that distinguishes Kieślowski's approach from Godard's more radical "hygiene of the gaze." *White* develops an equally subtle commentary on the prejudices of the cinematic gaze and narration.

In *White,* Kieślowski reverses the pattern of Godard's *Contempt:* it is the wife, Dominique, who destroys the communion of the marriage, reducing her husband to an object who, as such, has failed to fulfill her sexual needs. Although she explicitly tells the divorce court judge that she no longer loves Karol, when she finds him later in her hairdressing salon, she is clearly still enchanted by him and, finding that his sexual potency has returned, straddles him on a chair. When he loses his erection, however, she berates him and sets fire to the salon, telling Karol that every cop in Paris will soon be after him for arson.

However, Dominique's deception is revealed not just within the narrative but also at the level of narration. During the divorce proceedings, Karol is asked by the judge whether he did manage to consummate the marriage on one particular night. As Karol hesitates to answer, we see a flashback to his wedding, a subjective shot that seems to be his, as Dominique walks just ahead of the camera out of the church, then turns to it with a beatific smile. However, when we cut back to the courtroom, it is to a close shot of Dominique, who, apparently lost in this same memory, has failed to hear the judge's question to her. Thus, the editing develops a meaningful ambiguity, suggesting that a flashback that begins and is motivated as Karol's *becomes* Dominique's. In other words, the sequence reveals a genuine communion between them that is subsequently shattered by Dominique's denials to the judge. Dominique's deception is a kind of self-deception, and Karol eventually answers it in kind (and indeed, we see a similarly shared flashback toward the end of the film, after Karol has orchestrated Dominique's arrest for his murder).

That Kieślowski connects marriage to cinematic representation becomes apparent when Karol, smuggled back to Poland by Mikolaj, begins to orchestrate his revenge on Dominique. Like Tomek watching Magda through his telescope, Karol surveys Dominique at the scene of his own staged funeral through a pair of opera glasses, and the control that these lenses allow him is clearly a reflection of the voyeuristic detachment and illusion of control inherent in spectatorship. His contemplations of a two-franc coin, the sole salvage from his marriage, are followed by mysterious flashforwards of Dominique entering a darkened room, moments that are eventually revealed to be Karol's imaginings of his plan for revenge. Where Dominique has formerly been able to control the appearances of things so that she will defeat Karol under the French system of justice, Karol's increasingly cool and distanced vision allows him to gain control and, eventually, to imprison Dominique.[10] In the film's closing scene, the irony of Karol's ascendancy is revealed: he can now gaze at his leisure at his love object through his opera glasses, but she can only express her subjectivity in an essentially cinematic way, through a silent mime from the unbridgeable distance of her prison cell. Dominique has been reduced to a cinematic signifier.

Curiously, then, Godard and Kieślowski are united by their use of the figure of marriage as a symbol of cinema's attempts to present (rather than represent), and both are concerned with the possibility of cinema transcending its material and technical basis. As has been noted, Godard insists that "the cinema can and must transfigure reality" ("Shipwrecked" 38). Kieślowski, too, declared his need "to escape from this literalism" that is endemic to camera reality (Stok 195). Both Godard and Kieślowski use conventional images of transcendence—light sources or the sky—as a way of referencing that possibility.

In *Contempt,* not surprisingly, the "marriage" of the American producer Prokosch with the German director Lang for an Italian-based production of

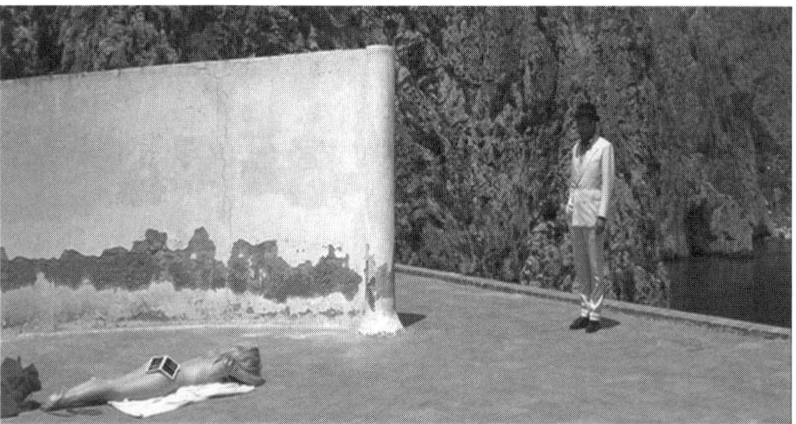

One of the many self-consciously stylized standoffs between Paul (Michel Piccoli) and his wife, Camille (Brigitte Bardot), in Godard's *Contempt* (1963).

an ancient Greek text is a dismal failure. The classical text remains as impenetrable and unknowable to the modern mind as Camille's motives do to her husband. Camille's death in Prokosch's sports car coincides with Paul's visit to the rooftop of the Casa Malaparte, where he witnesses Lang's crew filming the moment when Ulysses finally catches sight of the homeland from which he has so long been absent, a homeland conspicuously absent from the view of sea and sky that serves as the closing shot of *Contempt*. For Coates, the "emptiness" of that shot marks the separation of mind and body, of body and soul, as well as the consequent desacralization of art (*Cinema* 38). For Paige, this is another conspicuous instance of the "hygiene of the gaze": the closing shot of the graduated blues of sea and sky is "an image sublimely distanced from the weight of cultural tradition, of figuration, of content" (11), but which Godard has nevertheless flagged as a technological production, the blues a result of the apparatus of the camera and its film stock.[11] And for Douglas Morrey, while this closing shot, accompanied by Godard's call for silence, is "one of the most beautiful in all Godard," it paradoxically undercuts the film's nostalgia: "One can never locate an origin, Godard seems to suggest, much less return to it, for the origin is lost in that which comes after it, like the sea blending into the sky" (21). Typically, cinematic fictions are attempts to create the illusion of the original: we are to presume that we are watching the action *as it unfolds*. With the empty image, Godard denies this presentational possibility. In being divorced from the divine, Godard's Ulysses is closer to Dante's than Homer's, and Lang actually quotes from Ulysses' speech to Virgil in the *Inferno* in which Ulysses explains his need to leave home once more, making his final, one-way voyage beyond the Pillars of Hercules: "Night then saw all the stars. We were filled with gladness, which soon turned to tears, until the sea closed in on us." Being a pagan and having exceeded the rightful boundaries of the human, Dante's Ulysses is entirely removed from the divine. Godard's contemporary Ulysses, Paul Javal, must live in a world where the divine itself is a fabrication, as Lang reminds Prokosch: "Jerry, don't forget, the gods have not created man. Man has created gods."

The way that Kieślowski responds to the ontological and spiritual implications of Godard's film has been analyzed by Wilson in her book *Memory and Survival: The French Cinema of Krzysztof Kieślowski.* Of all Kieślowski's critics, Wilson gives the most sustained attention to Kieślowski's use of the *Contempt* poster in *White,* seeing it as exactly the kind of self-reflexive strategy Godard himself might use (and in fact in *Contempt,* we see a pan across a whole series of movie posters, for *Psycho* [1960], *Hatari* [1962], *Vivre Sa Vie* [1962], and *Vanina Vanini* [1961]). She notes, too, that as a fetishized object of desire, Julie Delpy is not far removed from Bardot, and she sees *White* as another installment in Kieślowski's own prolonged investigation of the issue of voyeurism, both as a method of surveillance and control within communist Poland and as a fetishizing strategy of commodity capitalism. But Wilson sees Kieślowski arguing against Godard, actually finding an equality in the alternating ascendancy of voyeur and exhibitionist: the exhibitionist can as easily assume a position of (sadistic) power as the voyeur (75–76). And implicitly disagreeing with Christian Metz's notion of the uniqueness and frustrations of the cinematic signifier, Wilson argues that "Kieślowski presents us with a drama which denies the failure and solitude upon which cinematic voyeurism has been seen to be based" (76). Kieślowski believes in a cinema of presences. That Godard does not—that presence can never be shown in the cinematic image—is evident through all of his films, but the denial is especially explicit in *Les Carabiniers* (1963) when one of the two soldier protagonists, Michel-Ange (Albert Juross), attends the cinema for the first time. Watching a train arrive at a station, he cowers in his seat and covers his eyes, his behavior recalling legends about audience reactions to the Lumières' first film screenings. Seeing an image of a naked woman in a bathtub, he approaches the screen and tries to peer down at her naked form, until the screen itself collapses. For Godard, the illusions of cinema must be broken as a precondition to the transfiguring of reality; they can never deliver that transfiguration themselves.

Kieślowski, by contrast, had long been attempting to evoke the supersensible realm *through* the phenomenon of cinema, and in doing so he was both following and redirecting the Polish cinematic tradition. Except for a brief, unremarkable period of socialist realism, Polish postwar cinema has been animated by the urge to describe reality as it is and dominated by an expressive-symbolist mode crucial to commenting on and moving beyond that often-grim reality. Kieślowski's international coproductions still hark back to this Polish context, even if the reality he describes and the solutions he proposes belong more to the realm of metaphysics than the bleak materialist fabric of our world. In this, Kieślowski's metaphysical cinema is clearly related to Bergman's and Tarkovsky's, but as Janina Falkowska has noted, it is also part of a Polish religio-metaphysical tradition, too, a tradition that ran underground in communist Poland with such films as *Mother Joan of the Angels* (1960, dir. Jerzy Kawalerowicz) and *The Life of Matthew* (1968, dir. Witold Leszczyŋski), that bubbled strongly to the surface with Kieślowski's work, and that continues in the differently inflected work of Jan Jakub Kolski (67).

If Kieślowski did aspire to evoke an immaterial realm, he was hampered by the materiality of the film medium, conditioned by his own spiritual uncertainty, and, as Paul C. Santilli has recently noted, bound by the Kantian prohibition that forbids piercing the veil of being, since direct knowledge of being would reduce us to mere puppets rather than subjects with free will and a moral sensibility. Kieślowski's films from *Blind Chance* (1981; released 1987) on deploy a wide range of strategies to try to negotiate this challenging terrain. However, when he moved beyond the Polish context, Kieślowski faced a new kind of artistic challenge. Leaving the relative insularity of the Polish cinematic tradition behind and embracing the French, Kieślowski was faced with the iconoclasm that is endemic to much French culture and absolutely central to Godard's work.

Godard has been more or less dedicated throughout his career to exposing ideological fabrications, not least those that are conjured up by cinema. As David Sterritt summarizes Godard's oeuvre, "The eccentricities and idiosyncracies of his work are a decades-long howl of protest against cinema that contents itself with reflecting instead of questioning the assumptions of the society around it" (23). Godard's work is an attempt to undermine or at least expose the epistemological grid that convinces us of the self-evident nature of our sense of reality. In some ways, Kieślowski shares this project, remarking of the abstract concepts liberty, equality, and fraternity at the heart of the *Three Colors* trilogy: "Debates and meditations about what these words actually mean seem appropriate to me, for we often use words whose meanings we have forgotten. They become merely symbols of certain events and so become detached from reality, life, the concrete" (qtd. in Coates, "The inner life" 171). However, a crucial difference between the two is that for Kieślowski, meaning can emanate directly from the concrete, without the mediation of an ideologically inflected system of signs. Furthermore, Godard, born into a wealthy family with a privileged upbringing, seems to reject the very notion of individual subjectivity that has been fundamental to the Western tradition of humanism. Kieślowski, born and raised in the Eastern bloc, working for most of his career within a communist-controlled and tightly monitored film industry, surrounded by Catholicism though never embracing Christian dogma for himself, remained committed to the sanctity of the subject.

Certainly not just *White*, but every part of the *Three Colors* trilogy ends with shots, scenes, or whole sequences suggesting a move toward recognition, communion, and transcendence: in *Three Colors: Blue* (1993), the lovemaking of Julie and Olivier is at once stiflingly subterranean and heavenly (the connection between the earthbound and the spiritual is addressed by Slavoj Žižek in *The Fright of Real Tears*); in *White,* Karol and Dominique may have to regard each other from a great distance, through the bars of a Polish jail, but Dominique nevertheless mimes her desire to remarry him; and in *Three Colors: Red* (1994), Judge Joseph Kern gazes out at us through a window, but one that is conspicuously broken.[12]

Such evocations of the transcendent can be traced backward through Kieślowski's earlier work, too. For instance, in the closing scene of *Decalogue 5/A Short Film about Killing* (1988), immediately after the scene in which the murderer Jacek has himself been killed by the state, we see a field at dusk punctuated by a flaring light. In *Decalogue 5,* the light holds as the camera pans to reveal a despairing and angry Piotr repeating the words, "I abhor it." In *A Short Film about Killing,* the light suddenly dims and the camera pans to show Piotr in mute despair. Despite these differences, we may interpret that light in both cases as simply the sun reflecting off an abandoned object or descending beyond the trees. However, given the immediately preceding death of Jacek and our awareness that this field may be the very one in which Jacek's sister was run over by a tractor, our material reading is balanced by a symbolic, spiritual one. This is but one particularly obvious example of what Joseph G. Kickasola has termed the "liminal image" in Kieślowski's work, an image balanced between "the articulable and the ineffable" in its abstraction, a vehicle that grounds us in the immanent while simultaneously intimating the transcendent (41). Kieślowski elaborated a whole range of means to produce such doubled, undecideable images and moments. For another instance, in *The Double Life of Véronique,* Véronique is disturbed by a piercing, warm light that comes through her window. Though the light is at first revealed to have a definite source—we see a child holding a piece of mirror in an apartment opposite hers—the light persists in playing across her wall even after that source is gone. Thus, Kieślowski shades natural objects and phenomena toward radiant symbolism either by hinting at an immaterial etiology or by undermining the rational etiology.

Another possibility for such symbolism open to Kieślowski was the simple dramatic gesture of looking at the sky, a gesture that, as Coates has argued, is central to spiritual experience and can be used particularly powerfully in the cinema "when it both contrasts with, and issues logically from, a film's entire visual system" (*Cinema* 36). As we have seen, Godard uses the look to the sky as a negation at the end of *Contempt,* and in fact, the gesture is surprisingly common in his work.[13] Kieślowski had hoped to use the gesture in a much more affirmative way in a film, based on a concrete experience he had in Poland: he had wanted to make a documentary about Poles watching Pope

John Paul II ascend by helicopter after his descent into their midst in June 1979. How curious, how Kieślowskian, that only after Kieślowski himself left this earth unexpectedly in 1996 would this motif of ascension be incorporated in a film that Kieślowski had fashioned. *Heaven* (2002) was ultimately directed by Tom Tykwer but was based on a screenplay completed by Piesiewicz from a detailed treatment written with Kieślowski.

The issue of how faithful Tykwer has been to Kieślowski and Piesiewicz's story and intentions is complex. The already-translated screenplay first handed to Tykwer went through at least two more transformations before being produced. As Tykwer explains,

> In an intuitive way, I absolutely know what it's about. I wasn't afraid to take it over. But it was difficult. If you've written it, you know every detail, so that was different. What I had to do to understand the story was that I did a complete rewrite in a way; I wrote the script one more time in my own words, and changed some of the dialogue. In typing in the 100 pages myself, but changing certain details along the way [sic]. Then I went over it again with Anthony Minghella, who was producing the film with us. (Qtd. in Kaufman)

Although Tykwer claims to have essentially rewritten the Kieślowski/Piesiewicz screenplay in his own words, the completed film follows very closely the contours and dialogue of the original screenplay.[14] Certainly, with added scenes, reductions in dialogue, and a relatively austere visual style, Tykwer does leave his own signature on *Heaven*. Nevertheless, the film extends the implications of the *Three Colors* trilogy, incorporates the idea of the Pope's ascent, and allows Kieślowski one final note of response to Godard from beyond the grave.

Heaven was supposed to be the concluding part of a trilogy that purportedly would reconceive Dante's *Divine Comedy* in contemporary cinematic terms.[15] Kieślowski and Piesiewicz's turn to Dante was doubtless motivated by many factors. The *Divine Comedy* is not simply a pure spiritual allegory but also a description and commentary on the complex politics of northern Italy and Europe of Dante's time, composed while Dante was in exile from Florence. The form of the *Comedy* is, then, perhaps an ideal cinematic vehicle through which the Christian Piesiewicz and the self-exiled Kieślowski could meditate on the ethical state of Europe in their own time, just as the Ten Commandments had allowed them to refract ten stories set in late-1980s Poland into more universal fables. However, it is fitting that Kieślowski began the process of refiguring this trilogy, and ended his life, with the writing of the final part. For the *Three Colors* trilogy (and the *Decalogue*) had already dwelt on the pains of purgation, and the idea of hell's endless and inescapable punishment was presumably anathema to Kieślowski, even if a pervasive idea in his Polish Catholic background.

Admittedly, *Hell* (*L'Enfer,* 2005, dir. Danis Tanovic) is the only other part of this trilogy to have been produced, but Kieślowski contributed less to its details. The revelation of pure malice at the conclusion of that film, a malice directed by a wife toward her husband and that entirely poisoned the lives of their three daughters, is certainly worthy of Dante's ninth circle of hell, reserved for those who betray their kin, but that revelation seems decidedly foreign to Kieślowski. Paradoxically, *Hell* is more recognizably Kieślowskian in style than Tykwer's *Heaven,* saturated as it is with images and scenes that are either unexplained, ambiguous, or seem entirely superfluous to the narrative: a pretitle sequence, later to be understood as a flashback, in which a young girl rushes into the office of her father only to find him there with a naked boy; a title sequence in which a hatchling cuckoo forces the other eggs out of the nest it has infiltrated; visual distortions through prisms and kaleidoscopes; an old woman who struggles to deposit a bottle in a recycling container; and a bee drowning in a glass of juice.

Perhaps the idea of heaven was as abstract to Kieślowski as the notion of hell. Certainly, *Heaven* corresponds more closely to Dante's *Purgatorio* than his *Paradiso,* starting with an extremity of suffering but gradually moving toward relief. As with many of Kieślowski's later films, it is built on a narrative fragment of an earlier film, in this case extending a subplot of *Red* concerning a wealthy and respected drug dealer whose crimes go unpunished. At the beginning of *Heaven,* Philippa (Cate Blanchett), an English schoolteacher living and working in Milan in northern Italy (the territory of Dante's wanderings in his exile from Florence; and Godard's film is, of course, set in Italy, though in Rome and Capri) decides to take justice into her own hands after children in her school and her own husband have died from drug-related causes and the police have ignored her information about the source of the drugs. She plants a bomb in the office of the drug dealer and carefully orchestrates matters so that only he will be killed. She returns home and sleeps, awaking to find herself surrounded by armed police. At her subsequent interrogation, she soon learns that the bomb killed not the drug dealer but four innocent people, including two young girls and their father. Distraught beyond words, she is accused by the police officers complicit with the drug dealer of being a terrorist. At the same time, she attracts the sympathy and then the love of Filippo (Giovanni Ribisi), the policeman who translates for her and records her testimony. Tykwer makes this connection believable through a close-up of Philippa's face as she is told the news of the deaths, the microphysiognomy of her face, quite brilliantly managed by Blanchett, marking her descent into a personal purgatory. (Tykwer evokes the connection between Filippo and his younger brother and father through similar extralinguistic means.) In the terms of Dante's Catholic schema, Philippa is guilty of the deadly sins of pride and anger.

Filippo orchestrates her escape from police custody, and together, he and Philippa travel across a gloriously lit, practically unpopulated Tuscan landscape while transforming themselves physically into androgynous mirror images of each other. After witnessing a wedding in a village square, they find refuge at the farmhouse of one of Philippa's friends and there, on a ridgetop, silhouetted against the sky, come together as a reborn Adam and Eve while the clouds flow in accelerated time behind them. Arriving at the Earthly Paradise, like Dante and his beloved Beatrice in Dante's *Purgatorio,* the characters must then ascend, and the means for them to do so are provided by the police who converge on the farmhouse by car and helicopter. Relying on the police's misdirected attention, the couple are able to climb into the helicopter, unnoticed for the few crucial seconds it takes Filippo to assume the controls and begin a straight vertical ascent.

It is with this closing of the film that Kieślowski, then, through Tykwer's agency, delivers a final, forceful response to Godard. As we have seen, the sky for Godard marks at best an emptiness, at worst a threatening absence, figuring both the vacuity of the cinematic image and the impossibility of intersubjective experience, including experience of the divine. Kieślowski and Piesiewicz indicate in their screenplay for *Heaven* that the final scene occurs at "night, right before dawn," and the ascending helicopter "disappears into the gray sky. Its lower light now looks like one of the stars that shine high above the heads of the gaping crowd" (89–92). The decision to end with an image of a star might have recalled, for some viewers, the opening scenes of *The Double Life of Véronique,* but it is also a reference to the image with which each part of Dante's *Divine Comedy* ends. The stars that are an image of hope at the end of *The Inferno* become a mark of divine love at the end of the *Paradiso,* a love that encompasses Dante himself. In a signal change from the screenplay, but of a kind that Kieślowski himself typically made, Tykwer chose to set the final scene of *Heaven* at dawn, and so the helicopter ascends and disappears into a blue sky, newly inflecting the apparent emptiness with an unseen presence.

Here, Kieślowski's discourse on the possibility of an unselfish love, a charity that would encompass liberty, equality, and fraternity—a love that has been frustrated in the earlier films by the urge for an illusory, selfish liberty (*Blue*), the failure of languages to bridge subjects (*White*), and the distrust of human motives (*Red*)—is completed. The instrument of the law becomes enamored with the apparent criminal. Captor and prisoner become equal through mutual regard, their differences of nationality, native language, and even gender eroded, disappearing by the film's conclusion as the pair rise on technological "wings." Philippa and Filippo have ascended from Mount Purgatory and have now become a part of the all-encompassing charity that, for Dante and perhaps for Kieślowski, defines heaven. The spectator, too, who bears witness to the ascension is given a new faith in the cinematic signifier, for though the final image of *Heaven* may be as empty as that of *Contempt,* the spectator

Androgynous mirror images of each other, Filippo (Giovanni Ribisi) and Philippa (Cate Blanchett) regard each other with complete comprehension before ascending from the earth in *Heaven* (2002).

invests the image with presences, an investment that Kieślowski insists is not misplaced.

In his DVD commentary for *Contempt,* Robert Stam refers to the "ephemeral, artificial, and polyglot style of transnational cinema." Kieślowski, however, was able to turn transnational filmmaking to his own ends. Rather than simply becoming hopelessly compromised "pidgin" texts, as the film version of the *Odyssey* clearly is in Godard's film—Fritz Lang sees the film as an homage to a long-vanished epoch of mythos, foregrounding the impenetrability of the text, while Prokosch sees it, just as Cecil B. Demille apparently saw the biblical epic in the 1920s, as an opportunity for a spectacle of sex and violence—Kieślowski used his French-language coproductions as the ideal vehicles for analyzing the human failure to connect. By embracing and absorbing foreign cinematic traditions and practices—the French into the Polish, Godard's into his own—Kieślowski was able to reassert cinema's power to speak of an immaterial reality. It seems highly appropriate, then, that his idea for *Heaven,* offered from beyond the grave, would find its way into the hands of Tom Tykwer. An article in *Variety* entitled "International Chefs Serve up 'Heaven'" described the production thus: "German helmer Tom Tykwer's first English-language picture features producers from France and the U.S., an Australian star playing an English teacher living in Italy, and a script by a late Polish filmmaker that was translated into French, then English." Kieślowski, I think, would have approved.

Notes

1. Obviously, Godard does provide some possible motivations for Camille's reaction. Camille herself implies that Paul practically prostituted her to Prokosch, and Camille also witnesses Paul's flirtation with Prokosch's assistant and translator Francesca Vanini (Giorgia Moll). Ultimately, though, Godard refuses such reductive psychological causality.

2. Moravia's novel had ended with the screenwriter having a fantastic encounter with what may have been the ghost of his wife. Godard avoids trying to create a cinematic equivalent for this equivocal encounter and thereby makes his film a more forceful denial of spiritual realities.

3. Admittedly, there is a difference, too. The exact reasons for Camille Javal's contempt remain obscure, while the reasons for Dominique's disgust with her husband are all too open, becoming part of Karol's public humiliation at the beginning of *White.* In the divorce proceedings, Dominique declares that their marriage has never been consummated.

4. Some critics claim that *Contempt* is coded in blue, red, and yellow, but this claim seems to be based on the first post-title scene, in which a naked Camille is lying on a yellow blanket but is photographed with a blue filter, with no filter, and finally with a red filter. Yellow does figure throughout the film, but not as consistently as the other three colors.

5. Note that Marin Karmitz, the producer of Kieślowski's trilogy, had not only distributed Godard's films but also produced Godard's *Sauve Qui Peut* (1980).

6. Fritz Lang's part in Godard's film also undoubtedly impressed Kieślowski deeply. Lang's *Destiny* (1921), in which a woman bargains with Death for the return of her fiancé, is echoed in a number of Kieślowski's own films. The woman in *Destiny* is given three chances to save her lover, being incarnated as more or less the same woman in three different places and time periods. The three parallel lives of Witek in *Blind Chance* seem to borrow this narrative strategy. And while the woman in *Destiny* fails to restore her fiancé to life, Death does agree to reunite her with her fiancé in death, as a reward for her self-sacrifice in saving a baby's life. The final scene of the film shows her walking and vanishing into death with her fiancé, a shot imitated directly in the final scene of Kieślowski's *No End* (1985).

7. With *Contempt,* Godard transposes Moravia's literary enigma—the first-person husband-narrator cannot narrate and thereby understand the interior of the wife who has come to despise him—into a meditation on cinematic voyeurism: the fetishized object of desire, played by Brigitte Bardot, necessarily remains an obscure subject for the voyeuristic camera.

8. Also in this scene, Godard mixes flashbacks to previous scenes (tentatively coded as evidence in the couple's argument) with flashforwards to the film's future scenes. Kieślowski employed a similar formal strategy, confusing flashbacks and flashforwards in *White.*

9. Of course, even within orthodox Christian thinking, Christ's relationship to the church is described as a marriage.

10. Indeed, the earliest step in his gaining of control is itself an allusion to the cinema: after losing everything, Karol gazes at a plaster bust of a young woman in a shop window, a scene borrowed directly from Charlie Chaplin's *City Lights* (1931).

11. Interestingly, although the technicians shooting Lang's film wear overalls with "Technicolor" printed on the back, Godard's film was shot in Eastmancolor.

12. This, the last image that Kieślowski himself was able to deliver to his audience, has been given great import and varied interpretation by critics, signaling "the end of representation" for Vincent Amiel, but for Joseph G. Kickasola suggesting "that transcendence (and redemption) remains the essential possibility" (321).

13. In the course of his long and dynamic career, Godard has repeatedly employed shots of the sky and dialogue about the sky as a commentary on the problem of the relation between matter and spirit. The film to deal most directly and persistently with the spiritual in terms of images of the sky is *Hail Mary* (1985), Godard's highly controversial yet ultimately very reverent consideration of the Annunciation and Immaculate Conception in contemporary terms, with Mary (Myriem Roussel) as a gas-station attendant's daughter. The fragmented narrative is punctuated with many shots of the moon in the night sky and the sun behind clouds. Interestingly, Godard originally wanted the last shot to have been of a helicopter flying over Joseph and Mary, with a TV salesman calling down, "Hail, Mary" (Godard, *Notes*).

More commonly, though, Godard mocks our tendency to confuse the sky with heaven, a confusion that clearly has implications for our manipulation by cinematic images. For example, at the end of *Band of Outsiders* (1964), Odile and Franz escape from a robbery and head south to catch a steamer to South America. A narrator comments in voiceover: "Three days later, Odile and Franz saw the sea. It looked like a theater, with the horizon as its stage, and beyond it nothing but sky. Before the gently spreading waves of this harmony, Franz and Odile saw neither limits nor contradictions." With the couple on board ship, the voiceover continues: "My story ends here, like in a pulp novel, at that superb moment when nothing weakens, nothing wears away, nothing wanes." This ironic conclusion at once exceeds anything the image can show us and draws attention to the cheaply won happy endings of mainstream cinema. But lest we think that the skepticism of early Godard has given way, after the polemical works of his midcareer, to a more reassuring positivism in films like *Hail Mary,* we should note that the negative implications of the sky in *Contempt* recur even in the relatively recent *For Ever Mozart* (1996), in which one character comments, "When I look at the sky, I only see what has disappeared."

14. My thanks go to Krzysztof Piesiewicz's agent, Nicole Cann, who very kindly provided me with the English translation of Kieślowski and Piesiewicz's version of the screenplay.

15. Moravia also wrote a version of *Paradise,* although the title of the short story is clearly ironic.

Works Cited

Bailey, Derrick Sherwin. *The Mystery of Love and Marriage: A Study in the Theology of Sexual Relation.* New York: Harper and Brothers, 1952.

Coates, Paul. *Cinema, Religion, and the Romantic Legacy.* Aldershot: Ashgate, 2003.

———. "'The inner life is the only thing that interests me': A Conversation with Krzysztof Kieślowski." *Lucid Dreams: The Films of Krzysztof Kieślowski.* Ed. Paul Coates. Trowbridge: Flicks Books, 1999. 160–74.

Falkowska, Janina. "Religious Themes in Polish Cinema." *The New Polish Cinema.* Ed.

Janina Falkowska and Marek Haltof. Trowbridge: Flicks Books, 2003. 65–80.

Godard, Jean-Luc. *Notes about* Hail Mary. *Hail Mary.* Dir. Jean-Luc Godard. DVD. New Yorker Video, 2006.

———. "Shipwrecked People from the Modern World." Interview by Yvonne Baby. Rpt. in *Focus on Godard.* Ed. Royal S. Brown. Englewood Cliffs: Prentice-Hall, 1972. 37–39.

Haltof, Marek. *The Cinema of Krzysztof Kieślowski: Variations on Destiny and Chance.* London: Wallflower, 2004.

Kaufman, Anthony. "Interview: Run Tykwer Run; From Lola to 'The Princess and the Warrior.'" *Indiewire* 8 February 2005. http://www.indiewire.com/people/int_Tykwer_Tom_010625.html.

Kickasola, Joseph G. *The Films of Krzysztof Kieślowski: The Liminal Image.* New York: Continuum, 2004.

Kieślowski, Krzysztof, and Krzysztof Piesiewicz. *Heaven.* Unpublished screenplay. March 1998.

———. *Three Colours Trilogy: Blue, White, Red.* Trans. Danusia Stok. London: Faber and Faber, 1998.

Lubelski, Tadeusz. "A Difficult Return to 'Freedom Cinema.'" *The New Polish Cinema.* Trowbridge: Flicks Books, 2003. 24–36.

Morrey, Douglas. *Jean-Luc Godard.* Manchester: Manchester University Press, 2005.

Nowell-Smith, Geoffrey. "Paris Match: Godard and *Cahiers.*" *Sight and Sound,* n.s., 11.1 (June 2001): 18–21.

Pagels, Elaine. *The Gnostic Gospels.* 1979. New York: Vintage Books, 1989.

Paige, Nicholas. "Bardot and Godard in 1963 (Historicizing the Postmodern Image)." *Representations* 88 (Fall 2004): 1–25.

Santilli, Paul C. "Cinema and Subjectivity in Krzysztof Kieślowski." *Journal of Aesthetics and Art Criticism* 64.1 (Winter 2006): 147–56.

Stam, Robert. "Commentary." Disc 1. *Contempt.* Dir. Jean-Luc Godard. DVD. Criterion, 2002.

Steiner, George. *Real Presences.* Chicago: University of Chicago Press, 1989.

Sterritt, David. *The Films of Jean-Luc Godard: Seeing the Invisible.* Cambridge: Cambridge University Press, 1999.

Stok, Danusia, ed. *Kieślowski on Kieślowski.* London: Faber and Faber, 1993.

Vaucher, Andrea R. "International Chefs Serve up 'Heaven.'" *Variety* 3 September 2001: 8. Infotrac. 24 September 2004.

West, Christopher. "A Basic Theology of Marriage." *Catholic Education Resource Center.* http://www.catholiceducation.org/articles/sexuality/se0096.html.

Wilson, Emma. *Memory and Survival: The French Cinema of Krzysztof Kieślowski.* Oxford: Legenda, 2000.

Žižek, Slavoj. *The Fright of Real Tears: Krzysztof Kieślowski between Theory and Post-Theory.* London: BFI, 2001.

III. The Global Legacy

9

Kieślowski's Visual Legacy

Charles Eidsvik

Very few narrative film directors create visual worlds that are strikingly and unmistakably their own. Those directors who do create such worlds usually either have a background in photography or visual art (Von Sternberg, Kurosawa, Kubrick, Lynch) or else work closely with only one or two cinematographers. Ingmar Bergman's early films use the graphics-based approach of Gunnar Fischer, his later work, the subtle light-sensitivity of Sven Nykvist. When critics write of Bernardo Bertolluci's style, they are usually referring to the distinct aesthetic of his cameraman, Vittorio Storaro. Krzysztof Kieślowski was an exception, an utter rarity, a director who worked with many cameramen and who prized collaboration but whose visual world remains clearly his own.

This is not to say that the lighting or camera work was the same from film to film. With very few exceptions, his Polish films (including *Three Colors: White* [1994] but with the two *Short Films* [1988] as exceptions) could be described as using a realistic photographic approach; each of his French films used stylized "art-cinema" camerawork and lighting. And each film was a product of the give and take with his team, and especially with his cinematographers. Kieślowski believed in collaboration. Not only did he choose cinematographers for their appropriateness for a given story, he expected them to be active cocreators of his films' visual worlds. Paradoxically, Kieślowski's visual signature depended on close collaboration: he believed that only people given creative responsibility are apt to bring new or original elements to a film. As Sławomir Idziak points out:

> And this is something about Kieślowski, he is open to any kind of risk, he really gives room for the cinematographer because he strongly believes that the look is more important than anything

> else. It's not so much what we are telling, but how we are telling it, because he understands to what extent the style affects the story. He understands that the style is the story itself. Changing the style changes the story. What I really like is not so much the shooting, which is challenging and interesting of course, but to work with Kieślowski before we start [shooting] we spend weeks or months on the script and this collaboration is the most interesting part. (Amos)

Idziak and other of Kieślowski's cameramen noted that he rarely even looked through the viewfinder during a shoot. He trusted his cameramen to invent, using lenses and lights. As Idziak explains, on-set discussions were "in general terms of style and atmosphere" (Amos). There is a huge difference between the visual world of a director and the technical details of lighting, camera position, and lenses. On the set, Kieślowski concentrated on the actors; his cameraman tried to provide the technical means through which the viewer could grasp the scene (Amos). In good part, I suspect, Kieślowski's collaborative style was supported and leveraged by his genius in the editing room. Idziak's description of Kieślowski is telling: "a great director, a great scriptwriter, he was talented, but he was absolutely unbelievable in terms of cutting." Idziak describes the first cut of *Three Colors: Blue* (1993) as the worst movie he had ever seen, but Kieślowski went back to the editing room and two months later delivered "something which people universally like" (Idziak). In Kieślowski's films, the cameraman's shots are not just descriptions of what happens but fragmentary clues to what the characters and their story is really about. Their essence and beauty is in their suggestiveness. To describe Kieślowski's visual world is not just to describe cinematography and its techniques but to show how Kieślowski brought the suggestiveness of shots into relation through editing.

This essay will attempt to describe Kieślowski's visual world and its legacy in films since his death. Primary among my concerns are films outside of the European art-cinema tradition. Kieślowski's legacy is only beginning: though his approach has little to do with (and little relevance to) hundred-million-dollar Hollywood films, it is perfectly suited for digital filmmaking. Digital media such as the DVD are making his work accessible to young filmmakers, not just through other filmmakers' interpretations or imitations, but directly. At film festivals such as Cannes, it is now common to hear young filmmakers mention Kieślowski; there are very, very few young filmmakers there who do not know his work. Most seem to have encountered his work on DVD rather than in the film festivals and art houses that introduced older generations to his films. As Sławomir Idziak argued in his lecture to the 2007 Berlinale Talent Campus, with digital tools, the bloated crews and costs of studio filmmaking are unnecessary; small crews and collaborative approaches are perfect for our digital age (Idziak). It thus is the job of this essay not just to assess past influence but also to describe the basics of Kieślowski's visual world clearly enough that we can recognize its legacy when it shows up in the work of young filmmakers in the future.

Kieślowski's visual legacy has taken many forms, forms related to his overall creative vision. Some elements of his approach are traditional; others are radical. I will begin with the traditional, that is, with the coherence of his visual world. His cinema is a hybrid of documentary, in which we do not know what will happen next, and fiction film, with its convention of the camera (and microphone) being in exactly the best position, and with the best shot size, for us to see what is happening. The excitement this hybrid quality creates is the visual constant in his films. But the "privileged" vantage point from which we see has as its field of vision a stylized universe, first because of scene design or art direction, and second, because of lighting that helps separate field from ground and that helps lead the eye.

In all of Kieślowski's work, location, scene, and costume design—together called "art direction"—are tightly intertwined with the cinematographer's lighting. The designer and cinematographer work together to create a film's world. A cinematographer and director can do little without talented art directors to make locations and backgrounds "speak" in a film's emotional terms. In the *Decalogue* (1988) and *Short Films* (1988), Halina Dobrowolska was art director, and Patrice Mercier was the art director for *The Double Life of Véronique* (1991). Claude Lenoir was art director for all three films of the *Three Colors* trilogy. Normally the director, art director, and cinematographer work together in planning the look of the film and of each scene, but in Kieślowski's French films, often the cinematographer dictated much about backgrounds, especially their colors. For example, Piotr Sobociński made sure that extras in *Three Colors: Red* (1994) would not wear jeans; there was to be no blue in the film (Pizzello 70). Masterful strokes, such as the mottled and crumbling blue paint on the wall behind the flautist outside the café in *Blue* and the red rust on the wrought-iron fence and gate outside the Judge's house in *Red* are typical collaborations, beautifully textured, stunningly lit and photographed. Simpler designs, such as the three different room colors in Julie's apartment in *Blue* or the carefully "aged" look of the Judge's house in *Red* or the creation of the two apartments from parts of seventeen interiors in *A Short Film about Love* are testaments to the importance of set designers for the "look" of Kieślowski's films (Stok 171). The designer creates a coherent world for us to see the characters in.

Three techniques are essential to Kieślowski's hybrid visual style. First, he borrowed techniques for separating a figure (usually, a main character) from his or her background from traditional painting. In painting, background tends to be blurred out, darker, or lit with a different colored light than the figure or foreground. In black-and-white sketches, still photography, and cinema, rimlighting, sidelighting, and backlighting help keep characters from being submerged muddily into their surroundings. Selective focus and depth-of-field limiting (via lens, aperture, and filter choice as well as lighting) is adjusted to modulate this separation. These techniques guide the eye and thus help make viewing more coherent. Further, such separation allows the filmmaker to make a "statement" about the relationship of characters to their environment or their surroundings. In customary lighting in movies, unlike the handling of light color in painting, the light-color temperature is relatively constant for the entire scene: backgrounds are lit with color temperature similar to the lighting on actors. This makes editing continuity from shot to shot within a scene easier. Kieślowski pioneered the use of multiple light colors within scenes. (His light-color techniques have become widespread in the time since his death, though they are rarely used as audaciously as in his films.) His most striking explorations of the light-color separation technique were with the cinematographer Sławomir Idziak in *Véronique* and *Blue*, in which light color or filters reflected the mental states and moods of the films' protagonists. At times in *Véronique*, subtle filters make the streets and sky ugly while Weronika's and other characters' faces are lit warmly, as if to contrast our emotional attachment to Weronika with the world she lives in. Kieślowski, of course, was also capable of bathing his protagonists in a colored background, reversing his usual technique for effect. In *A Short Film about Killing*, for example, green camera filters, often stacked in groups, gave the sense of a world infused with urine. The characters are tinted with the same hues as the backgrounds. Similarly, in the trilogy, images often go completely blue (or red) to expressionistically put us in characters' emotional worlds. The basic idea behind figure/ground separation and coloration is to help us see more easily and clearly; Kieślowski was capable of taking entirely opposite approaches, using immersion instead of separation when it suited his needs. Much of the *Decalogue* and parts of *White* use immersion to create a claustrophobic sense of the futilities of life in Poland.

Often a color palette and momentary color effects—striking deviations from that palette—are used in dynamic combination, thereby creating a visual drama parallel to the narrative drama. For example, as Idziak explains when his interviewer remarks on how much warm light there is in *Blue*:

> I decided to use the colour blue as a kind of dramaturgical colour—a colour which has a meaning; we tried not to exaggerate so we don't have too much blue on the actual locations. . . . So we keep the film with a warm atmosphere and having quite strong, very aggressive blue at important moments. The blue we are having is the strong, aggressive, artificial . . . which has nothing to do with the natural blue that is already around. (Amos)

Because we notice only the unusual, the striking, there is little red in *Red*'s sets; there is rarely bright blue in *Blue*.

Kieślowski's films were also deliberately visually evocative in lens choices and in use of shadows. He used macro cinematography to reflect images from the cornea of Juliette Binoche in *Blue*. In *A Short Film about Love*, Witold Adamek used shots through a telescope aided by backlighting and murky shadows to achieve a dialectic between the characters, their dreams, and their soulless dwellings. Piotr Sobociński used selective lighting and strong shadows to get separation effects in *Red*, especially in Judge Kern's house, where bright light through windows would silhouette the Judge but hit Valentine full-face. (The most striking of these scenes is the one in which Judge Kern and Valentine have a parting drink.) Often, of course, clarity was put aside in favor of suspense: Kieślowski was unafraid to silhouette his characters or put us behind their backs when he wanted us to have to wait to read their expressions clearly. The result is a rhythmical dance of mystery and revelation, in an adult and very sophisticated version of psychological hide-and-seek.

Each of the above elements had roots in and derived conventions from painting and from older decades of cinema. But still photography also informed Kieślowski's practice. Still photography—the art of capturing images that will grab and hold the eye—was drilled into students at Łódź. In film school Kieślowski learned to think in terms of the meanings of moments that can be photographed to tell a story (Stok 44–47), that crystallize larger activities or realities, and that can accrete into a mental collage in memory. (Strong individual moments are also part of the aesthetic of Wajda's films, of Roman Polanski's, and of other Polish directors.) Privileged image-moments, which Sobociŋski called "key moments" (Pizzello 72), modulate and punctuate Kieślowski's visual patterns and structures. For example, an old woman struggling to put bottles into a recycling bin is seen in each film of the trilogy. That moment is not only unforgettable, it recalls the roots of Kieślowski's documentary career in Łódź. In this essay I will use Sobociński's term *key moments* to indicate their motif-like function in the structuring of Kieślowski's narratives. These moments work two ways. First, they grab attention, and thus are mnemonically salient. Second, these image-moments can temporally organize a film in the same way that motifs in music can organize a composition. Especially given Kieślowski's closeness to his composer, Zbigniew Preisner, it is not at all surprising that he often used a music-like visual structure in his films—a structure that often counterpoints the music in the films.

Yet another kind of visual signature is the result of casting and of Kieślowski's handling of actors. Kieślowski taught that the three important parts of making a film are the story, the casting, and the editing. Kieślowski felt that lead actors had to be people you could not take your eyes off of, and whom you wished well. What your eye goes to first, traditionally called the "dominant" in a shot, is usually the lead actor; how the lead actor gets and holds attention is central to leading the viewer's eye, and thus to how the film is seen. A director cannot, of course, "make" an actor visually charismatic; as Kieślowski pointed out in *A Masterclass for Young Directors,* in any group of people, the eye is apt to fall on only one. That one can perhaps play a lead role in a film. To make "reading" his lead actors easier, Kieślowski tended to keep his camera close to them. Often the tension between dialogue and image central to his aesthetic is literally embodied by his lead actors.

All of the above techniques are versions of traditional filmmaking, modified for Kieślowski's stories. One technique that was not traditional was borrowed from documentary. Kieślowski's images, like those in documentary, show a world of chance, contingency, and unpredictable events with unforeseen consequences, whereas in Hollywood, the camera's job is to predict and explain the next image and the direction of the film. In Hollywood, the camera "knows" what will happen next. A pan begins before the actor in frame moves; a dolly starts before the people or vehicles in the frame. There is, thus, in traditional film watching, a sense of fate, a sense that the story we watch is in the past tense, that the camera is a storyteller who knows how it will end.

Documentary films, in contrast, foreground the unpredictability of real behavior by following action, even chasing it. The character moves, then a split second later, the camera follows. The effect is to create the sense of the film's world as nondeterministic and potentially surprising. Used discriminately in a fiction film, this increases viewer alertness and emotional tension; the technique puts the action into the present tense. Kieślowski often used this technique to add tension and an element of surprise, to make the viewer as uncertain of the future of the story as the characters are. For example, in *Blue*, when Julie asks her housekeeper why she is crying, the aged woman says, "Because you aren't." Julie, normally unresponsive to others, reacts by quickly embracing the old woman. The camera, hand held, reframes, moving in close. The moment feels like documentary, as if the cameraman were as surprised by Julie's sudden compassion as we are. When the camera follows the action, reacting to its presence and immediacy rather than leading it, tension tends to rise; conversely, when the camera "predicts" the action by reframing just ahead of the action, viewers tend to relax. Kieślowski used the documentarist's approach to raise tension and attention; he brought in more "predictive" camerawork to lessen or release tension. Few filmmakers use this technique; few cameramen without experience in documentaries can master it.

In a conventional Hollywood production, the spatial relationship between actors and camera is controlled by a production ritual often called *follow-focus.* In rehearsal, actors "walk through" each scene, while crew members mark the floor with tape at each position where an actor will need to be in sharp focus. The camera operator and focus puller establish exact focus for each of these positions, marking the correct setting on tape on the focus ring of the camera lens. During a take, then, actors must hit the marks while the focus puller shifts the camera's focus correspondingly. (The camera operator is busy with framing; the operator and focus puller work as a team.) In practice, the follow-focus procedure reinforces the sense of predictive camera movement; the focus puller hits the marked point on the lens just before the actor gets there. The ritualized procedure makes for reliable filmmaking but not for inspired acting or camerawork. Filmmakers (such as Robert Altman) who allow improvisation and variation to take advantage of the creative impulses of the actor in the moment usually must use greater depth of field and wider framing. Kieślowski, in contrast, believed that his cameramen and focus pullers were fast enough and intuitive enough to allow acting spontaneity. Idziak preferred to shoot with his camera on his shoulder and do his own focus work, just as documentary cameramen do. Juliette Binoche, in a television interview about her experience with *Blue*, mentioned that she had moved on impulse in one shot but had been certain a retake would be necessary. At the end of the take, she realized that Idziak had guessed her move and had moved with her, smoothly. Idziak has described this kind of actor-cameraman interaction as a "dance." Given Kieślowski's uses of documentary techniques and the skill of his collaborators, the results are innovations, not mistakes.

In studio-funded films, every visual element makes sense and advances the plot. In documentaries, all sorts of potentially distracting, peripherally noticed events just "happen"; they are part of what makes a documentary feel real. Kieślowski put such apparent anomalies into his scenes (e.g., the old people trying to recycle bottles in the trilogy). While his characters create meaning from the contingent by focusing on very limited details, we become aware of the expressiveness of the entire visual field, including its anomalous details. For example, in *Blue*, Julie (Juliette Binoche) is drawn out of her willed isolation when, while sitting in a café, she notices a flautist on the street playing her dead husband's composition. We, however, see more through the café's windows than what she notices: a mottled blue wall and a street with happy families. Both mirror Julie's inner world even though they are peripheral to the narrative event. Thus, Kieślowski's visual worlds at least partially mirror the inner worlds of his protagonists (Amos). This mirroring, a counterpoint to the film's music and the performance of the actors, creates moments that are striking and picturesque. It is as if the characters were seeing themselves in a film sympathetic to them but over which they have little control. Kieślowski's characters are aware of both watching and being watched. They deal with existential dilemmas and emotional needs beyond their ability to articulate or easily "solve."

The collaboration between those who have created the film ultimately continues in the film's "collaboration" with the viewer (Stok 152). At the story level as well as in the moment, the viewer is asked to put the film's story together, to make leaps of faith, to see intelligently and with curiosity. At the emotional level—the level probably most important to Kieślowski—the viewer is apt to have a kind of "fellow feeling" with the characters, not exactly identification but rather recognition of what it feels like in their world. Our seeing becomes a form of seeking. Kieślowski gave us the images. He did not give us what to think of them.

Kieślowski's approach to what we see of course transcends the description I have given. The most complex elements I have left out are his handling of actors within visual space, the ways in which characters' nonverbal behavior is more "telling" than the words in his dialogue, and the highly elliptical editing rhythms both within and between scenes. These rhythms, and the fragments we see of scenes, make parts of the films feel a bit like narrative photo essays but with the photos in motion, with dialogue and sound and music. Each of these elements affects his visual world. Unfortunately, to describe them using the written word is almost impossible.

Given the nature of Kieślowski's visual world, how might we trace its legacy? One impulse would be to trace the work of cinematographers who worked with him. The problem, of course, is that they were only part of a collaborative partnership. The most inventive of Kieślowski's lighting cameramen and probably the most important to his legacy was Sławomir Idziak. Kieślowski made three visually astonishing films with Idziak: *Decalogue 5/A Short Film about Killing*, *The Double Life of Véronique*, and *Three Colors: Blue*. Idziak has gone on to become a major international cinematographer, who manages, though sometimes only briefly, to bring aspects of Kieślowski's visual approach to widely disparate films. Most of these films have been seen by only a few people or just on cable or video. The large Hollywood studio films he has shot, such as *Black Hawk Down* (2001) and *Harry Potter and the Order of the Phoenix* (2007) have reached hundreds of millions and have had the ironic effect of spreading Kieślowski's name—Idziak is frequently referred to as "Kieślowski's cinematographer"—but have little to do with Kieślowski's approach. Idziak is clear that the collaborative process on which his work with Kieślowski depended is completely antithetical to Hollywood's large studio filmmaking structure. He describes the American system as a kind of "industrial" approach:

> They don't expect the cinematographer to decide anything. They expect the cinematographer to execute. The American director tells you where to put the camera, which lens to shoot with, and even if it is the most idiotic position you have to put it there. There is no discussion. . . . You have to understand it is a different system. . . . They are shooting everything. So if there is any potential position of the camera they put the camera there. . . . It is too big an investment to risk any kind of major disaster so they try to protect everything. (Idziak)

The only positive experience Idziak found in shooting for Hollywood was on *Black Hawk Down*, the director of which, Ridley Scott, Idziak praises as "incredibly visual" and "extremely collaborative" (Idziak). But the film was shot with fifteen cameras; although Idziak ran the team, working with fifteen camera operators is a very different process from putting a camera on your shoulder and shooting.

Idziak has shot at least eighteen features since he last worked with Kieślowski, with thirteen of these in English. John Sayles's *Men with Guns* (1997) is perhaps typical. The first half-hour of Sayles's film—mostly set in a central American city—gives almost no indications of Idziak's work with Kieślowski. Then the protagonist, a Central American doctor searching for students he trained to be doctors in the countryside, begins to encounter the brutal realities of a civil war in which the indigenous Indians are the victims of both rebels and government troops. The film begins to take on Kieślowskian stylistic characteristics. In a blind woman's hut, the figure-ground separation occurs with both color and luminance levels: the background is colorless and shadowed, the foreground warmer, brighter. In small jumps, as the ageing doctor goes deeper and deeper into the mountain jungles, lighting and camera surprises begin to crop up. Key moments occur and (in typical Sayles style) also get recycled in flashbacks. In one section, in which a disillusioned priest who calls himself a ghost tells of his last times with the village in which he was a priest, the film becomes visually exciting. It remains exciting to the end (except for brief interludes) as the doctor and those who accompany him search for a refugees' village that survives because it cannot be seen from the air or reached by roads. The worse the doctors' encounter with genocidal horrors goes, and the further into the jungle they travel, the more Idziak has the chance to use what he learned in Poland and France. Even with a director like Sayles, a storyteller with limited visual sense and a habit of relying on dialogue to propel his stories, Idziak had some opportunities for interesting work.

Similarly, in *Black Hawk Down* the images that introduce the film, heavily blue-filtered and with desaturated colors, announce the world of the film will be that of Idziak. As the film continues to describe the situation in Somalia and particularly in Mogadishu, the colors—often with green tones in black faces set against a world of brown dust and a crumbling social disaster of corpses, starvation, and war—remind one of *A Short Film about Killing*. As the story progresses, Idziak gives the faces of the American soldiers sent into Mogadishu saturated color; the world they are in borders on the desaturated. The scenes vary stylistically, with scenes of soldierly camaraderie on the base lit and shot with little stylization, whereas the brutal battles are handled as ugly portraits of a hell with little color except for the blood spattered on faces. The key moments of course are those one expects from a Ridley Scott war film. From the perspective of cinematography, it is clear that Kieślowski's vision can be brought to almost any serious filmic genre, provided that the director has enough of a visual sense to let it happen. Scott is a master of leading the eye, of utilizing what a cinematographer can bring to a film, and of treating style as statement. But Idziak hates action movies (Idziak) and has no interest in working on another.

Are all the films lit and shot by Idziak similarly expressive, using techniques honed with Kieślowski? Hardly. The life of a cinematographer breaking into the consciousness of the English-speaking world is inherently one of making do with available opportunities. Thus, of the two John Duigan films Idziak shot, one, *The Journey of August King* (1995), was a good film, competently shot but not visually stylized; the other, *Paranoia* (1997), had stylized visuals but in every nonvisual sense was a mess. *Gattaca* (1997) was a well-designed, well-lit and well-shot sci-fi piece that came and went without notice. Idziak has done extraordinary work in each film he has shot. Even *Harry Potter and the Order of the Phoenix* has moments that remind me of moments in Kieślowski's world. But they are only moments, not real documents of his legacy.

Perhaps more important to the future than the millions who have seen Idziak's studio work are the few hundred film students Idziak has taught in Europe (primarily in Berlin) and at the Australian film school. Kieślowski's films show what he could do. Idziak tells how it was done. The question of visual legacy in an art so dependent on technology is in part a question of learning how it was done and how to do it in new films.

Piotr Sobociński (*Decalogue 3* and *9* and *Three Colors: Red*) also had a strong international career after Kieślowski's death, albeit an unfortunately short one. In *Red,* Sobociński embraced the world of modern cinematic technology—steadicams, remote-controlled camera booms, and the like. He was in demand in America as a cinematographer, completing five features in five years—three thrillers, and two quiet "art" films (*Marvin's Room* [1996] and *Hearts in Atlantis* [2001]). His death in 2001, at forty-three years of age, cut short the influence he was bound to have had with more films in circulation. In his American films there are glimpses of his genius, as, for example, in the opening of *Angel Eyes* (2001) and the color tone shifts from present to past in *Hearts in Atlantis.* But the body of his work after Kieślowski was too small, genre-limited, and (except for *Ransom* [1996]) limited in distribution for his impact to be truly significant.

Others have been influential, but primarily in Europe, not my subject here. Edward Kłosiński (*Decalogue 2, Three Colors: White* [1994]) brought a sensibility bathed in subtle and almost repressed expressionism (most clearly visible in his later work like Von Trier's 1991 *Europa*—called *Zentropa* in the United States). Witold Adamek (*Decalogue 6/A Short Film about Love*) also clearly has had European influence, including in all probability on Kieślowski's work in the *Three Colors* trilogy; Adamek's creation of a world of longing and love seen (or imagined) through telephoto lenses is like nothing before it in cinema, but a perfect metaphor for Kieślowskian visual seeking. Alas for the international community, Adamek kept largely to Polish films until his death early in 2008.

It is, of course, easy enough to notice Kieślowski's visual world when one is looking at his cameramen or the world of European art cinema. But how would we recognize his world outside of his oeuvre or the work of his cinematographers? One way of appreciating a master's work is through looking at those who either "fake" the master's style (as in "fake" paintings, which are pedagogically useful in that they reveal what a particular period or culture found important in the original) or who deliberately attempt to utilize elements from that style. What would a film influenced by the ten-hour television series the *Decalogue* look like? One example lies in the Indian film *The Terrorist* (1999), shot and directed by Santosh Sivan. The lead actress, Ayesha Dharker, playing a guerrilla fighter who has been chosen as a suicide bomber sent to kill a politician, has said that the director made a point of showing the cast and crew the *Decalogue* during rehearsals for the film so that they would understand the style he was going to use (Dharker). Sriram S.'s art direction, carried out through Shyam Sunder's production design and Anu Radha's costume design, follows Kieślowski's approach closely. Santosh Sivan directed from his camera's viewfinder, his camera shoulder-mounted like Idziak's. (When Idziak has worked as a director, he has also done camera.)

Many Kieślowskian visual elements are present in *The Terrorist*. Santosh Sivan grasped what few other directors have about Kieślowski: the work must be edited elliptically, with room for the viewer to imagine what goes between the images. And the film must move as quickly as possible, so that we have the energy to put the images together in our imaginations. The subject of the film is the inner life of a would-be suicide bomber. The thematic civil war–based roots of the film leap at us even before the titles: Malli, dressed in red against a grey and black river background. In the opening scene, a young man who has informed on the rebels is about to be shot. His warm skin tones stand out against the green jungle background. The rebels wear cloth over their heads and faces, mostly in red. Malli, masked in pink, executes the informer with a revolver. The rebels leave, viewed in a lightly "dutched" (slanted rather than level) shot, shoulder-held. Malli washes her blood-spattered cloth mask in a river. A girl washes Malli's hair. Automatic weapons fire; Malli's cloth mask floats in the river current. Malli, in extreme close-up (ECU), then in medium shot (MS), fires her machine-gun carbine at the offscreen soldiers. As her friend watches, she (in almost ghostlike soft focus) runs toward a flaming dwelling. We see her primarily in shallow-focus ECU, warm-skinned; then we see a government soldier, in the red-beret of an officer, in ECU over the black barrel of Malli's weapon. Malli shoots. The film moves from key moment to key moment; together they are organized as leitmotifs describing action, what she sees, and what she remembers: a murdered brother, a dying sweetheart, murdered children. We see her eyeball in an ECU, looking down. Then we see what she sees: a teenaged boy is in the water. She pulls him out. In the blue-filtered darkness, she tries to care for the boy; flames punctuate the night. Then we are back to the river in long shot (LS). Then there is a cut to Malli in a camp being fitted for a body bomb. Then we jump to her trip through the jungle, led by a young boy named Lotus. In CU, we see her hands bringing up water to her face, then images of her night encounter with a dying young man, a key image-moment and, through flashbacks, a recurring motif throughout the film. As in Kieślowski, most key images in Santosh Sivan's film are the links between people and their inner lives. At the end, Malli chooses not to detonate the bomb. We are left to imagine what future, if any, is left to her.

Santosh Sivan studied Kieślowski because his methods would work, and be effective, for a cash-strapped production with only a small cast and crew. The inner life is cheap to film. What can be left to the imagination costs far less than what is shown. Small elements can represent larger environments and events, and if the director is also a highly skilled cameraman, that at least provides a visual context in which to build a film out of purely sensory elements. The art of film is, after all, the art of putting synecdoches into motion in time.

Is a Kieślowski legacy possible in America in the same way it is in Europe or in developing countries? Perhaps, but probably only in independent, small-budget "specialty" film. Kieślowski's French trilogy was financed by a producer who also was an exhibitor and distributor. Marin Karmitz's MK2 production company has few current equivalents in America. There are usually a half-dozen to a dozen small independent American production and distribution companies (such as Good Machine was in the 1980s and 1990s and Thinkfilm or Greene Street Films now) that resemble the production side of MK2 Productions and support independent filmmakers. But in the last decade most such companies in North America have become specialty film branches of major studios—for example, Good Machine became Focus Films, an art-film branch of NBC Universal. Technological change has made filmmaking relatively easy, especially on digital; distribution and access to movie screens (or even cable television screens) has not gotten easier, despite the success of the Sundance and Independent Film cable channels and the move of HBO into releasing some films as features. Very, very few directors in the United States have "final cut" on their films. Without final cut, Kieślowski would have been crippled as a filmmaker. (Censoring usually is less harmful to a film than loss of final cut; a censor clips a few "offensive" parts; an incompetent or unfriendly editor destroys the film's rhythms and thus its soul.) The result has been a gloving-over of stylistic and authorial fingerprints that might, a decade ago, clearly have shown Kieślowski's influence and legacy at work. In a world in which very few directors have final cut, how would a film made in the United States most obviously embody Kieślowski's influence? At

In *The Terrorist* (1999), Santosh Sivan adopts Kieślowski's practice of creating striking moments that mirror the inner world of the protagonist. Here, the would-be suicide-bomber Malli (Ayesha Dharker) strays from her single-minded purpose.

this moment in American film history, it is easy to describe such moments of influence in specific aspects or parts of individual films but rarely in whole films.

The obvious place to look is in films that echo Kieslowki's thematic obsession with chance, and his demonstration of how to put chance into stories, and into characters' dilemmas. The most striking of such echoes perhaps are Paul Thomas Anderson's films, which are done in collaboration with his cinematographer, Robert Elswit, and which are the unique product of a director who rethinks scenes as he shoots (as did Kieślowski)—for example, *Boogie Nights* (1997), *Magnolia* (1999), or *There Will Be Blood* (2007). Equally interesting are Steven Soderbergh's *Traffic* (2000), in which chance plays a large role, and in which director-cameraman "collaboration" was insured by Soderbergh doing much of his own camera work. Paul Haggis's *Crash* (2004) and Alejandro González Iñárritu's *21 Grams* (2003), shot by his longtime collaborator Rodrigo Prieto, also stand out.

Each reflection of Kieślowski is different from the others; directors used whatever was useful to them. For example, in perhaps twenty minutes of Paul Thomas Anderson's *Magnolia* (mainly involving Tom Cruise's scenes) the figure-ground separation in interiors often is reminiscent of *Decalogue*-era Kieślowski even though Robert Elswit has a style of his own that has evolved since the early 1980s, a style that shares little with Kieślowski's. Rodrigo Prieto's camera work in Iñárritu's *21 Grams* resembles Kieślowski's basic visual approach in the same way that Guillermo Arriaga's screenplay for the film echoes Kieślowski's structures and concerns for the unpredicted consequences of acts and accidents. Brigitte Broche's production designs on *21 Grams* function like those in Kieślowski's films, especially in locations in which poor people live. In many respects, Iñárritu's techniques for fragmenting and juggling time, along with the impenetrability that is part of Arriaga's and Iñárritu's approach to characterization, make the viewer active in a way similar to what happens in a Kieślowski film. There is, of course, more violence and a more dynamic acting style than Kieślowski used. But the interiors, especially the night-club scenes, look as if Idziak shot them; exterior nights also resemble his work. Prieto began working professionally in the late 1980s, developing during Kieślowski's best-known period. That this film's work looks so much like Idziak shooting for Kieślowski can hardly be an accident. But the style of *21 Grams* is a one-off: the other two films in the Arriaga/Iñárritu trilogy (*Amores Perros* and *Babel*) do not look or function visually like *21 Grams*. For contemporary filmmakers, emulation of Kieślowski's or Idziak's work is one choice among many.

Curiously, however, a number of films in the mid-1990s function very similarly to Kieślowski's. Julian Schnabel's *Basquiat* (1997), for example, leads the eye using figure/field separation and careful interplay between Ron Fortunato's cinematography and Dan Leigh's production design; though Schnabel's New York is more colorful than anything Kieślowski filmed, and though Schnabel used less backlighting than Kieślowski, Schnabel's painterly eye and devotion to visual energy make his film oddly Kieślowskian. Did Schnabel see Kieślowski's films? Probably: Schnabel's filmic and artistic literacy are unquestionable. But was he influenced cinematographically, or was he dipping into the same root sources as Kieślowski? There is no clear way of answering the question. Kieślowski was interested in the inner life; Schnabel clearly shares both this obsession and artistic techniques for getting at that life. Schnabel's latest film, *The Diving Bell and the Butterfly* (2007), especially in its first half, pushes the cinematic possibilities of getting inside a character beyond even what Kieślowski's films show. My reaction was, "that is how Kieślowski would have done it."

In technology-based art forms such as the cinema, access to the past increases in scope and ease with every decade, if not every year. New technology at both the viewing and filmmaking level is key to Kieślowski's visual world's long-term importance. Even when his influence seems sporadic or almost trivial, as when, for example, the television series *Six Feet Under* treated memories and nightmares stylistically as if they had occurred in the *Decalogue*, an homage is still a reminder. More profound of course is the simple fact that Kieślowski's work is available on DVD, which has made not only the "story" side of art filmmaking but also the stylistic elements visible and thus available for emulation. As James Monaco argues in *How to Read a Film*, DVD makes movies as portable and as easily accessed as a book. Just as time does not make great writers' books or great painters' canvases "age" in a damaging way, cinema's legacies are now carried forward far more by DVD than by

Watching and being watched: Julian Schnabel's *The Diving Bell and the Butterfly* (2007), especially in its first half, pushes the cinematic possibilities of getting inside a character beyond even what Kieślowski's films show. (Publicity photo by Etienne George)

what has happened in theaters since Kieślowski's death. And with DVDs (and the literate commentaries in sets such as *Krzysztof Kieślowski's Three Colors*), increased understanding of what Kieślowski was doing visually (and, equally important, how and why he was doing it) is readily available to young filmmakers. There are very few film students who do not know Kieślowski's films. Digital technology, both at mini-DV and HD levels, is cheap enough, precise enough, and sophisticated enough so that young filmmakers can emulate great films, working directly from the source films rather than from imitations. DVD has made it possible not to depend on the present quirks of film distribution and exhibition. Further, and most important, digital technology has made it possible for any film student or even film buff to learn how to edit films, how to record, mix, and manipulate sound, and, via the Internet, to get feedback on even fledgling artistic work. Only in the editing room can one truly appreciate the true singularity of Kieślowski's talent.

Digital technology has also revived the documentary. Just as Kieślowski came to fiction-filmmaking from a background in documentary, young filmmakers are attempting the form en masse. Some perhaps will eventually, as Kieślowski did, discover the limits of documentary but the virtues of repurposing some of its visual techniques. When those people begin making their own feature films, it is likely we will see them turning, with Kieślowski as a model, to hybrid stylistic forms. It is one of the ironies of film history that technology unavailable to Kieślowski is apt to make his legacy grow huge. One cannot but think he would have been as amused by this irony as he was by those of his own stories and his career.

Works Cited

Amos, Lindsay. Interview with Sławomir Idziak. January 1996. *moviexpress*. (Australia) http://moviexpress.tripod.com/id10.htm.

Dharker, Ayesha. Interview by Charles Eidsvik. 12 June 2000. London, UK.

Idziak, Sławomir. "'On Eyelevel with a View-Finder': A Lecture by Sławomir Idziak." Berlinale Talent Campus. 14 February 2007. http://www.berlinale-talentcampus.de/story/59/1559.html.

Krzysztof Kieślowski: A Masterclass for Young Directors. Videocassette. Editions a voir, 1995.

Monaco, James. *How to Read a Film*. New York: Oxford University Press, 2000.

Pizzello, Stephen. "Piotr Sobociński: *Red*." *American Cinematographer* 76.6 (June 1995): 68–74.

Stok, Danusia, ed. *Kieślowski on Kieślowski*. London: Faber and Faber, 1993.

10

Kieślowski Crosses the Atlantic

Joseph G. Kickasola

> [The Americans] care for the public's interests because they care about their wallets; so that's a different sort of caring really. What I'm thinking of is caring also for the audience's spiritual life. Maybe that's too strong a word but something which is a little more than just box-office. The Americans take excellent care of the box-office. And while doing so they make the best, or some of the best, films in the world anyway, also on the spiritual level. But I reckon that this realm of higher needs, of something more than just forgetting about everyday life, of mere recreation, this realm of needs has been clearly neglected by us. So the public's turned away from us because they don't feel we're taking care of them. Maybe these needs are disappearing. —Krzysztof Kieślowski, *Kieślowski on Kieślowski*

Krzysztof Kieślowski typically discussed America through tossed-off sardonic comments laced with grudging admiration.[1] Despite his cynicism, Kieślowski considered "third-rate American cowboy adventures" and various American films among his formative influences.[2] The epigraph to this chapter shows this vacillation, wherein he lambastes the materialism of American cinema even as he admires its spiritual potential.

The American "box-office" industry was mostly foreign to Kieślowski. In communist Poland, his films faced censorship, but they also had little pressure to make money or be "entertainment." Poles loved Kieślowski's films (particularly his early work) not because they were amusing but because they smuggled in truths about the difficulties of Polish existence. As Poland faced overwhelming political tensions in the 1980s, Kieślowski's concern for the spiritual took a more prominent role as he broadened his thematic material to address more universal questions of existence, morality, suffering, and God.[3] His philosophical vision presaged the needs of the Poland to come, as the fall of communism would usher in an overwhelming measure of freedom and responsibility, and a national search for unifying, common values. In this essay I propose that Kieślowski's new themes in this period might be summarized as a concern for "existential possibility."

Kieślowski also found experimental forms well suited to this new theme, and it is here that we begin to see how America may have developed a taste for Kieślowski: through various narrative devices hinging on the "design versus chance" ontological binary, such as "the mosaic film" (multiple plot lines and characters intersecting in significant ways), the "forking-path narrative" (one character, several potential/virtual plot trajectories), and so forth. Various names have been invented for this general collective tendency (though each critic nuances the definition differently). David Bordwell suggests a number of different terms for this "adventurous storytelling" impulse, including "the fates converging film," the "puzzle film," and "network narratives" (*Hollywood* 72–103). Glenn Man groups them all as "the aesthetics of intersection" (1).[4] At least one prominent American critic, A. O. Scott of the *New York Times,* has suggested that the "genre" (a debatable term) is still embryonic enough to be "unnamed" at present.

I propose the collective description "multivalent" cinema. This term, from chemistry, describes the combined power of disparate, ever-moving electron paths in any given chemical reaction. Some electrons remain random, some combine their paths with others—through intersection—to great effect. Within "multivalence," we have a defining relationship between randomness and order that is of primary concern, and this relationship is paramount in Kieślowski's later narratives and many contemporary American films.

Though such film structures have always been around (and they preexisted cinema in various literary forms), Bordwell notes they were not so common in American film between 1932 (when *Grand Hotel* came out) and 1990 ("Mutual Friends" 362).[5] Kieślowski employed these forms in nearly all of his films, from *Blind Chance* (1981) to his final work, *Three Colors: Red* (1994).[6] Since 1990, they have been commonplace in North American films; Bordwell highlights over one hundred examples, and that is an incomplete list ("Mutual Friends" 361). It appears that Kieślowski presaged a multivalent resurgence.[7]

I will begin with a discussion of multivalent structures and their reappearance in North American films after 1990.[8] I will then interpret these forms within the thematic framework of existential possibility. That is, the forms imply a continuum of randomness versus order in human interaction, and I will situate Kieślowski (via Richard Kearney's metaphysics of possibility) between Gilles Deleuze's rhizomatic position and the classic order of onto-theistic metaphysics. In a sense, Kieślowski might be seen as dialectic between these two poles, as he, at various times, suggests both randomness and an uncanny order in his films. Finally, I will survey examples of North American multivalent tendencies along the full range of existential possibility.

Multivalence and Existential Possibility

> But I think that there is a point at which all these trifling matters, all these little mysteries, come together like droplets of mercury to form a larger question about the meaning of life, about our presence here, what in fact went before and what will come after, whether there is someone who controls all this, or whether it all depends on our own reason or on someone or something else. That mystery is there all the time. Of course it has certain religious connotations, but those connotations fundamentally arise out of the existential questions, rather than the other way around. —Krzysztof Kieślowski, qtd. in Paul Coates, *Lucid Dreams*

Understanding the relationship between multivalent forms and existential possibility—which often represents the "little mysteries" that "come together" in Kieślowski's films—requires some more elaboration on both points. Remarkably, Kieślowski's films from 1981 on represent virtually all the most common multivalent forms, and I will detail them later on. Likewise, a more thorough understanding of existential possibility will help us understand the relevance of Kieślowski's offerings to the resurgence of such forms and themes in North American cinema.

Varieties of Multivalent Cinema

Multivalent structures can be roughly divided into three primary groups: the mosaic structure, the forking-path narrative, and the multivalent consciousness film. The first group is by far the largest and most varied on the subcategorical level and is roughly equivalent to what Bordwell labels "network films." The other two are not exactly "networks" as Bordwell has described the trend at issue, but they function in similar ways and evoke many of the same questions. This is, to my mind, a reason for calling them multivalent, because the term essentially provides a category that describes multiple trajectories of any sort that raise questions about the relationship between randomness and order.

The Mosaic Structure. The mosaic film, as it is often called,[9] represents this essential idea: small pieces of narrative, or smaller narratives, that come together to form a larger metanarrative. Inherently, this raises the question: are not most films with multiple characters of this structure? Bordwell addresses this issue succinctly: some films highlight the network more than others ("Mutual Friends" 359). To Bordwell's observation I would add that this "highlighting" most often manifests itself in a *reverse expositional structure.* That is, more-traditional narratives will show you an early event of synthesis and exposition where all the characters are introduced, complete with their relationships to one another, and the drama of the film is contingent on these relationships developing and changing throughout the course of the film. In the mosaic film, however, the relationship of the characters and their respective narratives is typically withheld until later in the film, and part of the appeal of the narrative is the "puzzle factor," the sheer joy of watching the elements come together to form a whole. This pleasure is augmented by the fact that our conception of these characters is often altered and recontextualized by the "revelation" of their relationships with each other.

For instance, one could make a film called *One Polish Family,* establishing, right up front, the constituents of the family, and then tell the stories of each of the members, building the drama on the interfamilial relations and tensions inherent within them. Or, one could choose a mosaic structure, as Kieślowski did in the short documentary *Seven Days a Week* (1988), where each day of the week (Monday through Saturday) is dedicated to a different Polish person (young, old, male, and female) who speaks about his/her primary social, political, and personal concerns. The final day, Sunday, shows all of these characters sitting down to one family dinner, their familial relationship revealed as an added, unifying component. The value of the structure is that we first apprehend these characters apart from each other, devoting our attention to individual aspects of their characters and seeing them as constituents of a "holistic" portrait of Warsaw society in 1988. Then, at the end, we must reconceive them in light of their formative relations with each other, reflecting Kieślowski's abiding concern for the individual-communal tension in society. Kieślowski employed this idea on a larger scale in the *Decalogue* series (1988), where the ten constituent films are gradually revealed to be playing out within one Warsaw apartment complex among neighbors who may or may not know one another. His final three films, the *Three Colors* trilogy (1993–94), also subtly and gradually reveal connections between the characters within them.

In all cases, mosaic films feature multiple protagonists in intersection with each other, with various degrees of contingency at play. In some cases, the intersection carries the weight of a cause-effect relation (that is, character one directly influences a narrative outcome for character two, despite their typical ignorance of each other). In other cases, the intersection simply provokes the thought in the spectator: what might have been, had these two characters known each other (as when Karol of *Three Colors: White* and Julie of *Three Colors: Blue* end up in the same Paris courtroom, yet never interact). Indeed, the "highlighting" often appears as an apparently random group of characters that are apparently disconnected are gradually revealed to be connected in some fashion (usually later in the film), causing the audience to experience something like serendipity and more intensely press these characters' trajectories and thematic developments into relationship.

Numerous examples of this sort of structure may be found in American cinema since 1990. As mentioned, Bordwell gives a rather lengthy (but not quite complete!) list, but some American examples are *Grand Canyon* (Lawrence Kasdan, 1991), *Traffic* (Steven Soderbergh, 2000), and *13 Conversations about One Thing* (Jill Sprecher, 2001).

Forking Paths. The Kieślowski film *Blind Chance* is a "forking-path" narrative, a form named after the archetypal Jorge Luis Borges story "The Garden of the Forking Paths" (1941).[10] Essentially, you have one character proceeding along a particular narrative trajectory that suddenly forks in several directions. One path may be the "true" story of the character and the others are alternate endings that hinge on the outcome of that moment of "contingency" (i.e., whether or not Witek catches that train at a particular moment), though in certain more experimental forking-path narratives (e.g., some films by David Lynch), it is not entirely clear which path is the "true" story.[11]

The most obvious imitators of *Blind Chance* have been European, namely, the blatantly derivative *Sliding Doors* (Britain, Peter Howitt, 1998) and the much more stylistically unique *Run Lola Run* (*Lola Rentt,* Germany, Tom Tykwer, 1998). In America, the most common use of the forking-path form has been in the science-fiction genre, where time travel accounts for divergent outcomes (e.g., *Donnie Darko* [2001], and *Primer* [2004]). Of course, science-fiction stories have always explored divergent futures via time travel (e.g., H.G. Wells's *The Time Machine* [1895] and Isaac Asimov's story "The End of Eternity" [1955]). What interests us here is the resurgence of the idea in films since 1990, including the ones just mentioned and the recent film adaptation of *The Time Machine* (Simon Wells, 2002).

Multivalent Consciousness. In essence, films of this variety posit the question: can one person actually, in some way or another, have two or more simultaneous modes of existence? This varies from the forking-path narrative in that multiple trajectories are imaginatively conceived as simultaneous realities, not *possible* outcomes hinging on a particular contingency.

Kieślowski employs this form through the doppelgänger motif. *The Double Life of Véronique* (1991) explores the idea of two people who may, in fact, be the same person: a doppelgänger story that suggests something of a forking-path narrative; though they are two distinct persons, we are pressed to think of them as the same person (particularly as they are played by the same actress, Irène Jacob) whose life outcomes were determined by various contingencies. That instinct is confounded, however, when we see the two women very briefly in the same scene. In this case, Kieślowski enticingly suggests that one might outmaneuver fate through some sort of secret intuition of the other "double" character. Kieślowski's film evokes a sense of mystical connection between these two characters, which both have sensed but not been able to articulate.

The doppelgänger, of course, has a long literary tradition, but its resurgence is quite interesting, from the straightforward doubles to be found in *Doppelgänger* (Avi Nesher, 1993) to the mysteries of *Mulholland Drive* (David Lynch, 2001), in which two characters may be distinct, doppelgänger, or one mind fractured in two (depending on one's interpretation). Likewise, we might consider the double lives that false consciousness can create, whether through delusion, virtuality, or fictional narrative paths. One variation is the "fiction writer" protagonist, which serves as a conceit for projecting alternative futures (e.g., Woody Allen's *Melinda and Melinda* [2004] and Spike Jonze's *Adaptation* [2002]). *Memento* (Christopher Nolan, 2000) hinges on a multivalence born of memory, or lack thereof. *A Beautiful Mind* (Ron Howard, 2001), *Schizopolis* (Steven Soderbergh, 1996), and *Fight Club* (David Fincher, 1999) stake much of their appeal on the multivalent plots born of psychological delusion. *Vanilla Sky* (Cameron Crowe, 2001) and *Eternal Sunshine of the Spotless Mind* (Michel Gondry, 2004) demonstrate multivalence à la techno-futurist meddling with consciousness.

For every film example in the three multivalent categories just given, many more could be listed. Remarkably, however, Kieślowski seems to have presaged nearly all of them, stylistically. Whereas there are many stylistic and tonal differences between Kieślowski and these filmmakers, the interest in multivalent structures remains. Likewise, I argue that Kieślowski's theme of existential possibility might be surmised in this trend.

Existential Possibility

Multivalent narratives naturally carry the idea of existential possibility. This is not merely the pessimistic existentialism so common in film and literature during the middle of the last century. Rather, out of the concrete immediate existential position, this theme offers questions regarding the orderliness of reality, tinted by varying levels of belief and doubt in such order, through a consideration of what might have been. Such a theme does not dogmatically require any postulate, such as an organizing person or principle, but it does, de facto, broach the possibility of such even as it acknowledges the simultaneous uncanniness and philosophical difficulties such a possibility entails. I argue that Kieślowski has put the issue on the table, so to speak, by explicitly highlighting the theme as it lurks in multivalent forms.

Existential possibility might be linked with the concept of "radical contingency," which is that pervasive sense in the contemporary world that the universe is extraordinarily vast, that reality is infinitely complex, and that the human instinct to ascribe meaning to given events paradoxically grows in light of these discoveries (Dupré 135). This theme may be conceived as the dialectic play between Enlightenment conceptions of order/telos and the postmodern Deleuzian rhizome of random connection. That is, in a now-"classic" bit of subversion, Gilles Deleuze and Felix Guattari announced the end of Western metaphysics by replacing the Enlightenment "taproot" model of reality with the "rhizome," where an unpredictable system of roots emerges in a given environment (common in some grasses, for instance, where there is no central organizing root for any of the others and none are necessarily more important than any others). In other words, for Deleuze, any sense of "significance" of connections should not be presumed, as connections are haphazard, aleatoric, and ever-evolving. We might revel in the connections in a shallow, postmodern way, but we should not have any illusions about connections leading us to a taproot, a single source of knowledge, or a single Truth.[12] Indeed, in Deleuze's view, we should not view connection as significant beyond the natural salience of the connection itself.

Multivalence evokes the question of whether one considers "coincidence" to be a teleological revelation or a rhizomatic, haphazard event. Indeed, the final, big questions mosaic films often encourage rise to the metaphysical level: does this connection evidence some sort of grand design related to human needs and the search for meaning where some extraordinary benefit or extraordinary tragedy comes about through the connection? Does the connection seem uncanny, and does the connection suggest something beyond mere chance? Some filmmakers push toward a "yes" answer (often in a romantic, unsophisticated manner), others toward "no" (often in a cynical, equally unsophisticated manner). Through forking-path narratives, we begin to explore something like divine "middle knowledge," the knowledge of all subjunctive conditionals, all the things that might have been in any conceivable chain of events.[13] This is partly why Bordwell, in a decidedly nontheological context, calls forking-path plots "multiple draft" plots (Bordwell, "Film Futures" 102); as Edward Branigan expounds, these films appeal to us because they appeal to the fundamental "what if" imaginative capacity upon which so much of our decision-making and humanness is based (Branigan 110). The multivalence-of-consciousness film is another means of thinking out "the possible" in any given existential context, and the "possibilities" presented typically give us occasion to consider the impact (moral and existential) of human choice in the world. The most "Kieślowskian" films of this type not only think out the possible but consider the *meaning* of what happens (as opposed to what *might* have happened) and thoughtfully reflect on human nature and action in these contexts, just as Kieślowski sought to do in *Blind Chance* (Stok 113).

Kieślowski's coincidences are fraught with enough ambiguity regarding causality that one cannot put him squarely in the "taproot" camp (particularly in the darker films of the early 1980s). In later films, when faced with the baldly aleatoric and postmodern philosophy that undermines significance of any sort, Kieślowski strains toward the miraculous. Though he never dogmatically embraced either extreme, his characteristic seriousness and earnest raising of the issue gives the issue itself significance and echoes Richard Kearney's recently articulated "metaphysics of possibility."

Kearney begins his book *The God Who May Be: A Hermeneutics of Religion* with the statement: "God neither is nor is not but may be" (1). Essentially, when faced with a choice of God who metaphysically is (in the strongest sense of being) and the God who is beyond being (the God of the negative theologians Jean-Luc Marion, Emmanuel Levinas, and others), Kearney sees a fruitful middle road in the category of *posse,* or potentiality. It is very difficult to conceptualize a God who neither is nor is not, of course, but this is where Kieślowski's ambiguous, dialectical musings on the question become most relevant. Neither Kearney nor Kieślowski wants to assert God's existence, nature, or action(s) in the world with any kind of concrete certitude. At the same time, they see the human search for meaning, promise, and hope as fundamental to our existence and impossible to ignore. Kearney even goes so far as to say God will eventually *come into being* at the eschaton, the final promise that He (who/what/wherever He is or may be) has given. In other words, Kearney seems to suggest that, in whatever sense we might say that God "exists," Western metaphysics has endowed Him with too much ontological weight. Yet, he holds such existence to be fundamental to the faith as the future *promise* that will rescue the past. As for Kieślowski, he never detailed his philosophy, but it is fair to say that he balanced his pessimism about God's existence with prayers for *jasnosc* (a Polish term Insdorf translates as "illumination," 81).[14]

The purpose of this essay is not to hash out all the complexities and difficulties of Kearney's creative argument. However, it provides a serious theological portrait (at a dialectical historical moment in which we are battling between modernist and postmodernist sensibilities) of what philosophical theology looks like in the wake of these massive questions. Existential possibility summarizes, precisely, the "spiritual needs" to which Kieślowski referred, and multivalent structures are the most natural of vehicles for this important theme. Not all "multivalent" filmmakers share Kieślowski's concern for the spiritual, but their use of multivalent forms implies they cannot escape the general discussion of the contingency/design question.

American Films along the Continuum

Some multivalent films revel in the Deleuzean rhizome. Others suggest a more definitive (if not clearly understood) cosmic order. This section will survey American films at both these poles. Kieślowski's dialectical position between them gives his films maximum stylistic, thematic, and philosophical range. A few filmmakers have emulated this position, and I will conclude the section by briefly discussing two of these kindred spirits across the Atlantic, the Canadian writer/director Paul Haggis and the Mexican filmmaker Alejandro Gonzalez Iñárritu.

Toward the Rhizome

Robert Altman, an American director who was a bit more pessimistic about order, made his reputation with his network films of the 1970s (e.g., *Nashville* [1975]). His work in the 1980s did not hold consistently to the network model (and it did not receive much box office or critical attention), but in the early 1990s he resurrected the model in full (*The Player* [1992], and *Short Cuts* [1993]). I argue there is a distinctly cynical tone to Altman's treatment of these themes that Kieślowski does not share. It deliberately squelches much suggestion of existential possibility and promotes a darker, random, existential feeling about any order in the universe, along the lines of French existentialism and the black, loaded humor of someone like Samuel Beckett. Perhaps Glenn Man sums it up best when he considers the narratives of

> Kieślowski and Iñárritu in contrast to Altman's closeted vision. Suffice it to say that the intersections that occur in *Blue, Red,* and *Amores Perros* offer transformations and possibilities out of even the most tragic of circumstances, while those in *Nashville* and *Short Cuts* neither offer their characters opportunities to transform nor reveal depths of internal struggle; instead, Altman's intersections function primarily to build associations between characters locked in their superficial and unexamined lives and living out their social or political roles among each other. (2–3)

As we move further toward the rhizome, consider the role of coincidence in Quentin Tarantino's *Pulp Fiction* (1994) and its many imitators (like Doug Liman's *Go* [1999]). It seems that Tarantino is interested in coincidence to the degree that it will make his story interesting, not because he philosophically invests in it. His view is mawkish, cynical, and detached, despite anecdotal evidence that Tarantino is a Kieślowski fan (Weinstein 35–37). Whereas Kieślowski encouraged his audience to look beyond the cinematic product to what it revealed about reality and human relationship to it, Tarantino sees possibility as a useful tool to other ends, namely, stimulating interest in the cinematic product itself and reveling in the immediate salience of connections (without fretting over philosophical implications). In the end, *Pulp Fiction* really is a story about a few groups of characters whose paths intersect, but they do not intersect in any uncanny way, and these intersections do not overtly encourage thought about a larger metaphysical frame. In this case, if the story is retold in linear fashion, it begins with some hit men who go after a target, and the job leads to complications that are eventually resolved (in ways both macabre and amusing). Later in the film, one of them is killed by his target. Plenty of other events happen with other characters, but those trajectories are not laced together in any way that would suggest any remarkable, fortuitous connection.

However, the nonchronological storytelling form gives the *appearance* of serendipity, and herein lies the rub. The multivalent structure offers up the question, so it cannot be entirely avoided. This is precisely why Samuel L. Jackson's character, Jules Winnfield, overtly talks about the spiritual significance of an apparently miraculous event, while his partner in crime, Vincent Vega, resists any suggestion beyond happenstance. One may choose to identify with Jules's interpretation, but the light tone of Tarantino's film and its refusal to follow through or even consider the ethical problems it raises suggests a casual, postmodern approach to existential possibility, closer to a rhizomatic approach than a teleological one. Even so, among the many things that made *Pulp Fiction* one of the most influential films of the 1990s, the nonchronological, multivalent structure was paramount, and the late "revelation" of the connections between characters created a novel, surface postmodern pleasure.

If we wish to consider the work of a filmmaker who embraces the rhizome with a bit more seriousness, it seems that David Lynch's films (including *Lost Highway* [1997] and *Mulholland Drive*) seek a deeper understanding of knowledge, synchrony, and significance in contemporary life and art. As Martha Nochimson has pointed out, Lynch's films are not traditional onto-theological musings, but neither are they about the "shallow" postmodern: reflexivity, representation, or "surface" pleasures. Rather, Lynch desires to "represent meaning by balancing the energy of the subconscious and the logic of the linguistic" (7). Along these lines, we might say that Lynch and Kieślowski have a lot in common in the sense that they are both interested in realms of meaning that are not bound by language. However, the hallmarks of postmodern style (pastiche, conflation of high and low culture, extreme violence, extreme artifice) are so prominent in Lynch that he seems more at home at the rhizomatic end of the continuum. All the same, Lynch's chief artistic virtue is that he defies most easy categorizations.

Metaphysics of Order

Many contemporary multivalent films approach existential possibility more positively. The ubiquity and variety of this theme of possibility in the contemporary resurgence of the form shows that something far more than postmodern "surface" is at stake in American culture; possibility works as a theme because it is assumed to have *potential* significance. One does not have to be an Enlightenment rationalist to use or enjoy this theme but need not completely surrender to postmodern play, surface, and a-signification either.

In 1990, the proverbial year that Bordwell designates as the beginning of the network narrative resurgence, we find *Flatliners,* a curious Joel Schumacher film containing a number of young stars (Kiefer Sutherland, Kevin Bacon, Julia Roberts, Oliver Platt, William Baldwin). To summarize the plot, a number of medical students dare each other to venture into death, experience the liminal life/afterlife state where they see many long-lost, yet significant memories, and come back (revived by each other through medical emergency procedure). After their rollicking, thrilling experiences, they start seeing their memories—that is, formative sins of their past—literally stalking them in their daily lives. Whether this is real or imagined becomes quite ambiguous, making one particular character cry out that what we do in our lives really does ultimately matter. I evoke this example because it functions something like a forking-path narrative (with various scenes and characters of the past revisited in revised form), and it declares a certain orderliness, a definitive cause-effect structure to the universe.

Nine years later, a cry for significance emerges in Paul Thomas Anderson's *Magnolia* (1999). The film's opening prologue blatantly asks the audience to consider a series of remarkable stories of uncanny coincidence (all of them involving tragedy of some sort): "It is the humble opinion of this narrator that this is not just 'something that happened.' This cannot be 'one of those things.' This, please, cannot be that. And what I would like to say . . . this was not just a matter of chance. These strange things happen all the time." The film then goes on to tell a multivalent story in which numerous characters intersect with numerous other characters. As each node of connection is revealed, the characters' portraits deepen and the pathos intensifies. On top of that, the significance of each connection is highlighted, and all sense of the uncanny and miraculous is blatantly amplified.

Magnolia, while stylistically distinct from Kieślowski in many respects, reflects the existential possibility theme, the multivalent structures that carry it, and a certain open, less-cynical tone on the issues of existential possibility than Tarantino or Altman. This is not to say that every story ends well, or that the "connection" is constantly rendered a sentimental deus ex machina. Indeed, some characters' lives appear to be damaged by the coincidences. What counts (in the context of Kieślowski) is not happy endings but a sense of uncanniness that leads to questions of order. Given a very extraordinary, undoubtedly supernatural miracle that occurs at the climax of the film (raining frogs, presaged by numerous biblical references beforehand), we might characterize this film as rather certain about the orderliness of the universe, though quite mystified about how to make sense of it from a limited, mortal perspective.

Kindred Spirits in the Dialectic

Some filmmakers embrace the existential possibility theme as explicitly as Kieślowski did and adopt something of his earnest, searching, dialectical tone within the multivalent framework. In addition, Haggis and (to a lesser degree) Iñárritu find his stylistic use of abstraction to be a means of amplifying and reinforcing many of the same themes.[15]

Paul Haggis's *Crash* (2005) opens with a visual strategy that is not so unlike Kieślowski's later style. In short, the film opens not with a typical "establishing shot" but a series of abstract images, ending, in focus, on a man's face. As he speaks, a woman comes into view next to him.

> Man: In L.A., nobody touches each other . . . trapped behind this metal and glass. I think we miss that touch so much, we crash into each other just to feel something.
> Woman (to policeman, looking in the car): I think he hit his head . . .
> Man: You don't think that's true?
> Woman: I think we got rear-ended. I think we spun around twice. And somewhere in there one of us lost that frame of reference. I'm gonna go look for it.

Character, setting, and context are all gradually revealed, but only after we've received this man's opening monologue in the widest possible interpretive terms. The film's initial images, moving, multicolored dots and slashes of light, are similarly "revealed" to be images of car headlights and other traffic-themed images rendered abstract. I have argued elsewhere that such ambiguity and abstraction is a key element in Kieślowski's style, and there are many reasons why these techniques suit themselves to the expression of mysteries.[16]

Having been denied the standard "control" feature of classic Hollywood poetics—the establishing shot—the audience is already placed in a position of vulnerability and bewilderment; the indeterminacy of abstract visuals only amplifies the effect. We do not know where we are, we do not know our context; we might be anywhere, and the conversation we witness must be understood in the widest possible context. As the dialogue suggests, the accident is a shock to the materialist system; a bracketing of the everyday approach, and an openness to insight. The man, Detective Graham Waters, gains insight from beyond the materialist frame. By the end of the scene, he is to witness a dark "coincidence" that may be conceived as judgment, or, at least, tragedy on a metaphysical scale. Throughout the rest of the film, the characters' lives are revealed to be intertwined in various ways. Likewise, there are several fortuitous

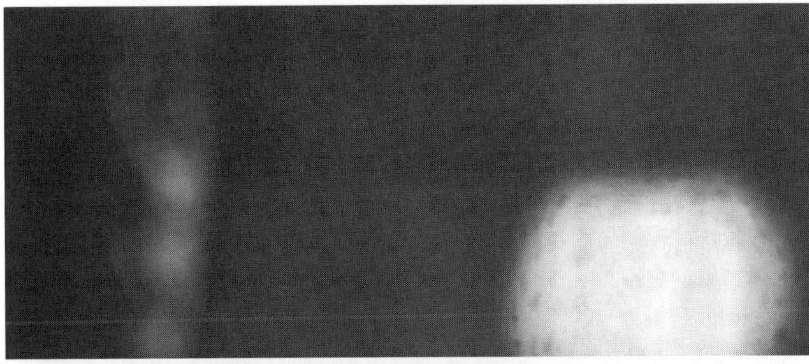

Abstract imagery and the face of Detective Graham Waters (Don Cheadle) in Paul Haggis's *Crash* (2005).

events, ("miracles," perhaps), often functioning as or arising out of the node of connection. The film ends with an overhead shot of Los Angeles at night, full of intersections and potential collisions. The appeal of the multivalent narrative is the synchrony, the way the goals and needs of each character are pressed into relation and connected. The intersections between them suggest they are all synechdochal of universal human needs.

Haggis does not argue that every connection is an index of divine causality, but he also, tellingly, leaves the door open for transcendent meaning. In one particular scene near the middle of the film, a "miracle" occurs that (unlike Anderson's miracle in *Magnolia*) can be understood in physical, material terms. A child is believed shot but survives as the bullets are revealed to be blanks. However, the status of the event *as miracle* is not completely diminished; it is ambiguous whether the event came about through the deliberate actions of another character in the film or through some astonishing coincidence of events that resulted in what the shooter considers a miraculous, life-changing moment. Indeed, it is the *significance* of the event that matters most, and it is significance (that is, the "meaning" problem) that Kieślowski, Haggis, and Iñárritu hold to be most important. This is Kearney's god who "may be," embodied in the sincere, multivalent dialectic.

All Alejandro Gonzalez Iñárritu's films employ multivalent structures. In his first, highly regarded film *Amores Perros* (2000), numerous characters are linked by a single car accident, though it is hardly clear in the beginning that this will be the case. Deeply tragic ramifications flow from this accident, but the judgment, evil, and treachery in this film are always peppered with kindness, selflessness, and minor miracles of virtue. As our assessment of these characters shifts and changes with their own evolution throughout the film, the dialectical pull between randomness and order makes itself plain. The thrust of the film is to exercise our moral instincts, to reveal to us how the *search* for meaning in this tragedy is fundamental to who we are and how we see the world.

Perhaps it's fair to say that Iñárritu's connections are nearly always tragic, but they are shown in such a way that we are forced to decide what meaning we could possibly derive from the tragedy. In other words, the connection is preserved as meaningful, but the problem of evil nearly always looms large. He does not cynically suggest that the search for meaning is a fool's errand, but he despairs of the search all the same. This agnostic outlook is reflected in the four stories of *Babel* (2006). The film ends with two "happy" endings and two "tragic" endings, but they are nearly all mixtures of both. Richard and Susan's stories (as realized by Brad Pitt and Cate Blanchett) begin tragically and end happily (though they are scarred). The Japanese girl's story is the same, though "hopeful" is, perhaps, a more accurate term than "happy." The Mexican woman's story ends tragically (her deportation), but her young charges survive the nightmare they have to endure. The Moroccan story remains unambiguously tragic. The characters and storylines are connected more "emotionally" than "physically," Iñárritu says (Gilchrist 2), with only strands of relational connections between them (the Japanese family is connected to the Moroccan family through the gun that is used to shoot one of the Americans, who employ the Mexican woman as a caregiver for their children). The stories do not have cause-and-effect relations, and so the film is less strictly "multivalent," as I have defined it, but they do have thematic affinities: in each case, the parent-child relationship is a central theme. Thematic unity between stories is often the central lesson of multivalent narratives.

The film *21 Grams* (2003) is more structurally demanding. The film is told in a chronological jumble—though it takes some time to figure this out—with various characters pictured together early in the film that are clearly leading lives apart from each other later. It is not clear through much of the film whether the ensemble scenes are part of the story's past or the future, and the truth of these characters hinges on where these chronological events "actually" take place. The result is a fascinating bit of narrative reflexivity, but (in my opinion) a weaker drama. The performances are unquestionably brilliant, but the viewer has a difficult time relating to the characters because we don't know their past for certain. If, in fact, the ensemble scenes prove to be the past, we will see the "present" scenes as largely falsehoods, characters pretending to be who they are not. If these scenes prove to be the future, we will see them as tragic foreshadowing. The ambiguity kills the possibility of identification. Roger Ebert and other critics had similar reactions to the multivalent technique, which has all the innovation of *Pulp Fiction* but not enough of the rewarding serendipity of *Magnolia*.[17]

But perhaps Iñárritu also has bigger philosophical fish to fry in *21 Grams*, namely, a struggle with the idea of serendipity and meaningful connection itself. Sean Penn's character, Paul Rivers, speaks of the mathematical fractals of the universe creating an overwhelmingly complicated, romantic, orchestral sweeping of two characters together. The film's narrative tinkering has led us to believe that the fortuitous circumstances in the film do, indeed, bear the marks of miracle. From our limited perspective, we might ascribe the intersection of characters to fate, God, predestination, and so forth. Indeed, one of the characters, Jack Jordan (played by Benicio del Toro) is a direct theo-fatalist, proclaiming it was God's will for him to have accidentally run over a man and his two small children in an accident (a family, it has been revealed, who belong to another character in the drama). In the end, however, the revelation of the "true" story proves most (not all) of our suggestions of providence to be misguided, mimicking Rivers's own construction of fate (as it is revealed that he actually researched and sought out his new love, his ascription of serendipity to the event being, ultimately, a come-on). As the film closes, most of the mysteries have been explained. These characters' lives have intersected for mostly understandable and logical reasons. Some of the tragedies are man-made; others are assigned as nonsensical "acts of God," though Jordan's wife has told us that "life must go on, even without God."

Yet we've felt the necessity of meaning, of possibility, and over this final, Euclidean union of stories hangs Rivers's final, somber soliloquy: what is lost and what is gained when a person dies? This is the metaphysical question, the "significance" question, the only question. Iñárritu has appealed to our sense of faith, forced us to consider God's potential behind the story, brutally yanked it back to the level of rational explanation, then slapped us with the question: can you afford to give up the designer? This tension between the need for belief (and order) and the rhizomatic play of possibilities appeals to the most fundamental aspects of our existence. The "second" Witek of Kieślowski's *Blind Chance* asked "only one thing" of God: "to be." This may be the same prayer of these filmmakers in the dialectic, but Kearney's "may be" is the most honest answer their multivalent dramas can suggest.

Conclusion

> I'm afraid of America. Whenever I'm in New York I always have the feeling that it's going to cave in and all I can think about is how to avoid being there when that happens. . . . Everybody runs around too quickly. There's too much commotion, too much uproar. Everybody pretends too hard that they're happy there. But I don't believe in their happiness, I think they're just as unhappy as we are, except that we still talk about it sometimes but they only say that everything's fine, that it's fantastic. . . . When Americans asked me "How are you?" I said "So-so." They probably thought somebody in my family had died. But I simply had jet lag because I'd been flying for seven hours and didn't feel particularly well. But it was enough for me to say "So-so" and they immediately thought that something tragic had happened. You can't say "So-so." You have to say "Well" or "Very well." The most optimistic thing I can say is "I'm alive." So I'm not cut out for America for that reason. —Krzysztof Kieślowski, *Kieślowski on Kieślowski*

But perhaps America is cut out for Kieślowski. The Polish filmmaker could not have predicted the horrific events of September 11, 2001, or the horrendous global conflicts and anxieties that would follow, but there is now a dramatic sense in the United States that there is an essential need for discussion of ultimate, metaphysical issues. Like Kieślowski, the United States cannot easily decide the *answers* to all these questions, but the ubiquity and complexity of global political, technological, and social networks have made the questions seem that much more important, and overwhelming.

In his discussion of the contemporary rise of the network narrative, Bordwell eschews talk of a philosophical "zeitgeisty" cause and looks for more conventional explanations, all industry-related (e.g., the rise of independent film, the rise of "film school education," creative solutions to budget problems, other media, like video games) (*Hollywood* 73). Those are, indeed, the "more proximate causes," but what Bordwell avoids in the service of scholarly precision, Kieślowski considered of utmost concern. He became known for his address of these social and philosophical issues (and his novel stylistics in addressing them) well before 1990. Many institutional and cultural trends in

America may have churned up a need for the network narrative, but trends endure and flourish in an ideological milieu. So, it seems that whatever "more proximate causes" may exist, the social and ideological conditions were also ripe for Kieślowski's narratives and the philosophical discourse they encourage.

Why multivalent narratives in America now, and why should Kieślowski lead the way? I don't know that we can give definitive answers here, but we might begin to speculate on future research into this multivalent trend. It seems to me that the central issue to which the rhizome-order continuum yields is one of control, whether God or some other force has it, and to what degree we have it. Given the revolutionary and sudden, blinding rise of what Paul Virilio has called "technological space-time" in American life[18]—something of the "commotion" and "uproar" Kieślowski references in the quote opening this section—the binaries of randomness versus order, purpose versus chaos, and possibility versus nihilism have never been more relevant to American culture. James Beniger characterizes our age as beset by a "Control Revolution" and sees the rush of the latest technology as symptomatic of the exponentially growing need to control information since the Industrial Revolution (7).

Undoubtedly, control is a central issue in technology as well, and that nuance did not escape Kieślowski. Technology plays a role in nearly all of his films, and the central theme of control is always nearby.[19] There is not space here to survey all of the fascinating ways Kieślowski approaches technology throughout his films, but in short, he held a certain fascination for it even as he viewed it with a wary eye. The only Poland Kieślowski ever really knew was run by a government obsessed with control over its citizens, often using technology to pursue this end. Kieślowski recognized the need for technological prudence, to view technologies as tools to help us to do good and promote justice. Yet, like Joseph Kern of *Red,* he questioned how much we can actually control, for good or ill. This question is often manifested in his films as a coincidental scenario that science is needed to explain but cannot (e.g., *Decalogue 1*).[20]

The ubiquity of the technological in our age may explain why so many of the contemporary multivalent films take place in science-fiction genres. The contemporary realities of virtual reality (read forking paths), indeterminate online identities and human cloning (read doppelgängers), rapid technological acceleration and expanded reach (read complicated, mosaic-like social networks) all beg for sci-fi treatment. A television show like *The X-Files* took advantage of this rising question of the uncanny and posited it within the modernist/postmodernist dialectic: things that science can explain quite powerfully versus ways in which science can be built on shaky presuppositions and Foucauldian power games. This show (inspired by the *Twilight Zone* episodes of the 1960s) gave rise to a host of contemporary television shows dedicated to the uncanny as it exhibits the natural/supernatural tension (e.g., *Lost, Supernatural, Ghost Whisperer,* and others).

When we consider how theoretical physics has upended our sense of the stable, knowable, and measurable universe, this trend is not a surprise. We now have the rise of chaos theory, complexity theory, and synchrony theory in the sciences,[21] and it is not difficult to see how multivalent narratives might flourish in this milieu. Contemporary communications have heightened our sense of control over local problems, but they have also dramatically expanded our scope of what needs controlling. Some prominent scientists have even left the safety of modernist paradigms to pursue more speculative, "supernatural" (and, I should add, highly contested) theoretical avenues like Jungian synchronicity (e.g., the physicist David Peat) and paranormal studies (e.g., the Nobelist and Cambridge physicist Brian Josephson), and it is not surprising that a number of films emerged along these lines: *Donnie Darko* and *Primer,* among others. A part-fiction, part-documentary film *What the Bleep Do We Know?* (2004) takes relativity theory (and, hence, possibility) to be an explicit focus.

In his article "Film Futures," Bordwell treats forking-path films as clues as to how our minds handle (or rather cannot handle) too much possibility. Most forking-path films, he demonstrates, consider very few alternative futures and offset the ambiguities surrounding the "true" plot with rather clear, logical conventions to guide the audience in its interpretation. Edward Branigan's response to this article extends this idea to the essential human quality of imagining possible outcomes in *any* circumstance or film, the fundamental and defining "what if" capacity of human beings (108, 110). The insight of these articles only amplifies a particular cultural question: why are we so concerned with our imaginative limits in this area? Why all these multivalent films? Perhaps it is because we sense the thrill and the terror of possibility more than previous generations did, precisely because we have so much access to information, and so little way to truly control it.

Ultimately, whatever the overarching, multiple reasons we see multivalent forms en vogue in America, Kieślowski's influence across the Atlantic is not that he "invented" multivalent forms but that he delivered/revived the entire "package" of concerns at an important historical moment. As the quote opening this essay suggests, he worried that the spiritual needs of the audience were disappearing, at least in Poland, but this survey indicates that is far from the case in the United States and elsewhere. Kieślowski's influence is felt in the work of many filmmakers who have continued these themes after him, revealing an ongoing conversation about contemporary existential significance. For the perpetuation and advancement of that conversation, we are in his debt.

Notes

1. See Stok 205–7 for a few examples.

2. Kieślowski had unusual access to American film in communist Poland by virtue of being in film school. There, he says he saw *Citizen Kane* "a hundred times" (Stok 32–34).

3. See my discussion of this transition in *The Films of Krzysztof Kieślowski*, 12–26.

4. My thanks to Glenn Man for permission to cite his paper.

5. My thanks to David Bordwell for permission to cite this unpublished essay.

6. *No End* (1985) is not, technically, a multivalent film, but the theme of existential possibility is consistently threaded throughout.

7. I do not staunchly argue for a singular "Kieślowski effect." He was, and is, influential, but North American filmmaking is nearly always a large confluence of multiple cultural streams. The techniques I have itemized did not begin with Kieślowski, nor did the cinematic treatment of existential or metaphysical themes. Regardless of any "direct" connection between Kieślowski and North American filmmakers, I argue that all the dimensions of the Kieślowski "package" (themes of existential possibility through multivalent forms) are abundantly present in American cinema since 1990, when Kieślowski started to get the attention of Western audiences. Remarkably, they were not so abundant before that time.

8. I say "North American" because I will incorporate one Mexican filmmaker (who often coproduces his films in the United States): Alejandro Gonzalez Iñárritu. I also consider Paul Haggis, a Canadian, but he has essentially made his career in the U.S. film industry.

9. This term has become common in film discussion, as acknowledged by Bordwell, "Mutual Friends," 365 (e.g., http://www.joblo.com/forums/showthread.php?threadid=102332).

10. It's worth mentioning that Bordwell traces the forking-path narrative to a much earlier, though less radical, source: Dickens's *A Christmas Carol* (see "Film Futures" 89).

11. One of Bordwell's major points in his article on forking-path narratives ("Film Futures") is that truly open-ended, ambiguous forking-path narratives (such as those by Lynch) are very rare, and for good cognitive reasons.

12. See chapter 1 of *A Thousand Plateaus* for an extended discussion of this topic.

13. The idea of "middle knowledge" was first put forth by Luis deMolina, a sixteenth-century Jesuit, as an attempt to explain Divine foreknowledge while still preserving human free will. See the entry on Molina in *The Oxford Companion to Philosophy*, ed. Ted Honderich (Oxford: Oxford University Press, 1995).

14. The original quotation is from a Kieślowski interview in the film *Krzysztof Kieślowski: I'm So-So* (Krzysztof Wierzbicki, 1995).

15. Abstraction is not a fundamental part of Iñarritu's overall style, but it plays a powerful role in many of his best scenes (e.g., the dance club scene in the Japanese chapter of *Babel,* 2006).

16. In *The Films of Krzysztof Kieślowski: The Liminal Image,* I argue for a conception of "liminality" as a stylistic designation for Kieślowski's use of various techniques (including visual abstraction, multivalence, and editing strategies that promote certain

ambiguities) to evoke a certain liminal position between the material world and the transcendent possibility. Abstraction, in particular, carries traits that lend itself to this evocation: ambiguity, primary epistemological impact, and an expanded view of time and space. For a full treatment of this topic, see chapter 2 (pp. 38–89).

17. See Ebert's review, where he says, "But in the closing passages, as the shape of the underlying structure becomes clear, a vague dissatisfaction sets in. You wonder if Iñárritu took you the long way around, running up mileage on his storyteller's taxi meter. Imagining how heartbreaking the conclusion would have been if we had arrived at it in the ordinary way by starting at the beginning, I felt as if an unnecessary screen of technique had been placed between the story and the audience" (http://rogerebert.suntimes.com/apps/pbcs.dll/article?AID=/20031125/REVIEWS/41005002/1023).

18. "Technological space-time" is a concept that Virilio explores throughout *The Lost Dimension.* In short, it observes that space and time are radically altered in light of new, fast, and virtual technologies.

19. For example, the ominous surveillance cameras in the early documentary *The Station* (1980) mirrored his own attempts to penetrate reality, to see into areas normally hidden from view. It was precisely this parallelism between the communist government's "control" technology and Kieślowski's own distaste for manipulation that caused him to abandon the documentary form. In a telling scene, those cameras in *The Station* reemerge in *Decalogue 3,* but in this case, no one is at the controls when someone very well should be (as a man has escaped from a mental institution and is wandering in the station, and a woman is on the verge of suicide in the station).

The gadgets that Werner brings back from the West in *Blind Chance* don't amount to much at first; the most prominent of these is a slinky, which accomplishes little work but does teach something of a prophetic lesson about being "flexible" in times of impossible choices and tensions. Yet in the end, the rise of Solidarity becomes known to all the characters in the film, precisely through the technology of radio.

The computer (and related devices) that so charm and educate Pawel in *Decalogue 1* prove powerless to warn against the ultimate tragedy. In *Red,* Joseph Kern sought benevolent control in his courtroom as he sought to promote justice. In the end, discouraged by his inability to bring about such an end, he's reduced to a bitter shell of his former self, using surveillance equipment to spy on his neighbors, gaining the insight he never had as a judge but lacking the power to do anything good. In a double irony, however, he regains some hope through an uncanny coincidence, beyond the control of any technology, as mediated through technology (a television). It is an uneasy hope, though; the sudden storm that provided a unique, hopeful scenario of providence for a character he loved also caused the death of several hundred people. His final image, an ambiguous tear rolling down his cheek as he stares through a broken window, proved to be one of the last images in Kieślowski's career.

20. It is interesting to note that the uncanny breaking of the ice in *Decalogue 1* was scientifically explained in the original script, but Kieślowski quite deliberately excised that explanation from the film, leaving its cause mysterious.

21. See Steven Strogatz, *Sync: The Emerging Science of Spontaneous Order* (New York: Theia Books, 2003), and Duncan J. Watts, *Six Degrees: The Science of a Connected Age* (New York: Norton, 2003).

Works Cited

Beniger, James. *The Control Revolution.* Cambridge: Harvard University Press, 1986.

Bordwell, David. "Film Futures." *SubStance* 97, 31.1 (2002): 88–104.

———. "Mutual Friends and Chronologies of Chance." Unpublished Essay.

———. *The Way Hollywood Tells It.* Berkeley: University of California Press, 2006.

Branigan, Edward. "Nearly True: Forking Plots, Forking Interpretations, A Response to David Bordwell's 'Film Futures.'" *SubStance* 97, 31.1 (2002): 105–14.

Coates, Paul, ed. *Lucid Dreams: The Films of Krzysztof Kieślowski.* Trowbridge, Wiltshire, England: Flicks Books, 1999.

Deleuze, Gilles, and Felix Guattari. *A Thousand Plateaus: Capitalism and Schizophrenia.* Minneapolis: University of Minneapolis Press, 1987.

Dupré, Louis. *Religious Mystery and Rational Reflection.* Grand Rapids: Wm. Eerdman's, 1998.

Gilchrist, Todd. "Interview: Alejandro Gonzalez Iñárritu." http://movies.ign.com/articles/742/74207.html.

Insdorf, Annette. *Double Lives, Second Chances: The Cinema of Krzysztof Kieślowski.* New York: Miramax Books, 1999.

Kearney, Richard. *The God Who May Be: A Hermeneutics of Religion.* Indianapolis: University of Indiana Press, 2001.

Kickasola, Joseph G. *The Films of Krzysztof Kieślowski: The Liminal Image.* New York: Continuum, 2004.

Man, Glenn. "Robert Altman's Multiple Narratives." Annual conference of the Society for Cinema and Media Studies. Vancouver, Canada. 3 March 2006.

Nochimson, Martha. *The Passion of David Lynch: Wild at Heart in Hollywood.* Austin: University of Texas Press, 1997.

Scott, A. O. "Emotion Needs No Translation." *The New York Times:* 27 October 2006. http://movies2.nytimes.com/2006/10/27/movies/27babe.html?adxnnl=1&adxnnlx=1166455966-iCIAPc8UcL9yRZ/HIhfP0w.

Stok, Danusia, ed. *Kieślowski on Kieślowski.* London: Faber and Faber, 1993.

Virilio, Paul. *The Lost Dimension.* Trans. Daniel Moshenberg. New York: Semiotext(e), 1991.

Weinstein, Harvey. "To Smoke and Drink in L.A." *Premiere* June 1996: 35–37.

11

Kieślowski and Kiarostami

A Metaphysical Cinema

John Caruana

Introduction

Kieślowski has been described as a metaphysical filmmaker on more than one occasion. That designation certainly becomes evident when his work is compared with that of other filmmakers who similarly strive to represent the ineffable features of human reality. Recently, Kieślowski's style has been fruitfully juxtaposed with a quintessential metaphysical director, Andrei Tarkovsky (Kickasola). I would like to attempt something similar here by comparing certain elements of Kieślowski's cinema with the films of one of his contemporaries, the celebrated Iranian cineaste Abbas Kiarostami. What unites both of these filmmakers, despite their obvious cultural and ethnic differences, is a firm intuition that reality conceals within itself the invisible markings of our nature as desiring, moral, and spiritual agents.

At first glance, the juxtaposition of these two auteurs might seem odd. It is not immediately apparent what connects the two: they seem, on the surface of things, to inhabit very different universes. Kieślowski's world combines several of the unique and often contradictory elements that characterized Poland during the second half of the twentieth century. This period, of course, was marked by the tensions between the communist regime and various forces of resistance that would eventually cohere as the Solidarity movement, and the powerful influence of the Catholic Church (which also played a vital role in Solidarity). As Kieślowski represents it, the characters inhabiting this world frequently appeal, directly and indirectly, to their Catholic heritage in their struggle against the despondency fostered by communist rule. Despite his own major reservations with official church doctrine, the major staples of Catholic thought—moral law, sin, guilt, free will, angels—infuse Kieślowski's world. This is clearly evident in the *Decalogue* (1988). Even the non-Polish films make recourse to the unmistakable influence of Catholicism. *Three Colors: Blue* (1993), for instance, is punctuated with such Catholic iconography and themes as crucifixes, the obligation to forgive, and Paul's famous words about the nature of love. Kiarostami's universe, on the other hand, is set squarely in the midst of the world's first modern theocracy. His characters also have recourse to a long-established spiritual heritage, but one that seems light-years away from Kieślowski's. Kiarostami's spiritual points of reference are rooted, of course, in Persian culture, especially in its storytelling and mystical traditions. This spiritual influence, which can be discerned in much of his work, is particularly pronounced in his critically acclaimed Koker Trilogy.

There are other differences between the two filmmakers. Kieślowski's world feels cramped, not surprisingly, given that virtually all of his films are set in urban environments; some of these in the soul-destroying Soviet-style housing that defines this period. Kiarostami's world, on the other hand, consists primarily of wide open landscapes; interior shots are almost nonexistent in his films. Kieślowski's universe is often interrupted by music. His films frequently employ diegetic and nondiegetic music to signal a moment of transcendence or rupture. *The Double Life of Véronique* (1991), for example, excels at this technique. By contrast, it is poetry, more so than music, that serves to disturb the inertia of life in a typical Kiarostami film. This is not surprising, given that poetry was and continues to be a major art form in Iranian culture. These differences between the Polish and the Iranian directors are certainly not minor. But with great filmmakers of this caliber we ought not to let such differences get in the way of seeing possible shared deeper currents. Despite the obvious differences, there are some significant similarities between the two that I will map out in this chapter. These similarities, as I hope to show, warrant the label "metaphysical cinema." As we will see, both Kieślowski and Kiarostami share (1) a Bazinian-like passion for cinematically representing the truth about the world; (2) a vigilant gaze that is directed not only toward the world around them but more significantly, and, more uncommonly, at least with respect to the history of cinema, toward their own selves; and finally, (3) a desire to catch a glimpse of the ways that we attain transcendence in the midst of the mysterious intertwinement of life and death.

Searching for Truth in the Postmodern Age

Kieślowski and Kiarostami share a refreshing refusal to tarry with the reigning intellectual paradigms of our times. Despite the unfashionableness of speaking about deeper universal truths within academic circles today, it is precisely the search for such truths that motivates both Kieślowski and Kiarostami. Our present age celebrates irony, pastiche, and aesthetic cleverness, such as one finds, for instance, in the films and screenplays of Quentin Tarantino or Charlie Kaufman. We are by and large suspicious of any sign of moral seriousness.

Behind such seriousness we are apt to discern untenable claims about the way things really are, that is, capital *t* Truth. In the film world, we associate such high-mindedness with an earlier era, one that was dominated by the likes of Carl Dreyer, Robert Bresson, and Roberto Rossellini. Those filmmakers who embodied André Bazin's ideal of a cinema that reveals the sacred and moral substratum of human reality seemed by the close of the 1960s to be, at best, quaint and, at worst, ideologically compromised. Rather than "Truth" and "reality," postmodern intellectuals and artists have inclined us to think in terms of relative truths and socially constructed realities.[1]

Today, however, visible cracks are forming in the postmodern shell. Increasingly, a number of prominent voices have appeared on the scene to question some of the unquestioned shibboleths of postmodern discourse. One of the more powerful of these voices belongs to Terry Eagleton. In his recent book *After Theory,* Eagleton cogently expresses his concerns with what he takes to be the jaded cynicism of certain postmodern trends:

> Cultural theory as we have it promises to grapple with some fundamental problems, but on the whole fails to deliver. It has been shamefaced about morality and metaphysics, embarrassed about love, biology, religion and revolution, largely silent about evil, reticent about death and suffering, dogmatic about essences, universals and foundations, and superficial about truth, objectivity and disinterestedness. This, on any estimate, is rather a large slice of human existence to fall down on. It is also rather an awkward moment in history to find oneself with little or nothing to say about such fundamental questions. (25)

But lest one mistake Eagleton for a naïve realist, it should be pointed out that reality for him—as it was a half-century ago for Bazin and the filmmakers mentioned above—is infinitely more complex than we could ever imagine, and that while there can be no question of a (naïve) one-to-one correspondence of image to reality, we nevertheless have an obligation to testify to its complexity.

After more than a quarter-century of what Eagleton calls "a strong current of anything-goes-ism" in cultural theory (*Idea of Culture* 65), a growing number of theorists, critics, and artists—one thinks of the likes of Charles Taylor and Jean-Luc Marion in philosophy and Geoffrey Hartman in literary theory—are once again eager to return to concepts that can do justice to universal phenomena like moral awareness, the experience of conscience, and the remarkable capacities of love, hope, and forgiveness. At least for these individuals, Bazin's realism, suddenly, does not seem so antiquated. The merit of Bazin's thought lies in its unyielding desire to grapple with the fundamental questions without succumbing to the rigidity that characterizes some of the truth-discourses of the past. Despite what his critics have claimed, Bazin's realism is focused not so much on the possibility of duplicating the content of physical reality as it is with revealing the underpinnings of *human* reality. That explains why Bazin could admire a phantasmatic film like Vittorio De Sica's *Miracle in Milan* (*Miracolo a Milano,* 1951). The fact that the film's protagonist possesses the unrealistic power to fly is incidental to Bazin's understanding of realism. What matters for him is that the film as a whole transcends the particularities of ideological parochialism in order to express some universal facet concerning our humanity, in this case, the hunger and demand for social justice. As Bazin himself puts it, *Miracle in Milan* manages to "reach down to deeper layers than the consciousness cultivated by partisan ideologies" (2:70). In this fashion, the film says something very "real" about the human condition. For Bazin, realism has more to do with our ability to represent the fundamentals of human existence than with the camera's capacity to accurately register the physical dimensions of its subject matter. If Bazin emphasizes—as he frequently does—the powerful indexical character of film and photography, he does so to underscore his conviction that these technologies are remarkably suited to accomplish the moral imperative to "offer witness to [our] final and irrefutable humanity" (74)—a task fulfilled by a select number of directors, like De Sica.

For Bazin, the pursuit of truth and objectivity is not the clandestine basis of oppression in general, as the postmodern antirealists have taught us to believe. It is our faith in the perfectibility of others and ourselves, the possibility of transcending the narrowness of the present in the hope of a better future, and the powerful sense of an ideal justice that can right the wrongs of the past, that fills our lives with meaning and purpose. Far from being the very root of oppression, the quest or belief in higher truths has been humanity's liberating grace. This faith in truth forms the bedrock of our reasonable understanding of the world and interaction with others, and not, as Nietzsche said, the most dangerous and sophisticated lie ever concocted. For Bazin, art, at its best, reveals or highlights those moments that testify to this faith. How it does so, however, will vary from artist to artist. In this regard, Bazin encouraged a plurality of styles that could voice or represent the passion for truth. Bazin's pluralism belies those critics who insist that any realist theory of culture is, by definition, totalizing, or monolithic in its implications. This criticism of Bazin is difficult to square with the fact that he wrote so glowingly about such different and diverse filmmakers as Charlie Chaplin, Orson Welles, and F. W. Murnau. Bazin understood quite well that behind these dissimilar aesthetic sensibilities lies the same ancient and noble desire to tell the truth about who we are. Kieślowski and Kiarostami, I contend, belong to this same group of visionary artists that Bazin so passionately admired. Like them, Kieślowski and Kiarostami employ their own unique idiom in telling the truth, to the degree that this is humanly possible, about our astonishing reality.

Kieślowski and Kiarostami have not forgotten the "fundamental questions" that, as Eagleton laments, no longer form an essential part of our intellectual horizon. The Polish and Iranian filmmakers are two of the increasingly rare artists today who resist the seductiveness of postmodernism's radical skeptical view of the world. Thus, Kieślowski can state unapologetically: "Today the truth about the world, which for me continues to be a basic precondition, is not enough. One has to search out more dramatic situations, postulates that reach beyond everyday experience, diagnoses that are wiser and more universal" (qtd. in Coates, "Kieślowski" 45). For Kieślowski, there is no question that the idea of truth is not a simple one. As a concept, it is deeply problematic, inevitably prone to distortion, error, and miscommunication. But for all that, it is incumbent on artists and intellectuals alike, Kieślowski maintains, to live up to the difficult challenge of representing the complexity of reality. With similar conviction, Kiarostami observes in an interview given to the French weekly *L'Express,* "I struggle for the search for truth" ("*La vérité*" 60).

The notion of truth here, as with Kieślowski, is not limited to the immediately perceptible. Kieślowski and Kiarostami share a strong desire to represent both the visible and invisible dimensions of reality. Indeed, it is worth noting in this context that both filmmakers made the shift from documentary to fiction filmmaking and, at least in the case of Kieślowski, part of the motivation for doing so was to overcome the documentary's limitations in capturing what remains hidden in reality. For both directors, the imperceptible current of everyday life is equally "real," just as real as the phenomenal world that is recorded by the documentarist's camera. In their own distinct fashion, they have bequeathed to us a cinema that registers glimpses of such mysterious aspects of our universal reality as life, death, and spiritual yearning. For this reason, it would not be inappropriate to characterize their cinema as "metaphysical film-making" (Nancy 45).

There is in both Kieślowski and Kiarostami a deep appreciation for the complex intricacy of reality and the fact that cinema, like language, cannot fully grasp its profoundly dense character. Artists who are aware of this challenge feel themselves, nonetheless, impelled to devise various techniques to glimpse the more tenebrous features of reality. In this regard, both Kieślowski and Kiarostami are aware of the possibilities and limitations inherent in cinema to represent the unrepresentable. This recognition accounts for the ingenious techniques that one finds in their films to articulate cinematically what would otherwise go unnoticed by the camera. Thus, Kieślowski observes that film is very materialistic:

> all you can photograph, most of the time, is *things*. You can describe a soul, but you can't photograph it; you have to find an equivalent. But there isn't really an equivalent. Film is helpless

> when it comes to describing the soul, just as it is describing many other things, like a state of consciousness. You have to find methods, tricks, which may be more or less successful in making it understood that this is what your film is about. (Qtd. in Andrew 82)

Some critics have succumbed to the temptation of interpreting the manipulation of narrative and formal structures in their films—for instance, the use of Kieślowski's signature "conditional" story-telling in *Blind Chance* (1981, released 1987) and *Three Colors: Red* (1994), or, in Kiarostami's case, the subtle magical realism that one sees in the final half of *Where Is the Friend's House?* (1987)—as an expression of a postmodern sensibility, the desire to play, for its own sake, with the image in novel and unforeseen ways. Such interpretations, however, involve a serious distortion of these filmmakers' ideas. If both are inclined to exploit what Siegfried Kracauer calls the technical properties of film, then they do so—to use Kracauer's vernacular once more—in the basic service of the realist impulse. Rather than abandoning or setting aside "reality," both filmmakers set out to make their viewers aware that there is much more to reality than what first meets the eye. As Kieślowski fondly repeats in *I'm So-So* (1995): "there are more things in heaven and earth." If the formalist traits of narrative and filmic construction are exploited, they are so because they offer the wonderful possibility of aiding the imagination to "see" what lies immediately beyond the perceptual field.

The possibility for misinterpretation is perhaps even more of an issue in the case of Kiarostami's work. Films like *Close Up* (1990) and *Taste of Cherry* (1997), which deliberately challenge how audiences view cinema, have led some critics to conceive of Kiarostami as a quintessential postmodern artist who, in the absence of "reality" per se, is content with playfully uncoupling, reassembling, and juxtaposing a multiplicity of surfaces, appearances, and perspectives. But as Alberto Elena rightly points out, the "complex mirror game created by Kiarostami, so often short-sightedly seen as a device of a 'film within a film,' consistently breaks from the mannerist dimension from which these experiments with form usually suffer" (89). If Kiarostami employs aesthetic devices that seem to depart from the dictates of realism, he does so not so much to question the idea of reality itself as to draw our attention to its ineluctable knottiness. If Kiarostami intentionally blurs the distinction between reality and fiction, it is to establish a deeper point about the world, and in the case of *Close Up,* the human condition. Thus, *Close Up* is according to Kiarostami himself a film about "the need that people feel, whatever their material circumstances, for respect and social recognition. . . . Ultimately, what the film is dealing with is the difference between the 'ideal self' and the 'real self'" (qtd. in Elena 85).

In addition to upholding the value of truth-seeking, both Kieślowski and Kiarostami have also avoided another postmodern pitfall, namely, the identification of politics with reality. Here, too, we find a powerful kinship with Bazin's thought. In the context of a discussion of De Sica's neorealism, Bazin notes that a "political explanation does not cover the whole drama" (2:73). In a similar vein, Kiarostami notes in an interview that the artist must be on guard against the imperative to view the world primarily through a political prism. In a concise and articulate statement that combines both a clear commitment to the pursuit of truth and a refusal to bow to the pressure of politicizing reality, Kiarostami warns that "[a] fast and emotional reaction against social and political issues reduces the film to newspaper with an expiry date. And when those particular social intricacies change or end, the film becomes worthless. If the filmmaker creates a work with some raw and undigested ideas in his agenda, the film becomes an animated slogan." He quickly adds: "I believe true art should be timeless. In a country like Iran, where social and political issues are constantly shifting, the artist should focus beyond these mundane issues, on more fundamental realities like humanity itself, which is more universal" ("Talk").

This kind of language will undoubtedly get under the skin of those critics who are wed to the idea of cinema as a form of political engagement. Kieślowski's and Kiarostami's views on politics and art will probably strike such critics as a lack of concern with political life. But what these critics view as the problematic lack or neglect of politics in Kieślowski and Kiarostami is in actual fact a deliberate reaction against the tyranny of reducing the complexity of reality to the immediacy of the political—or to be more precise, a narrowly defined notion of the political. The relative absence of politics in Kieślowski and Kiarostami is not motivated by ignorance or neglect but is in fact quite intentional. The almost obsessive preoccupation with politics that characterizes a significant segment of the intellectual and artistic landscape today frequently obscures the more difficult task of probing deeper, asking more fundamental questions. Kieślowski's and Kiarostami's suspicion of the political does *not* come at the expense of understanding the politics of our times, a task that remains essential for both directors, but perhaps should be understood as a way to see the messy world of politics in a new and different light. Thus, Kieślowski could say when the topic of politics and cinema was broached in a conversation: "During martial law, I realized that politics aren't really important. In a way, of course, they define where we are and what we're allowed or aren't allowed to do, but they don't solve the really important human questions. They're not in a position to do anything about or to answer any of our essential, fundamental human and humanistic questions" (Stok 144). Kieślowski goes on to note that even his films that involve political content are ultimately not political films, or not political in the first place: "Politics were never the subject" (144). Kiarostami articulates a similar reservation about the imperative for the artist to adopt a political perspective: "I have a strong feeling against films which are 'ideologically' political and lose their function in a short period. The real political truth can be found in films that don't claim to be 'political'" ("Meeting"). Both directors are keen on reclaiming the notion of the political so that it resonates with the full spectrum of human life, much in the way that Aristotle famously meant when he defined the human being as a political animal. Their films invite us to adopt an expanded notion of politics, one that encompasses social, ethical, and even metaphysical concerns.

An Ethics of Seeing

A realist aesthetics always risks a certain hubris—overextending itself, claiming for itself an objective perspective, absolutely accurate representation, and a corresponding clear and unprejudiced judgment. The conscientious realist corrects for this egoistic tendency by subjecting his or her own inner world to the critical gaze of the camera. One does not have to look very hard to find such an ethics of self-recrimination in the films of Kieślowski and Kiarostami.

The point I am trying to establish here can be easily misconstrued. I am not simply claiming that Kieślowski and Kiarostami are morally engaged directors. That they possess an ethical awareness there can be no doubt. Their films frequently deal with characters who are confronted with moral dilemmas. One need only think of the complex and highly nuanced approach that Kieślowski adopts in relation to the Ten Commandments of the *Decalogue*. Similarly, films like *Ten* (2002) or *Taste of Cherry* demonstrate no lack of nerve on Kiarostami's part in grappling with thorny moral dilemmas. Of course, in this respect, Kieślowski and Kiarostami are not all that different from many other directors whose films also tackle moral issues. But what sets them apart from other conventional filmmakers is the fact that Kieślowski's and Kiarostami's ethical concerns tend to go beyond merely exploring moral content. Their heightened ethical awareness requires them to turn their moral gaze as much toward themselves as toward the characters that populate their films. Their scrupulous self-analysis often takes on the form of a critical examination of their own personal investments in the cinematic process.

Kieślowski claims that one of the reasons he stopped making documentaries was for fear of the harm it might cause his subjects (Stok 81, 86).[2] In *Camera Buff* (1979), a film that at times comes across as a thinly veiled autobiography, the principal character's initial love affair with his newfound camera seems to come at the expense of his most intimate relationships. It is only after he learns that his soon-to-be-released documentary will result in the firing of a well-liked supervisor that he becomes distressingly aware of the potential violence inherent in the gaze of the camera. The film's closing shot accentuates his guilt-ridden conscience as he turns the camera on himself, feeling for the first time the vulnerability of being on the other side of the lens. One place where Kieślowski may have turned the camera on himself is in *Red.* As Annette Insdorf and others have already pointed out, it is possible to interpret the fascinating character of Joseph Kern, the self-incriminating judge, as Kieślowski's "double" (177). Kern, like the film director, is a powerful figure, eavesdropping on the private world of other human beings—even succeeding to a certain extent in directing their behavior. Kern eventually turns himself in to the authorities for illegally eavesdropping on his neighbors' telephone conversations. His conscience betrays him, but in the process, it also awakens him to the reality of others and to the limitations of his own narcissism. Though Kieślowski's other films do not seem as self-reflexive as *Camera Buff* or *Red,* it is quite possible that the Polish director has cleverly hidden his presence. When Krzysztof Wierzbicki asked Kieślowski, "If you were to turn the camera on yourself, what would you say?" Kieślowski responded: "I turn the camera on myself in all my films. Not all the time, perhaps, but often. But I do it in a way so nobody can see it" (*I'm So-So;* see also Stok 112).

Likewise, Kiarostami is troubled by the power and privilege that the camera affords him. Like his Polish counterpart, the Iranian director feels morally ill at ease behind the camera. In *The Wind Will Carry Us* (1999), the mysterious protagonist, the Engineer (Behzad Dorani), who is really a photographer (we should not forget here that Kiarostami himself is an accomplished photographer) and perhaps even a member of a film crew, arrives in the remote northern Iranian village of Siah Dareh, where he hopes to photograph an exotic mourning ritual in which the female villagers scar their faces in sympathy for the deceased. In one scene, the Engineer attempts to photograph a woman who runs the local tea house. She chastises him for his presumptuous gesture. This disapproval is signaled again later in the film when the photographer tries to record the procession of women who, at least we are led to believe, are beginning their ritualized mourning for a recently deceased old woman. The grieving women return his objectifying gaze with their own reproachful looks. In another telling scene, the Engineer asks a young boy, who has served as his guide in the village, "Do you think I'm bad?" Kiarostami has confessed that it was in fact he who asked the boy this question as he stood behind the camera (Rosenbaum and Saeed-Vafa 111). In this reflexive moment, Kiarostami reveals to us the contents of his own troubled conscience. What one finds in both Kieślowski and Kiarostami is a moral preoccupation with the powerful intrusion of the camera and, specifically, with their own personal complicity in the camera's potential for violence.

The Desire for Transcendence in Life and Death

As "metaphysical" directors, Kieślowski and Kiarostami are intent on exploring the invisible ethical and spiritual traces of human existence. Not surprisingly, both are particularly fascinated with the question or problem of death. I qualify the term *death* here as a question or problem in order to underscore that for both directors, the word refers to more than the dissolution of biological life. The scientific worldview has conditioned us to construe death as an empirical event: termination of brain activity, the absence of a heartbeat, the presence of a corpse, and so on. In this way, we have, increasingly, forgotten that "death" is but a marker for a radically unknown event or experience. The category "death" is at best a provisional signpost meant to represent an experience that cannot by its very nature be known by the mind. Death remains a profound enigma of human existence, an irreducibly ambiguous and inaccessible threshold, gesturing as it does to both the possibility of the promise of something beyond this finite world and, at the same time, the void of an absolute nothingness. Death, in this way, taunts and befuddles both atheists and believers alike—in other words, all of us. By naming this enigma *death,* we give ourselves over to the falsely comforting illusion of believing that we understand what it entails. In his philosophical meditation on death in *Time and the Other,* Emmanuel Levinas writes: "the unknown of death signifies that the very relationship with death cannot take place in the light, that the subject is in relationship with what does not come from itself. We could say it is in relationship with mystery" (69–70). Death represents a region of our being that simply cannot be mastered or accommodated. What is most unsettling about death is not so much that it bodes the end of physical existence but rather that it remains, despite all of our attempts to domesticate it, a mystery, an oppressive shadow that stalks us from we know not where. Forugh Farrokzad captures this disquieting facet of death in her poem *The Wind Will Carry Us,* whose title Kiarostami adopts for his film:

> A moment
> and then nothing,
> night shuddering beyond this window
> the earth
> screeching to a halt
> something unknown watching you and me
> beyond this window
> (Qtd. in Rosenbaum and Saeed-Vafa, 34)

In their own attempts to grapple with the question of death, Kieślowski and Kiarostami call attention to its enigmatic character; they prod us to question the various stratagems that we employ to blunt the unease associated with death. If they do so, it is not because they delight in making us squirm or suffer more intensely. If death features so prominently in their art, it is, in large part, to make us more aware of the taken-for-granted graces of life. But that awareness necessarily involves enduring the mystery of death, accepting that death's time is not our time. Some of the parallels between the two directors in this regard are quite striking. Death, of course, features significantly in several of their films. But nowhere is the connection between the two of them more conspicuous than in how they choose to represent suicide, that is, the desire to achieve the death that eludes us. Badii (Homayon Ershadi), Kiarostami's protagonist in *Taste of Cherry,* shares an uncanny resemblance to the character of Mikolaj (Janusz Gajos) in Kieślowski's *Three Colors: White* (1994), released just three years before. In both instances, we are faced with an amicable but clearly burdened middle-aged male who has decided to terminate his life for reasons that are never properly disclosed. In neither case do we have any indication as to why the character wants to end his life. Mikolaj, it is true, does say "I wanted less of it" in response to Karol—the protagonist and the person whom Mikolaj enlists to help him die—when he makes the trite comment that "we all know pain." But even this response fails to locate a concrete motivation for desiring to opt out of life. One might venture here that these two characters express a kind of universal existential unease with life. Badii and Mikolaj are everyman, everywoman. The suicidal character in both films solicits strangers with lucrative financial offers to help him carry out his plan: Mikolaj requires someone to kill him, while Badii is prepared to kill himself but nevertheless desires someone to confirm his death. In each case, however, the plan to exit life is delayed and then finally thwarted. Mikolaj, after what seems like certain death, lives on, while Badii's "end" is entirely suspended by what is itself a suspended film ending. Kiarostami breaks the fictional thread of the film by turning the camera on himself, the crew, and the actors, but not before we are made to witness Badii's wide-open eyes in the murky hole in which he has chosen to spend his last moments, or so we are led to believe. This scene seems to suggest an eternity, as if death, from his (or the viewer's) point of view, is never accomplished, never grasped, never simply a matter of an event that transpires on this side of life. Death eludes him entirely, preserving its mystery, even at the moment that he feels he has it firmly in his grasp.

To convey the idea that death is perhaps much more than the empirical fact of the cessation of biological life, Kieślowski and Kiarostami frequently blur the line between life and death. In Kieślowski's *No End* (1985), for instance, Ulla, the film's principal character, successfully takes her own life, only to reappear as a ghost, rejoining her dead husband, whose spectral apparition is shown clinging to being from the start of the film. Death so understood is not simply an end. The title of the film declares as much. The same can be said of Kiarostami's aptly titled *And Life Goes On* (1991)—a film that captures the perseverance of life in the aftermath of a devastating earthquake. Here death is not an end point or a release from life, for life returns; being perseveres, even in the midst of death. In *The Wind Will Carry Us,* death is never far away: the seemingly interminable dying of Mrs. Malek; the disembodied voice of a laborer digging a hole beside a cemetery, suggesting a voice from the other world; a bone found in the cemetery that the Engineer carries on his dashboard. But the most significant reference to death's shadowing of life involves Farrokhzad's complex poem about death, solitude, and erotic longing. The poem is recited during a critical scene, after the Engineer descends into a cavernous room with a young woman whose face he desires to see but that is obscured by the darkness. The Farrokhzad poem he recites to the woman weaves together the theme of human anxiety about death with the anticipation of a lover's caress—as if to suggest that the promise of the latter is conditioned, or at the very least accentuated, by the fragility of the former. This scene, taking place as it does in an underground location, is also reminiscent of Orpheus descending to the dead to bring back his beloved Eurydice to the world of the living. But as we know, Orpheus's impatience to see Eurydice causes her to slip back into the irretrievable darkness of the unknown. The Engineer—who is each of us—is also an impatient person, most notably in his insistence that the young woman—who has every reason to maintain her modesty, given her culture, her age, and the fact that she is engaged to someone—show her face in the light of her lantern and his inability to let death enter the world on its own time.

The shadow of death undermines our confidence, our sense of control. Death can also, paradoxically, awaken us to the urgency of life's ephemerality, compelling us to enter life more fully, more engagedly. The painful confrontation with the question of death that we find in the films of Kieślowski and Kiarostami also brings home the unseen gifts that life harbors. Indeed, in *Decalogue 1,* Pawel's aunt says to her young nephew, "Being alive is [itself] a gift"—a reminder that has brutal significance given the brevity of Pawel's own life. So many of Kieślowski's films, with their focus on death, serve as a kind of memento mori, reminders of the fragility of life, prompting us to take heed of life's possible joys before it is too late. The stark reminder of our mortality awakens both the characters and viewers to life's treasures, much like the exhilarating euphoria felt by Mikolaj and Karol after Mikolaj realizes that he no longer wants to die: "I feel like a kid again. . . . Everything is possible." Kickasola appropriately describes the intensity of this scene as "among the greatest moments in all of Kieślowski's films" (288). Paradoxically, Mikolaj's awakening to life comes precisely at the moment that he almost succumbs to its finality. Similarly, the old taxidermist in Kiarostami's *Taste of Cherry* recounts how he too had once desired to end it all, but having then savored the taste of a luscious mulberry, he rediscovered his passion for life. In *The Wind Will Carry Us,* this message is repeated again, this time by the village doctor who advises the existentially derailed Engineer to look more carefully at the extraordinary delights and gifts that are omnipresent in nature—alluding to and paraphrasing the evocative words of the Persian mystical poet Omar Khayyam: before that death that I will never know—because I never have it as a concept to grasp—I must learn to patiently wait, to pay attention to the marvels of ordinary experiences. Nancy writes in connection to Kiarostami—though this could apply equally to Kieślowski—that death is the "blind spot that opens up looking" (18). It is as if both Kieślowski and Kiarostami wish to communicate that the giving made possible by the gift of life is inextricably intertwined with the giving of death; one might even be tempted to say, the gift of death.

The inaccessibility of death returns us to this world, to others, to the wonders of nature. It is certainly interesting that both Mikolaj and Badii seek out others in their moments of greatest despair. That they, for the most part, seek out sympathetic characters as their accomplices makes one wonder if what they really desire is a way to connect with others rather than to die. This is to say that what they perhaps truly desire is transcendence. Kiarostami seems to find the source of such transcendence ultimately—and if there is any hint of the divine in Kiarostami, it is here—in the sensualism of nature. If other human beings play a role in this desire, it is to redirect the existentially adrift soul, like the Engineer or Badii, to nature's bliss, that is, heaven on earth, which is for the Iranian director possibly the only heaven we have.[3] In Kieślowski, that transcendence is sometimes prompted by the sublimity of music, but more often than not, it is effected by the presence of other human beings. For Kieślowski, the presence of the Other, to use Levinas's language, strongly hints, in turn, at an even deeper presence, namely, the role of the divine in the world. Many of Kieślowski's characters are weighed down by a terrible loneliness, an oppressive atmosphere that threatens to suffocate the self. What finally "saves" these characters, if anything does, is the encounter with other human beings. Virtually every major character in the *Decalogue,* for example, is trapped by solitude or narcissism. It is the rubbing up against other person-

Kiarostami's existentially adrift souls, like the Engineer (Behzad Dorani) in *The Wind Will Carry Us* (1999), are redirected by their meetings with others toward nature's bliss, that is, heaven on earth, which is for the Iranian director possibly the only heaven we have.

alities in their midst that brings about solace or prompts a painful period of self-reckoning, thus challenging the self-centeredness that imprisons them. Quite often it is the Other's own fragility that transfigures the self. The Other in this case appears to be invested with an almost divine power to redeem the ego. In *Blue,* the principal character, Julie, sinks into a numbing depression after her husband and daughter die in a car accident. Even the passage of time fails to bring solace to her. It becomes evident as the film unfolds that she has retreated into a desolate form of self-isolation. Among the circumstances that finally help Julie to see beyond her own pain is a series of conversations that she has with a tenant in her building, Lucille (Charlotte Véry), whose vocation as a stripper establishes her as an outcast in the narrative context of the film; she is, in other words, an exemplary Other. Remarkably, Lucille's vulnerability acts as the catalyst that draws the young widow out of her anguish. The correlation between the vulnerable Other and the transformative grace of the divine, of course, is an essential feature of both the Jewish and Christian traditions. Lucille in this instance is an example of what the New Testament calls the "least of these"—that is, the marginalized among us—who bear the trace of the divine (Matt. 25.35–40).

Kieślowski and Kiarostami represent today two of the most important articulations of the kind of responsive and flexible realism that was originally espoused by Bazin. Their metaphysical cinema speaks to the part of our humanity that transcends geography, culture, and time. As different as they are, one is nevertheless impressed with how both filmmakers manage to pierce the shell of the prosaic to uncover the most fragile, but no less essential, facets of our shared humanity: the need to be understood by others, the narcissism

In *Three Colors: Blue* (1993), the young widow Julie (Juliette Binoche) is drawn out of her anguish and toward a transformative grace by one of the lowly and the marginalized, the stripper Lucille (Charlotte Véry).

that traps us and our convoluted attempts to overcome it, as well as our existential struggles to give meaning to our solitude and mortal existence. They reveal a sense of the transcendent even in the most ordinary subjects and affairs. In this manner, the charity of their camera epitomizes Bazin's remark that "the cinema more than any other art is particularly bound up with love" (2:72). This realist film philosophy ought to compel us to see that the transcendent moments of human experience are neither "socially constructed" nor "discursive conventions"—as postmodernism would have us believe—but part of the very horizon of our fundamental reality that conceptual language strives to, but cannot fully, articulate. It is left to such artists as Kieślowski and Kiarostami to give us a sense of the transcendent through other means and through their own unique voices.

Notes

1. Paul Coates does not exaggerate when he notes that "historical materialism . . . has dominated Film Studies" (*Cinema* 50) in the past few decades and that "Film Studies continues to be firmly rooted in anti-metaphysical positions" (178).

2. During the communist years, Kieślowski was concerned that footage from his documentaries could be used by the police against his subjects.

3. For an interesting discussion of the influence of Persian mysticism on Kiarostami, see Elena (184–95).

Works Cited

Andrew, Geoff. *The* Three Colours *Trilogy.* London: British Film Institute, 1998.

Bazin, André. *What Is Cinema?* Vol. 1. Trans. Hugh Gray. Berkeley: University of California Press, 1967.

———. *What Is Cinema?* Vol. 2. Trans. Hugh Gray. Berkeley: University of California Press, 1971.

Coates, Paul. *Cinema, Religion, and the Romantic Legacy: Through a Glass Darkly.* Aldershot, England: Ashgate, 2003.

———. "Kieślowski and the Antipolitics of Color: A Reading of the 'Three Colors' Trilogy." *Cinema Journal* 41.2 (2002): 41–66.

Eagleton, Terry. *After Theory.* New York: Basic Books, 2004.

———. *The Idea of Culture.* Oxford: Blackwell, 2000.

Elena, Alberto. *The Cinema of Abbas Kiarostami.* Trans. Belinda Coombes. London: SAQI, 2005.

Insdorf, Annette. *Double Lives, Second Chances: The Cinema of Krzystzof Kieślowski.* New York: Hyperion, 1999.

Kiarostami, Abbas. "Meeting Abbas Kiarostami." Interview with Peter Rist. *Off Screen* 6 March 2001. http://www.horschamp.qc.ca/new_offscreen/kiarostami.html.

———. "A Talk with the Artist: Abbas Kiarostami in Conversation." Interview with Shahin Parhami. *Synoptique,* 14 June 2004. http://www.synoptique.ca/core/en/articles/kiarostami_interview/.

———. "*La vérité en jeu.*" Interview with Eric Libiot. *L'Express.* 17 May 2004: 60.

Kickasola, Joseph G. *The Films of Krzysztof Kieślowski: The Liminal Image.* New York: Continuum Books, 2004.

Kracauer, Siegfried. *Theory of Film: The Redemption of Physical Reality.* New York: Oxford University Press, 1960.

Levinas, Emmanuel. *Time and the Other.* Trans. Richard Cohen. Pittsburgh: Duquesne University Press, 1987.

Nancy, Jean-Luc. *The Evidence of Film: Abbas Kiarostami.* Brussels: Yves Gevaert, 2001.

Rosenbaum, Jonathan, and Mehrnaz Saeed-Vafa. *Abbas Kiarostami.* Urbana: University of Illinois Press, 2003.

Stok, Danusia, ed. *Kieślowski on Kieślowski.* London, Faber and Faber, 1993.

12

The Decalogue *and the Remaking of American Television*

Sean O'Sullivan

What is the *Decalogue*, and what is its legacy? When critics discuss Kieślowski's 1988 series, they often discount or ignore its status as a work of television. Instead, the program is described as "ten films" or "an extraordinary cinematic achievement" (Kickasola 161, Insdorf 69), terms that labor to elevate Kieślowski's narrative, to redeem its lowly incarnation as a product of the small screen. From its first major international success at the 1989 Venice Film Festival, the *Decalogue* has been fêted as something greater than its origins—just as the televisual works of Ingmar Bergman are inevitably given aesthetic and formal dispensation. Even when the provenance is acknowledged, the stories are sometimes categorized as "loosely connected television films" (Haltof 75), as an anthology that groups dissimilar items by means of a broad premise rather than a series driven by a tight cluster of characters and events with a consistent dramatic and thematic progression.[1] Consequently, the *Decalogue* has acquired artistic significance chiefly as a critical turning point in Kieślowski's career—between the documentary emphasis of his early work and the auteurist art cinema of his final films—or as a portrait of Poland at the end of the cold war, or as a cross-cultural exploration of eternal moral problems. Whether the series might represent a critical turning point or influence in the development of narrative *television* seems of little or no concern. Kieślowski himself stressed the *Decalogue*'s putative failure as a work of television art, effectively by critiquing the limits of the medium: he writes that he made a "mistake" in not "following the conventions" of television when he allowed established characters to return only glancingly and sporadically, and that he made "another mistake" in ignoring the rule that "the same thing has to be repeated several times" on television in order to make the complex clear to the television viewer, apparently a more distractible, less focused species than her cinematic counterpart (Stok 155).[2]

I will argue that the *Decalogue*'s greatest artistic significance is *as* a television series and that part of that import lies exactly in the elements that Kieślowski, surely with a degree of false modesty, calls mistakes. The "great attention" (Stok 155) that the director argues the series requires from its audience emphasizes narrative qualities of distinctiveness and nuance—elements in which television programs may dabble but that are often subordinated to the prime directives of familiarity and repetitive emphasis. Likewise, Kieślowski planned to deploy ten different directors of photography (settling eventually for nine), ranging greatly in age and experience, so that "these ten stories should be narrated in a slightly different way" (Stok 156). But despite this degree of collaborative variation, relatively unusual in the traditionally uniform photography and mise-en-scène of television programs, Kieślowski admits that "the films are, all in all, extremely similar visually" (Stok 156). Of course, different-but-similar is exactly the basic recipe for serials, which must inscribe reliable routines and systems (through cast, structure, and style) while also providing the frisson of variation, however slight, from episode to episode. And for all his emphasis on the collective approach of television—the comforting company afforded by the return of known people, places, and events—Kieślowski also makes the essential point that "the television viewer watches alone," that "television means solitude while cinema means community" (Stok 154). But it is precisely the allure of a regular, knowable community—a regular, knowable community that might be found in a bar in Boston, or a hospital in Chicago, or a crime lab in Las Vegas—that keeps television series popular for so long. So the paradoxical synthesis of solitude and community defines any serial's appeal.

Furthermore, the *Decalogue* takes the interplay of the connected and the disconnected—the blueprint of television serial—as its very subject. The central ordering device of the Warsaw apartment complex serves as the connective infrastructure for the stories, a physical emblem of organizational unity to match the textual source of organizational unity, namely, the Bible, and specifically the Ten Commandments found in Exodus. Another unifying device is the character that is sometimes, misleadingly, called an angel but whom Kieślowski labels "this guy" (Stok 158), a chameleon who appears at moments of ethical or behavioral crisis for the protagonists of each episode. Given that he never intervenes in the situations he observes and that his very presence is vague rather than clarifying, the moniker "this guy" aptly connotes the simultaneous familiarity and unfamiliarity of his appearances as registers of iteration and variation. Kieślowski offers a crucial translation of this conflict between the unified and the sundered in his introduction to the scripts of the *Decalogue*. On the one hand, he insists from the beginning, "fate is an important part of life" (Kieślowski and Piesiewicz ix). "Fate" here functions as an analogy for the formulaic mandate of serial television, the fixed and plotted scheme that keeps the subject, pace, and trajectory of a narrative within prescribed bounds. On the other hand, Kieślowski reveals that the scheme of the program was to "suggest that the lead character had been chosen by the camera almost by accident, as if one of many" (Kieślowski and Piesiewicz xiii). The accidental, as opposed to the fated, illustrates not only a central element of virtually all drama, which requires at least some element of the random as plot device, but also the energy of the unpredictable (or at least the illusion of the unpredictable) that persuades viewers to return, on a regular basis, to a program whose outlines and motor become, over the course of many installments, entirely predictable. Through these defining tensions—the determinism and arbitrariness of the apartment block, the reliability and mystery of the "guy," the clarity of fate and the opacity of accident—the *Decalogue* does more than simply spin ten stories; it provides an examination of the very logic of serial narration.

But the *Decalogue*'s legacy goes beyond its ambition as a formal experiment, reaching an artistic milieu quite different from that of communist Poland. The early twenty-first century, it is commonly asserted, represents a golden age, perhaps *the* golden age, of American serial narrative on television. Such novel enterprises as *The Sopranos*, *Deadwood*, *The Wire*, and *24*, to name just a few, provide levels of storytelling or characterological complexity, and varieties of experimental approaches previously unfamiliar in the United States. For observers like Steven Johnson, the cognitive effort required by these programs stands as a triumph of popular culture, exercising the minds of the viewers, in particular their ability to master an intricate social network. Johnson traces this increasing complexity exclusively through homegrown American fare, from the utter simplicity of *Dragnet* through the developing sophistication of *Hill Street Blues* to the recent complications of *The Sopranos* (Johnson 65–72). This approach, however helpful in providing a national genealogy, is essentially one-dimensional, emphasizing informational density—such as challenging dialogue and story arcs—over everything else as an indication of success. For Johnson, it matters neither what these serials are about nor how they explore psychology, emotion, or ideas. This methodology may demonstrate that we have been schooled by a new curriculum of television to expect and embrace such departures as the multiple competing screen images of *24* or the linguistic pyrotechnics of *Deadwood*, but it does not interrogate the particulars of subject matter, or the choices or effects of character, or the tenor of thematic preoccupation. It is precisely these elements—a sophistication of subject, character, and theme—that most sharply define the touchstone series of our American moment, and it is precisely these elements that have their televisual precedent in the *Decalogue*.[3]

The two series that most clearly manifest their ancestry in Kieślowski's program are *Six Feet Under*, which ran from 2001 to 2005, and *Lost*, which began in 2004 and is scheduled to end in 2010. On the face of it, these two shows would seem to have as little in common with each other as they do with the

Decalogue. *Six Feet Under* was produced by HBO, the most celebrated storytelling brand name of the new millennium, a pay-cable channel synonymous with the televisual avant-garde. The series investigates the lives of the Fisher family, repressed proprietors and inhabitants of a Los Angeles funeral home, juxtaposing the traumatic with the mundane, dwelling in small shifts of consciousness and relationships, tilting more patently toward character than plot in its episodic and year-long arcs. *Lost* is produced by ABC, an over-the-air network that had been more recently associated with low-budget primetime game shows than narrative innovation. The series began with the jolt of a plane crashing on a remote island and has made mortal danger and exotic adventure its foundation while spreading its attention far beyond the pale Anglo-Saxon Fishers to incorporate a broad spectrum of ethnicities, nationalities, and social backgrounds. The differences extend to issues of censorship and public taste, as *Six Feet Under* indulges in explicit drug use, sexuality, profanity, and alternative lifestyles, while *Lost* hews to the more restrictive and sanitized parameters of "free" television. Yet, as we shall see, the series share some crucial preoccupations; these linked preoccupations serve not only to conjoin two seemingly disparate series but, most important for our purposes, to illustrate the scope and consequence of the *Decalogue* as a theory and practice of televisual narrative.

Specifically, the *Decalogue* and these two series share three main elements: the collision of accident and design, the manufacture of doubt, and something that I call the "absent middle." Each of these elements speaks not only to a distinct narrative trait but to an investment in broader questions about and approaches to serial narrative; these three elements, as a particular strain of narrative DNA, had been absent on American television before *Six Feet Under* and *Lost*, but their synthesis also serves as the recipe for the *Decalogue*. I will soon sketch out how each of the elements operates across the series, but it is worth emphasizing first that the elements function both as systems and subjects; in other words, the elements define both the particular narrative infrastructure of each program and the central content of each program. The series both *feature* and *are about* accident and design, the manufacture of doubt, and the absent middle. (By the "middle," I mean the narrative work of many television dramas, where the little—details, clues, evidence—is translated into a middle, that is, explained solutions, resolutions of the uncertainties upon which all plot propulsion relies. This middle then frequently points to the large, that is, to a broad issue or preoccupation of the human experience. The series I am examining here, by contrast, often deliberately and disorientingly omit that labor of translation into resolution.)

Beyond this triad of narrative elements, I would describe the central subjects of all three series as religion, death, and memory—with religion construed not narrowly as an organized church but as a belief, or questions about beliefs, in ideas, values, and stories that transcend the here and now, and that transcend pure reason. The distinctiveness lies not only in this grouping but in the way that each theme in the group has shaped the programs. It is not that death, for example, has been ignored, in either American or European television; consider the countless corpses that festoon the dark alleys and hospital morgues of routine dramas. But the attempt to make sense of death, and the way in which death alternately knits together and splits apart the past and present of existence, marks these series from their inception as death has never quite done before. Each of these series is concerned with the notion of wake, with all its implications: as the funereal rite that translates life into death and death into life; as the ripples produced by a boat or plane or car cleaving its environment; and as the array of changes, and the temporal distance between cause and effect, that every action produces. Wake invokes the past's lien on the present, as a synthesis of religion, death, and memory. And while religion, death, and memory may certainly have formed the center of untold poems, films, and novels, the particular consequences of an extended televisual narrative have transformed these subjects from postulates in these older and shorter genres—that is, as concerns presented and resolved within a limited time frame—into lived anxieties played out for both characters and viewers over the alternating gaps and appearances of serial stories. In this way, the shorter *Decalogue* almost served as a trial run, something closer in length to a single novel than to the sprawl of *Six Feet Under* (sixty-three episodes) and *Lost* (eventually to be over one hundred episodes), offering a scale model for them to develop more completely. This is, in part, where both the stuff and style of religion is relevant: Alan Ball, the creator of *Six Feet Under*, has called storytelling and the process of writing "probably the closest I come to having a religion" (Havrilesky). The weekly regularity of a hypnotic television series, its ability to make us believe in stories both about and beyond ourselves, the strange conjunction of the logic of drama and the illusion of metaphysics—these speak to the equivalence of, or even substitution for, religion in everyday life that Kieślowski intuited and played out in the *Decalogue*.

Accident and Design

Each of the three series begins with an accident, a devastating accident that not only precipitates the major plot arcs of the show but also makes the accidental a central part of the narrative—or, more broadly, that nexus of the random, the coincidental, and the destined that accident calls into play. In the case of *Lost*, it is the crash of Oceanic Airlines Flight 815, many hundreds of miles off its intended course from Sydney to Los Angeles, onto the shores of an uncanny island. The opening moments of the pilot (in this case, an ironic name for the first show in a series) seem to emphasize the arbitrary as passengers die or survive based on where they happen to be sitting on the plane, or where they happen to stand near the wreckage. As the series has evolved, one central open question has revolved around whether this initial accident is in fact an accident or part of some stratagem of mysterious authorship, perhaps located on the island.[4] More specifically, the series begins in the moments after the crash as the male lead, Jack Shephard (Matthew Fox), tries to interpret what has happened; this narrative choice introduces memory, specifically wake and retrospection, as an operative technique of the series, presenting the aftermath of trauma as the site where we choose to name something as accidental or designed, with all the things that this choice implies. Beyond the ontological matter of the crash as design or accident are the particular dynamics of the accident, which splits the plane into three distinct parts: the central section of the fuselage (which holds all the survivors apparent in the first season), the nose and cockpit (whose occupants perish in the opening episode), and the tail (whose fate, or even existence, is not addressed until the second season). This combination of accident and fragmentation articulates, in large chunks, the physiognomy of serialized fiction, that is, *part-publication,* as it was termed and established in the heyday of nineteenth-century Britain: namely, an array of bits and pieces (monthly or weekly parts) governed simultaneously by the forces of accident and divine (authorial) plan. As we shall see, each episode of *Lost*'s first three seasons further makes use of the paradigm of bits and pieces by pursuing a bifurcated trajectory, both tracing the collective story of the characters on the island and focusing on a single flashback story of a specific character, or a pair of conjoined characters. (The end of the third season would introduce flashforward as an analogous technique.) Each episode, in other words, is composed of narrative shards, a strategy that accentuates the programmatically interrupted nature of commercial television, in contrast to the idiosyncratic rhythms of HBO programs. Even more precisely, the design of these shards involves the breaking of one into several, the plane into distinct parts, the narrative of the group on the plane into the many narratives of the members of the plane.[5]

Six Feet Under reverses this particular narrative design. Its inaugurating accident is much more mundane, since it involves not a spectacular midair disintegration but that most routine of modern catastrophes, a collision between two motor vehicles—specifically, a bus and a hearse. Just as the mysterious nature of the plane's sundering seems triggered by, or at least analogous to, the mysterious nature of the island itself, so the car accident of *Six Feet Under* mirrors the constitution of its location, in this case the most famously automobile-dependent city in the world, Los Angeles. And just as the fragmentation into parts serves as a fitting introduction to the connected-but-fragmented infrastructure of *Lost*'s narrative, so the details of *Six Feet Under*'s accident foretell its storytelling system. A bus, a device that collects many disparate people in one large machine, rams into a hearse, a device that holds one living person—the hearse's driver—in the front and a dark space in the back, which contains vestiges of people's bodies and memories. We have, in other words, an enactment of Kieślowki's thesis-antithesis of community and solitude, or cinema and television, here figured by a bus and a hearse. This formulation offers a violent meeting of individual and group that will be *Six Feet Under*'s trademark, as each episode after the pilot will collide an individual death (in the first few minutes of the show, known as the "cold open") with the ongoing group dynamic of the Fisher family. In this case, by contrast with the narrative logic of *Lost*, the several become connected rather than the connected becoming several. This movement from the naturally scattered to the unwieldy whole underlies the drama of the inaugural accident as the death of the driver of the hearse, Nathaniel Fisher (Richard Jenkins)—husband to Ruth (Frances Conroy) and father to Nate (Peter Krause), David (Michael C. Hall), and Claire (Lauren Ambrose), a psychologically, geographically, and emotionally scattered group—forcibly reintegrates the family. The design of *Six Feet Under* traffics quite frequently in accident as cause (as cold-open victims suffer electrocution, asphyxiation, head injuries, workplace mishaps, and other variations on the aleatory) but more broadly on accident as meeting, as the separate worlds of the cold-open victims and the Fishers collide. The show often flaunts the designed nature of accident by illustrating thematic or emotional parallels between the colliding worlds—hardly original in serial television but expressly self-conscious here, since the nature, or ruse, of accident is the series' stock in trade. One final aspect of the show's initial design is the seasonal moment of the accident: Christmas Eve. The dead father and the date of the event both provide links to the accident that serves as the starting point of the *Decalogue*.[6]

Decalogue 1 does not present its accident in its opening moments, as do *Lost* and *Six Feet Under*. Rather, the first episode begins obliquely, with aftermath—far deeper into aftermath than *Lost*, in some uncertain time after the event, an event the viewer does not yet know has occurred. We start with a lake caught halfway between slushy ice and gelid water, a man ("this guy," played by Artur Barcis) shedding a tear in the snow, a grieving woman (Maja Komorowska) looking through a store window at a television program featuring young boys running through a school. Clearly, something has happened, and we are looking at wake—to use a term appropriate to the lake—just as the other shows' accidents are appropriate figurations of their locales. This beginning-as-retrospection is structurally atypical for the *Decalogue*, whose episodes much more commonly immerse us in the middle of an ongoing story; the past is explored not through manipulation of screen time but through dialogue and conflict.[7] This atypicality might seem to work against what I am arguing for as the serial, or deeply interconnected, quality of the *Decalogue*'s narrative apparatus, but in fact that atypicality, in terms of narrative mechanics, is often a defining feature of serial pilots. The pilot of *Lost*, for example, has the atypical length of two hours and, more importantly, spreads its flashbacks among several characters (rather than limiting them to one) while making the subject of those flashbacks the precrash moments on the plane itself rather than, as in subsequent episodes, picking up threads of lives lived long before the flight took off. The pilot of *Six Feet Under* features, in its opening images, not the future hallmark of the show, namely the cold open, but a mock advertisement for a hearse, part of a series of minisatires of the "death care industry" scattered through the hour; these nondiegetic interventions will never return in the series.[8] Pilots often function not as narrative blueprints to be imitated precisely but as frameworks of seeing and thinking to be entered, as initiation rituals for viewers and artists alike. It is central to my claim for the *Decalogue* as an ancestor for these American serial fictions that the first episode works as just such a pilot, establishing a thematic and narrative vocabulary, and an intellectual template, that defines our reception of the remainder of the episodes in a way far more influential than the initial installment of an anthology show would.

System, or structure—two synonyms for design—serve as the primary interests of *Decalogue 1*, especially of its protagonists, Krzysztof (Henryk Baranowski)—a professor of linguistics and computer science, focused on artificial intelligence—and his intellectually precocious son, Pawel (Wojciech Klata). The first words we hear them speak, indeed the first spoken words of the *Decalogue*, are "eleven, twelve, thirteen"—the push-ups they are doing in the living room of their apartment. In a series whose title requires its viewers to count from one to ten, this initial gesture suggests a self-consciousness of the process of seriality and connection; this self-consciousness will be echoed in the very last words of the *Decalogue*, when two brothers look at two rows of identical stamps and declare, "A series!" Pawel, as a spin-off of his father, is particularly keen to explore systems, as he asks to solve physics problems on the family computer and joins with his father in playing, and beating, a chess champion at a group tournament; recognizing their opponent's design, he exclaims, "See, she's using a system!" In a ten-episode series full of fractious or maladjusted relationships, the bond between Krzysztof and Pawel is by far the most harmonious—their almost ideal life scored by the music of design. Hence the shock of the accident that removes Pawel from the series, an accident that follows the most meticulous of mathematics and the most banal of scientific numbers: air temperature. After checking, more frequently than apparently necessary, the frigidity of the winter as a measure of the safety of the ice on the local lake, Krzysztof allows Pawel to go skating. Pawel falls through the ice, shattering the illusion of rational governance not only for Krzysztof but for the *Decalogue* as a whole. Crucially, we see neither Pawel's misfortune nor the recovery of his body; this boy, who represents a tenacious and tested faith in the infallibility of design, simply disappears.[9]

In a conclusion that has tempted some critics to read the series as turning away from science and the systematic, the desperate Krzysztof ends up alone in an outdoor church, where he dips his hand in the baptismal font. The confirmed atheist pulls out a chunk of ice and applies it to his forehead. But this moment, far from representing the comfort or solution of religion—as either a counterdesign or as a realm of unexplained accident—pushes the series into a space where neither the logical (the designed) nor the mystical (the accident) makes sense. The final image of *Decalogue 1* returns us to the beginning, to Pawel's black-and-white TV image running in school—the image we saw at the start through the gaze of a grieving woman whom we now know to be his Catholic aunt, the counterpart to her unbelieving brother. We end with the process of television itself, the repeated image offering a loop, a miniature series or design, underscoring serial narrative as neither a hard science nor a spiritual vision but as a cycle oscillating between the two. Paul Coates has observed that Kieślowski's "most characteristic phrase" was "I don't know" (Tasker 212) and that agnosticism, as subject and structure, is made manifest at the end of *Decalogue 1*. Unlike his American successors, Kieślowski keeps the actual scene of the accident completely offscreen, rendering accident itself a consequence not of mechanical laws suddenly failing (an airplane separating in midair) or of mechanical laws logically carried out (the impact of a moving bus on a moving car) but of the absence of law—an ironic counterpoint to the series' interest in the alternating presence and absence of God's law. The *Decalogue* will rewrite, as it proceeds, the interplay of design and accident in less Platonic terms than those implied by the pilot, where science and religion are characters more blatantly than anywhere else in the series. Rather, we begin to see that interplay emerge in moments such as one at the beginning of *Decalogue 3*, when we notice Krzysztof, the father in the first episode, leaving the building as Janusz (Daniel Olbrychski), the father in the third episode, enters. As in the beginning of *Six Feet Under*, it is Christmas Eve, and fatherhood and violent death are brought together. This is the first time that we see a character from an earlier story appear, tangentially, in a later story, and it marks the *Decalogue*'s investment in designs and plans (such as rituals of family holidays) and chance meetings (one parent passing another in a lobby) that bring the diurnal in contact with the theoretical. That collision will be the one that marks all three series; what happens when they come into contact will be a deliberately unresolved mystery.

The Absent Middle

Perhaps the most consistently popular and successful series structure in American television narrative has been the procedural. Procedurals traditionally appear in three guises—the medical, the investigative, and the legal—although a fourth, the forensic, has been dominant recently. These programs function by presenting bits of evidence—such as a diseased body, a collection of crime clues, a case defined by facts and precedents, or scientific minutiae—and then illustrating how, over the course of an hour, trained professionals translate those little things into a solution. That solution, which represents the rationalizing of those little things into a plausible series of linked facts, might then very well gesture to some broader social concern or ethical question—about the perils of drug use, or the quandary of abortion, or the responsibility of parents. We might schematize this as the transformation of the little into the big, of evidence into issue; but the real interest, for any viewer, is not really the little or the big, but the middle. Namely, will that patient be saved? Who committed the murder? How will the judge rule? What makes sense of the evidence? The satisfaction of such programs lies in the gradual route to the middle, a middle whose only real aim is to solve the arithmetical problem posed at the start of the hour. We might contrast this with another popular strain in American television, the family drama. The family drama begins in the middle and stays resolutely in the middle, from beginning to end. In other words, the governing logic of events and information is not mysterious at the start of each episode—as it is in the procedural—but neither does the hour seem to lead inexorably to an answer that points both inward (as explanation of information) and outward (to some larger question beyond the confines of the program). The satisfaction of the family dramas lies in their wallowing in middle events, such as who will sleep with whom, whether a sibling will discover a secret, how a troubled character considers suicide. The procedural and the family drama, consequently, tend to enunciate the difference between series (one-hour stories that can stand alone) and serials (extended narratives evolving over time, possibly, as in soap opera, without end).

Lost and *Six Feet Under*, taking their cue from the *Decalogue*, invoke the fascination with detail, with the little things that might be ignored or forgotten, that characterizes the procedural, and the investment in a small tribe, connected by shared needs and desires, that characterizes the family drama. The missing crucial stage, however, is the middle—that is, the space where the inchoate makes sense, or the space where things stabilize. This schematic approach is crucial to the *Decalogue*—and indeed to Kieślowski more broadly—as we get close-ups of such details as a bee climbing out of a glass (*Decalogue 2*) or a teabag being pushed into a glass (*Decalogue 5*) with no diegetic explanation as to why the camera is lingering on such minor incidents of everyday life. Or, we see a young boy peering at his father in a lecture hall, closing one eye and then the other, framing his view through an obstructing object (*Decalogue 1*), or a young man craning his head to look through the trapezoidal crook of his arm at a taxi queue (*Decalogue 5*)—moments that imply subjectivity without in any way clarifying how that subjectivity matters to the narrative events of the moment. The detailed views we get—of hands, of faces—do not present us with evidence to unpack, as in the procedural; rather, they present detail as a category in and of itself, free of context, without the route to explanation we might expect. Sometimes, details magically come together—such as when the young woman, Anka (Adrianna Biedrzynska), in *Decalogue 4*, taking an eye exam, is asked to identify the letters F-A-T-H-E-R, in effect spelling the identity (in English) of the person with whom she is most consumed; but there is absolutely nothing to suggest that the examiner, who chose these details, knows anything of the young woman's thoughts. This scene offers not just another inexplicable confluence of accident and design but a moment where interpretation of details yields a result that does not lead to an explanatory perspective—to a clarifying middle. Consequently, the emphasis on detail, linked to the concurrent interest in large questions as expressed by the Commandments, without a middle space, illustrates that interpretation itself, and not solution, is the series' subject. The *Decalogue*, from first episode to last, queries how and why we assign meaning, and how and why we negotiate between the empirical and the abstract.

The deliberate problem of the absent middle makes itself plain in *Six Feet Under* through the opening credits, which enact this strategy literally. The first image is an abstract blue of sky—indeed only recognizable as sky when a bird, far too distant to be identifiable, flies through it. The camera then moves down to show a horizon line and a single tree in the distance, again more abstract than specific; the tilt ends by revealing in the foreground two intertwined hands that immediately break apart. This sharp foreground/background distinction (which will become a recurring visual gesture of the show) depicts in a single image the tension between close-up and long shot, between the object at hand and the view in the distance. There is nothing to connect them, either graphically or thematically; the how and why of meaning are left open. This alternation between the close-up and long shot, or between the detail and the big picture, continues throughout the titles as we get tight shots of two more hands rubbing together; two feet on a gurney; the turning wheel of a gurney, which may or may not be the same as the gurney we have already seen; the gurney proceeding down a white corridor, away from an abstractly figured, unknown standing person; a vial of embalming fluid; a cotton ball swabbing the brow of a corpse; the hand of a pallbearer; a crow, which may or may not be the bird we saw in the first shot of the titles. All of these details are simultaneously precise and vague, corporally specific but belonging to no individuated beings. And we see, interspersed, a long shot of clouds, and then a return to the tree/sky vista with which we began. Credit sequences for dramas before *Six Feet Under* as a rule presented images, moving or static, of the principal players of the series, or offered scenes of the relevant locale, or in some way situated us in the middle space, where bits and pieces become distinguishable humans without turning them into concepts. The entrance to *Six Feet Under* gives us parts and ideas but nothing between, no recognizable landing place to move from micro to macro. For a series that is as invested in the particular consciousness and emotions of particular characters as this one, the removal of any traces of these characters in the credits is as shocking, in its own way, as the removal of Pawel thirty minutes into *Decalogue 1*. The rules of engage-

The opening credits of *Six Feet Under* (2001–5) emphasize the recurrent foreground/background tension of the series, and the absent middle. Here, the precise close-up of the gurney and the vague human form in the distance articulate the detail and the idea, the empirical and the abstract, leaving a nebulous white space between, always open for unresolved interpretation.

ment, not only as we are generically familiar with them but as these series seem to recreate them for themselves, refuse to be pinned down.

Grief and memory, *Six Feet Under*'s main subject, are offered as similarly slippery enterprises, ones that produce effects highly resistant to the smoothing ambitions of the rational. Claire's responses to the deaths of her father and her brother Nate, the events that bookend the five seasons of the series, demonstrate this resistance. In the pilot, on the morning after Nathaniel's death, Claire reminds her mother of the stuffed dog that she threw, as a young girl, on the roof of the house, and that to teach her a lesson, her father refused to fetch. Ruth reacts angrily to this anecdote, because she (perhaps familiar with the conventions of television drama) reads this as a story castigating Nathaniel's coldness and indifference, as an explanatory (i.e., middle) device. Claire, taken aback, defends herself by saying: "I just remembered it"—she offers the story as an unexplained detail, not processed hermeneutic. Likewise, in the wake of her brother's death, near the end of the fifth season, Claire complains to her boyfriend Ted (Chris Messina) that she keeps thinking, unwillingly, of unpleasant occasions, such as the time that Nate—for no apparent reason—refused to help her with an English paper. "It's not like it was some big traumatic thing," she states, before breaking into tears (episode 5.10, "All Alone"). Death in *Six Feet Under* is not a riddle, as it is in *Law and Order*, or *E.R.*, or

CSI, a cluster of signs to be worked over until they are ordered and rescued from chaos; rather, it is a fact that requires interpretation but yields no correct answers.[10] This difficulty is shared by the characters in the show and the viewers of the show, since the procedural work in question here is not the systematic methodology and training of a doctor or a detective or a medical examiner but the guesswork of characters and viewers trying to decide what makes sense and why. The details of life, and of narrative, require us to assign meaning to things; but what happens when we deem the assigning of meaning to be arbitrary, when the supposedly middle, stable space between the little stuff and the big stuff seems a mirage? Brenda Chenowith (Rachel Griffiths), Nate's off-and-on fiancée, expresses this view late in the second season as she describes her thought process in "crossing a line," namely, engaging in the latest in a series of inexplicable and arbitrary sexual encounters, all of which jeopardize the stable middle space of her life: "You know what? The lines are only in our heads. In actuality, there are no lines at all, which is really fucking terrifying if you think about it" (episode 2.10, "The Secret"). Her epiphany here speaks not only to the vital unwritten parts of human social contracts but to an anarchic world composed entirely of interpretation, where detail and big picture obey whatever meanings we take pleasure in assigning them. *Six Feet Under*, like the *Decalogue*, is sensitive to the existence of ancient moral codes; but, as Piotr (Krzysztof Globisz), the new lawyer in *Decalogue 5*, recognizes, "People ask themselves whether what they do has a meaning. The meaning's becoming increasingly evasive."

The world of *Lost*, by contrast, may look a lot more like the world of *Law and Order* and *CSI* in the sense that its characters engage in defined quests—searching for a radio signal, rescuing companions, trying to survive the island—that require the metamorphosis of evidence into action and result that governs the realm of the procedurals. But *Lost* undermines those traditional predecessors by multiplying the evidence, the details, and making their interpretation susceptible to many simultaneous, and competing, meanings. One example of detail is the close-up of an eye with which the series begins. Unlike the details of *Six Feet Under*'s title sequence, or the teabag of *Decalogue 5*, the connection (the middle space) of this eye quickly reveals itself in the face and figure of Jack Shephard. This eye trope, however, reduplicates itself as an opening gesture as eight of the first season's twenty-four episodes begin with this image, each time attached to a different castaway—or in one case, to a younger version of Jack—then returning as the opening image of the first episodes of seasons two and three. *Lost*'s version of the relativity of meaning may seem less disturbing than that of the other two series, represented here through the iteration of different life stories and perspectives, but it similarly undermines the procedural's claim to clarifying explanation. Furthermore, and at the center of *Lost*'s enterprise, are the hieratic numbers 4, 8, 15, 16, 23, and 42, which exude a mysterious power not only over individual lives but over the entire structure of the island. This sequence, or series of unexplained gaps and connections, stands not only as the lottery numbers that the happy-go-lucky Hurley (Jorge Garcia) played and won, to his eventual chagrin—markers of luck, or accident, as a force that as easily turns bad as good—but as an ineffable underlying design of some kind, since in the second season someone must type these numbers into an ancient computer every 108 minutes to avoid an implied but unknown calamity. The character who craves to fill the gap between detail and interpretation is John Locke (Terry O'Quinn), who is certain that the aftermath of the accident represents a rehabilitative destiny for him; he chooses to believe, to interpret, the round-the-clock task of typing in the numbers as a life-saving measure even though this necessity cannot be confirmed. Late in the season, when he believes that he has been set up as part of a psychological experiment, he decides that the typing is in fact meaningless and that he has been investing his belief in an arbitrary meaning. Events prove him to have been correct in the first place—but the numbers' refusal to coalesce into meaning make Locke's dilemma as terrifying as Brenda Chenowith's. Numbers are evidence-gathering at its most basic, most attentive—as an assembly of bits and pieces into coherent units, into middle spaces. But these six numbers don't gather anything, don't represent counting as such—they are at once precise and abstract, specific pieces of a rationalizing system but also emblems of Something Big, without any of the infrastructure to connect one with the other.

Lost, again more familiarly than the *Decalogue* and *Six Feet Under*, draws on the conventions of known genres, such as science fiction, horror, and mys-

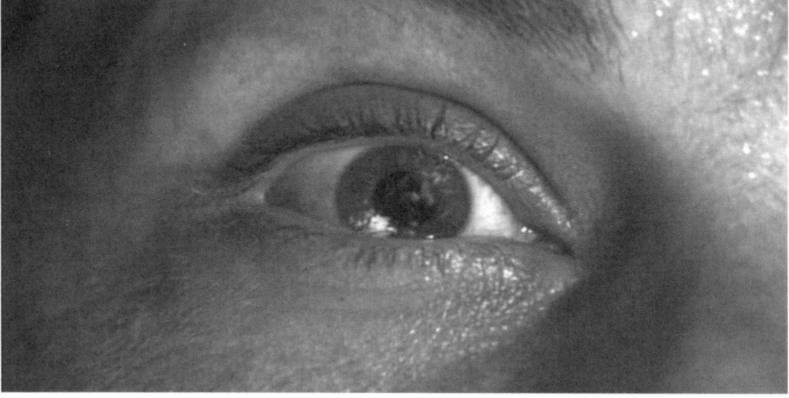

The first image of the pilot episode for *Lost* (2004–) shows a close-up of Jack Shephard (Matthew Fox) opening his eye. The eye motif will recur throughout the series, signalling both the organ of epistemological scrutiny and a classic marker of subjectivity, both knowledge and speculation. The volatile mixture of these antitheses recalls a similar defining feature of the *Decalogue* (1988).

tery, to populate the island with juxtaposed civilizations, little-seen monsters, and puzzles to be examined. But this hodgepodge of competing narrative systems creates problems of interpretation analogous to the problems created by the *absence* of such systems, or the skepticism about such systems, in the other two series. Are the dangerous Others, who may either be a parallel society or a vampiric sect, connected to the fatal black fog that swoops in from the jungle, and/or to the set of absurdly unlikely coincidences (another collision of accident and design) that establish vital connections between the apparently random collection of passengers on flight 815, or that reveal implausibly, to Mr. Eko (Adewale Akinnuoye-Agbaje), the wreck of his brother's plane from Nigeria across the distance of several years and thousands of miles? The interpretive challenge of *Lost* lies not so much in the amount of evidence, or tantalizing clues, as in the array of interpretive systems that these clues call into action, from Sherlock Holmesian deduction to conceptual symmetry to B-movie logic. Even the device that defines the narrative structure of the series—the selection, each episode, of a story within the back story of a castaway, or a conjoined pair of castaways—a device that would seem to provide a clear interpretive bridge by suggesting how past behavior or actions shape present behavior or actions, functions less as a source of limpid explanations for how things are and more as a justification for arbitrary, or self-justifying, codes of conduct. Kate Austen (Evangeline Lilly), the female lead, appears to us in a series of flashbacks as a collage of personas and ruses, an assembly borrowed from Alfred Hitchcock's *Marnie* (1964) and other tales of thieving and mercurial women. Is this assembly borrowed by the writers of *Lost* or by Kate herself? Should we read these back stories as objective information to be processed by the viewer or as subjective memory, interpretations of self, illusions of identity created by each character as a temporary middle space? The arbitrary values of meaning that were externalized as a problem in the *Decalogue* and *Six Feet Under* become internalized in *Lost* as each castaway creates a foundation of character and motivation that holds only so long as we don't consider any other character's foundation—at which point any consistent and shared process of meaning-making is shown to be "increasingly evasive."

The Manufacture of Doubt

Doubt, as both a subject and process of each of these series, in some ways can be seen as a byproduct of the two categories already discussed. What is the contest between accident and design but an instance of uncertainty about how we determine causation, or about the limits of systems or the presence of an author? And what is the problem of interpretation, or the arbitrary nature of meaning, but a specific manifestation of the force of doubt? But doubt can be both broader and narrower than these. Its etymological variants—to be undecided, to suspect, to anticipate with apprehension—all speak to the basic process of narrative, and especially serial narrative, which labors to instill indecision, suspicion, anticipation, and apprehension in its consumers to maintain interest from installment to installment or within installments. In this last sense, doubt (unlike the absent middle) is just as central to programs like *Law and Order* and *CSI*, which toss us red herrings or veiled clues to keep us somewhere on the sliding scale between ignorance and knowledge throughout the length of a program. These shows, and most narratives, use doubt as a mechanism, as the energy that we consume in moving from A to B, the primal craving for narrative satisfaction. The *Decalogue*, by contrast, makes doubt a central player of the drama from the first episode—not a means but an end. Krzysztof's eminently reasonable refusal to doubt—his refusal to doubt basic and seemingly fixed laws of physics—precipitates the tragedy of *Decalogue 1*, throwing him into the gelid aporia of the story's conclusion. *Decalogue 2* also stages a clash between certainty and uncertainty, or at least a belief in certainty, as a woman (Krystyna Janda) queries a doctor (Aleksander Bardini) about the prognosis for her ailing husband. His refusal to provide her a clear-cut answer, a refusal justified by medical grounds, proves irritating to her, since she—like Krzysztof before his peripeteia—wants science to offer a solution to doubt. The doctor ends up lying to the wife about her husband, telling her that the condition is fatal to prevent her from aborting the child she is carrying, a child conceived with another man. The moment when she realizes that she has been deceived, like the moment when Pawel falls through the ice, occurs offscreen; our knowledge of her reaction can only be guessed, exiled to the province of doubt. These two opening episodes, and Kieślowski's choices in omitting explanatory and concluding incidents, make that province the real estate of the *Decalogue*, as much as the apartment building that links the characters.

The story that raises the conflict between certainty and doubt most strikingly and abruptly is *Decalogue 5*, the episode that stands in many ways as the summa of the three elements that I have been tracing. Its narrative of three men—a newly minted lawyer, a surly and misanthropic cab driver, and an unstable young man traumatized by his accidental role in the death of his younger sister—connects people who would otherwise have nothing in common, who represent the collision of fate and chance that Kieślowski saw as the central logic of the series. The young man, Jacek (Miroslaw Baka), decides to kill someone at random, and only chance brings him into contact with this particular cab driver (Jan Tesarz) at the deciding moment. But the chain of causation in Jacek's mind is never made clear; we are given none of the systematized, persuasive psychological data—the middle space between details and consequence—that would suggest how or why he thinks this act of murder corresponds with, or atones for, or explains the death of his sister. The feature-length version of this episode, *A Short Film about Killing* (1988), teases us more explicitly into divining connections among these characters, in the manner of the secret linkages of *Lost*'s castaways. In the television version, we see Jacek eating a pastry at a café before embarking on his death errand; in *A Short Film*, the lawyer, Piotr, is also present at the café, suggesting a greater degree of convergence. *Decalogue 5* adheres to the more austere requirements of the television series by removing the connective space, by forbidding us the middle ground where the atomized characters might come together, in whatever mystical way, to make common meaning. In no other episode is the link between commandment and story so blatant as in this one, not least because there are two killings—Jacek's execution of the cab driver and the state's execution of Jacek. But in no other episode is the yawning gap between proscription (the big) and individual act (the small) so wide, since both murders are made to seem senseless, to lack a direct meaning or purpose. And accentuating this extreme experiment in the crash of accident into design, and the segregation of commandment and act, is the problem of doubt, which Piotr voices in the first moments of the episode as he asks, in voiceover, "For whom does the law avenge?"

Here we have a Kieślowskian irony: the episode begins, like no other in the *Decalogue*, by baldly announcing its thematic preoccupation, thereby making us feel scientifically certain as to the subject of the story to come. And yet that thematic preoccupation is precisely the opposite of scientific certainty. Piotr then expresses ambivalence about a question, one he says he's been asked twice before, and whose answer he says has become much more doubtful for him. Yet we do not even know what that question is; it might be the problem of the avenging law, but the cross-cutting between the three protagonists in the first phase of the episode removes Piotr's words from context, providing yet another moment of doubt on our part, or absence in the narrative's, as with Pawel's accident or the wife's realization that she has been tricked. "We have more and more doubts about what we do, even about what we'd like to do," Piotr observes. He has already realized what Brenda Chenowith and John Locke will realize—that interpretation may always be an arbitrary and futile, if absolutely necessary, act. Piotr says that the chief appeal of the legal profession, for him, is the opportunity "to meet and come to understand people I'd never meet otherwise"—the same appeal, in other words, that a series of stories about people living in an apartment block has to a viewer of television, or that any extended narrative about a collection of people has. That viewer, and Piotr, will find the desire to "come to understand" to be thwarted, deliberately and repeatedly, by what unfolds before them as understanding remains partial, or temporary.

If *Decalogue 5* offers doubt as crisis, emphasized by the final image of Piotr shouting his despair alone in a field, *Decalogue 4* offers doubt as a regular condition of experience—and this more measured story of the uncertain balances the question in a way that will find resonance in both *Lost* and *Six Feet Under*. This episode involves Anka, a theater student, who discovers, or seems to discover, that the man she has always believed to be her father may not be her father after all; Anka's mother died shortly after giving birth, leaving a sealed letter with a message for her daughter. When the father, Michal (Janusz Gajos), is off on a business trip, we are led to believe that Anka has opened the letter—which Michal has coyly enclosed in an envelope that he covertly wants her to open—and has discovered that she has no biological connection to him; consequently, she decides to act on the sexual feelings she has long harbored toward him. Only after he rejects her advances and after she believes he is about to leave does she confess that she has replaced the original letter, copying her mother's handwriting. The story ends with the shared act of burning the actual letter, unopened in its envelope; after Michal blows out the flame, Anka looks at a corner that has not yet turned to cinders and pulls out the letter. "'My dear daughter,'" she reads. "'Michal isn't . . .' It's burnt." The conclusion leaves us in as much doubt as we have been all along as to Michal's paternity. The crux, however, lies not simply in this refusal of resolution. We do not actually see her reading the words we have been waiting to see her read for an hour, since the camera is panning across her unoccupied bedroom—yet another refusal of diegetic knowledge, along the lines of Pawel's accident. Most important is the final image of the episode, a black-and-white photograph of a small group of men and women; one of the women is Anka's mother. This is the third time we have seen this photo, and on the second occasion, which occurs in the wake of Anka's fake revelation of the letter's contents, Michal tells Anka that one of the two men in the photo could be her father. This final iteration is different, in one detail, from the first two: what had been a picture of two men and two women is now the same picture with a fifth head floating in the top left corner; the head may be a refracted version, through glass, of the image of Anna's mother, but the quality is deliberately too blurry for us to be certain. This change in the status of the object has surprisingly gone unremarked by Kieślowski's critics, considering the significance of this alteration. If this is a different photograph, where did it come from, and how does it change the equation? If this is one of Kieślowski's manipulations of light, what purpose might that manipulation serve? Not only are we in doubt, but we are in doubt as to what we are doubting: is it the nature of the thing itself or is it the motivations of the director? This carefully crafted doubt is not the absence of final meaning—as expressed by Piotr, John Locke, and Brenda Chenowith—but a doubt of "and/or," of concurrent possibilities that solicit interpretation without the promise of confirmation but without the promise of nihilism, either.

The photographic image that concludes *Decalogue 4* is a machine of doubt, though a less visible and less noisy machine of doubt than the one that dominates *Lost*—namely, the island that is the castaways' new home. Locke, who had been confined to a wheelchair before his fall from the sky, now finds himself able to walk; another character, Rose (L. Scott Caldwell), who was suffering from terminal cancer, seems fully recovered. These two survivors believe that the island has somehow cured them—even if the how and the what (the middle space) of that miracle cure remains completely ambiguous. Is this an accidental result of the island's properties, a designed consequence of the island's forces, or some unseen controller of the island's forces? Locke is not the only one to doubt the accidental nature of the accident, given that so many people survive a crash that should most likely have killed them all. In *Lost*'s own version of irony, John Locke becomes not a philosopher of empiricism, as his namesake might suggest, but a dealer in mysticism; and his epistemological antagonist is Jack Shephard, whose surname might suggest a Christological transcendence of the explicable world but whose worldview as a fiercely pragmatic doctor puts him squarely in the line of Krzysztof, the professorial father of *Decalogue 1*. The ongoing dialectic between Jack and Locke (spelled out in the title of the second season opener, "Man of Science, Man of Faith") governs the audience's array of responses as well, since the oscillation between the verifiable and the unknown mirrors the series' oxymoronic methodology; *Lost* simultaneously invites us to believe that all its events can be contained within the plausible and forces us to digest coincidences and extravagances that push that plausibility past the breaking point. (The series' chief producers, Damon Lindelof and Carlton Cuse, have repeatedly insisted that *Lost*'s many mysteries are all grounded in the world of the explicable, while acknowledging their debt to horror, science fiction, the Gothic, and other traditions where science is sacrificed to faith, or to that which goes beyond science.) I would suggest that the tension between certainty and doubt that the series, and more specifically the island, generates can be linked to what John Keats famously called negative capability, "that is when man is capable of being in uncertainties, Mysteries, doubts, without any irritable reaching after fact & reason." Keats has just described *Lost*'s John Locke, at least as Locke would like to see himself for most of the first two seasons; and Keats has also described half of the series' appeal, since the success of the program must depend to a large degree on the willingness of so many people to be untethered to explanation or resolution for so long. But negative capability is most applicable to lyric poetry, which is focused not on plot progression or resolution but on reflections and questions mediated by experience. The innovation of *Lost*, and of the *Decalogue* and *Six Feet Under* before it, is to marry negative capability (the mode of the lyric) to the relentless thirst for events and answers (the mode of serial narrative). It is an uneasy marriage, one perhaps previously unattempted in popular culture, since it requires that two opposing structural and interpretive models be yoked together.[11]

The counterparts to Locke and Shephard in *Six Feet Under* are Nate Fisher and Brenda Chenowith, a fractious couple both as man and woman and as representations of faith and science. When Brenda considers returning to college, she is intrigued by a class on genetics, while Nate tries to persuade her to pursue religious studies. Their alternating attraction and repulsion is rarely as blatantly schematic as that moment would imply, and indeed the parallels become more complicated the closer we examine them. If Locke is a dogmatic mystic, Nate is a drifting seeker of the spiritual, squinting earnestly but with little conviction that he will find plain solutions. In many ways, Nate is the closest avatar to the figure of the television viewer in all three series, since he combines a deeply rooted interest in the pleasures and habits of the lived moment with a vaguely active concern with a big picture that will make sense of things; likewise, the viewer returns for the satisfying familiarity and amusement of each episode, while always craving an understanding of the arc of serial narrative. Brenda, by contrast, is a force of negation, of fear disguised as conviction, unlike the ceaselessly (and sometimes destructively) positivist Jack Shephard. Later in the episode in which she and Nate discuss her curricular choices, he asks whether she thinks there is any kind of design in the universe, or at least in human endeavor. "There's definitely no plan—just survival," she insists, using a lexicon apt to the world of *Lost* (episode 2.3, "The Plan"). Nate and Brenda represent a doubting believer and a believing doubter—two modes that storytelling requires, often in equal measures, from its consumers. More broadly, *Six Feet Under*'s concentration on the epicenter of doubt in human existence—namely, the meaning, purpose, and result of death—makes the Fisher home, in a more familiar way, a synonym of the uncanny island, a place whose business it is to process and display doubt. And both of these environments devolve from a Warsaw apartment block and a not-quite-frozen lake nearby, where doubt asserts its will over reason and hope alike.

The most controversial story in *Six Feet Under*'s run was a fourth-season episode called "That's My Dog," which depicted the harrowing journey of David Fisher after he picks up, and finds himself terrorized by, a young hitchhiker. The passenger, who calls himself Jake (Michael Weston), successively clubs David from behind, threatens him at gunpoint, forces him to smoke crack, and pours gasoline on his head as an apparent prelude to setting him on fire—before he takes off in David's van, abandoning the victim in an alley. Many loyal viewers expressed outrage at this treatment of a beloved character—drawing an at least implicit analogy between Jake and the show's producers as agents of motiveless malignancy—and termed this the nadir of the series, the manifest instance when it had lost control of its tenor and direction by engaging in cheap sadomasochism. The real source of anger, however, has its roots not so much in the violation of the character of David as in the violation of the rules and regulations that viewers assumed the series to be following; as one critic put it, "regular watchers rely on continuity . . . there's a structural trust few creators ever mess with" (Nussbaum). The broken rules and regulations in this case illustrate precisely the three elements—design, doubt, and the absent middle—that I have been detailing. First, absolutely no hint of this dominant storyline had been introduced in any of the previews, thereby violating a crucial part of the design of serial narrative; in addition, the last twenty-five minutes of the episode were devoted entirely to the nightmare ride, without returning to any of the other series principals, breaking a design convention not only of *Six Feet Under* but of virtually all multiarc serial dramas. Second, the meandering, seemingly improvisational nature of Jake's hijacking left viewers in a state of profound doubt—not only about what was going to happen to David, and when, and how, but about what was going on with the rest of the characters, who had inexplicably, and in unprecedented fashion, disappeared from the face of the show. And third, the relentless presentness of this storyline—the way it required viewers to focus on the details of the moment without the luxury of processing them, like a detective or pathologist, from a distance—marked this as perhaps the most antiprocedural hour in American television, since we are left, like Krzysztof in *Decalogue 1*, bereft not only of any specific procedures for processing this set of details but also of the very structure of procedure itself. In a sense, the series was nowhere more itself—nowhere more attuned to its central elements—than in this apparent violation of those elements, even down to the reversal of the collision of single and communal at the heart of *Six Feet Under*'s narrative logic; in this case the communal (the crowd of characters that define the show) was removed from the single (David, cut off from the group), in effect undoing the trope of the show's inaugurating accident.

Alan Poul, the director of this episode and Alan Ball's partner in running the series, addresses the violent reaction to "That's My Dog" in a DVD commentary, in part by underlining the broader preoccupations of this installment, the issues that linked the apparently separate halves of the hour. Pointing out David's good deed in offering help to what seemed to be a helpless young man by the side of the road and connecting it to similar efforts of benevolent connection in the episode, Poul observes, "You put stuff out there, in order to get a reaction from the world, with the best of intentions. And what you get back is often not what you expect, or deserve, or even consider to be an answer . . . But all of that added up doesn't mean that we're not living in a moral universe." Poul's attention to the lack of correspondence between effort and result, or desire and satisfaction, speaks to the central frustrating dynamic that governs not only *Six Feet Under* but the *Decalogue* and *Lost* as well—all series that undermine the apparatus of serial narration without ever dismissing it, that make undermining a particular way of exploiting the serial situation. It is fitting that Poul's perhaps half-hearted attempt at consolation—"all of that added up doesn't mean we're not living in a moral universe"—should be expressed through the rhetorical gesture of litotes, a negation of negation that makes doubt and not assertion the controlling instrument. The sense of the tenuous potentiality of design, the complicated way in which the detail connects to the global, the language of agnosticism: these three elements, interwoven, write a fitting epigraph for the ambitions and effects of three series that willfully challenged the laws of television.

Notes

1. Anthology shows such as *The Twilight Zone* and *Alfred Hitchcock Presents* featured most prominently in the first generation of American television narrative, emphasizing self-contained stories linked only by a general unifying concept—such as the inexplicable or the macabre.

2. Paul Coates does make reference to Kieślowski's "serial aesthetic" and its play between "familiarity and defamiliarisation, enticing viewers to return to the next variation." But Coates's use of seriality here incorporates both the *Decalogue* and the *Three Colors* (1993-94) trilogy, as if these very different enterprises somehow manifested analogous expressions of the rhetoric of "series." Space does not permit a lengthy inspection of Coates's intriguing collation, but some differences are central and apparent: the length of the *Decalogue* (significantly stretched beyond the conventional shape of a trilogy), the unifying devices (the apartment block, the mysterious visitor, the interlocking characters), and the televisual context—the latter being no small matter when we consider the how and why of narrative (Coates 7).

3. Johnson's benign nativism in tracing the evolution of American television is replicated, somewhat less parochially, in Lynette Porter and David Lavery's *Unlocking the Meaning of* Lost. This "unauthorized guide" cites twenty-two "ancestors" of the series; of these, ten are American television series, seven are "classic" American or British novels and stories, three are popular American novels (including two by Steven King), and two are films. The authors do not travel beyond this Anglo-American axis to discover potential narrative sources (Porter and Lavery 107–55).

4. The conclusion of the second season, and most of the third, suggest that a powerful, and accidental, electromagnetic surge caused the plane's disintegration; but the wealth of coincidences linking the passengers on the plane with each other and with the mysteries and properties of the island makes a diagnosis of pure accident impossible to justify.

5. The "cinematic" qualities of *Lost*'s plane crash, a term used by several first-season DVD commentators as praise for the show's ability to transcend the small screen, illustrate the cultural give-and-take among these series, as the questions of what the "cinematic" and the "televisual" entail become progressively more complicated.

6. Nathaniel Fisher will return many times after this moment, and indeed several times in the pilot—but as a psychological projection of various members of the Fisher family. These competing, and occasionally incompatible, iterations of the Nathaniel Fisher each of the characters constructs over the course of the series offer an analogue of "this guy." But this is analogue as opposite; rather than an unknown, purely external figure whose provenance and purpose are opaque, Nathaniel is a familiar entity, the result of an internal attempt to negotiate past and present, or self and family, or any number of daily questions of doubt.

7. There are ambiguous film-noir shots of the protagonists of *Decalogue 4* at the beginning of that episode, shots that suggest that the father and daughter are absor-

bing the revelations of the story; but these are not nearly as specific as the opening images of *Decalogue 1*. The more prominent exception might be *Decalogue 8*, where we see a young girl being led down a dark street; this will turn out to be the memory of Elzbieta (Teresa Marczewska), the adult Jewish survivor of the Holocaust. But this merely places an earlier event as prelude to a collection of contemporary events; it is not retrospective in the manner of *Decalogue One*.

8. *Six Feet Under* begins to open up the psychological space of the cold open later in the first season when the young brother of Claire Fisher's boyfriend inadvertently shoots himself at the start of the ninth episode ("Life's Too Short"). But the little brother had not existed within the show before that moment, so that the cold open has a similar effect of the individual-colliding-with-the-group, or the unknown-colliding-with-the-known, that is constitutive of the device. Only in later seasons does the cold open start to show someone whom we know, or whom the central characters know; these developments indicate *Six Feet Under*'s transition to its baroque phase.

9. As Annette Insdorf points out, the filmed episode veers critically away from the script at this moment. The script presents a scene where Krzysztof discovers that a power station had released hot water into the lake at night—a cause that would explain, firmly within the realm of science, Pawel's death. Insdorf's attempt to re-solve the problem—by suggesting that the fire that "this guy" uses to warm himself may be the new cause—misses entirely the effect of Kieślowski's maneuver. The removal of any kind of causation is central to the project of the episode, since it spotlights the issue of doubt, and the absent middle, that the rest of the series will follow (Insdorf 74; Kieślowski and Piesiewicz 24).

10. Claire seems to summon a more conventionally satisfying memory during Nate's burial as her mind drifts back to a moment in 1994, when Kurt Cobain died and a grieving Nate offered her what may have been her first joint. Her smile, as we return from past to the present, advertises this as an instance that appears to redeem the unsettling memories that have previously attended familial death. This flashback is one of the most unconvincing moments in all of *Six Feet Under*—on the level of performance, dialogue, and character consistency—and I would argue that this unconvincingness is deliberate. This reads much more plausibly as a false or screen memory, as a fiction that Claire's psyche conjures as the balm of consolation—not unlike the fictions of self that populate the backstories of so many of the principals of *Lost*.

11. In fact, one could say that it's not so much a marriage as a ménage à trois—since the series include all three of the traditional poetic modes: the lyric, the epic or narrative, and the dramatic, given that these are enacted stories.

Works Cited

Coates, Paul, ed. *Lucid Dreams: The Films of Krzysztof Kieślowski*. Trowbridge, UK: Flicks Books, 1999.

Haltof, Marek. *The Cinema of Krzysztof Kieślowski: Variations on Destiny and Chance*. London: Wallflower Press, 2004.

Havrilesky. Heather. "An Alan Ball Postmortem." *Salon* 20 August 2005. http://dir.salon.com/story/ent/feature/2005/08/20/alan_ball/index.html?pn=3.

Insdorf, Annette. *Double Lives, Second Chances: The Cinema of Krzysztof Kieślowski.* New York: Miramax Books, 1999.

Johnson, Steven. *Everything Bad Is Good for You: How Today's Popular Culture Is Actually Making Us Smarter.* New York: Riverhead Books, 2005.

Keats, John. John Keats to George and Tom Keats, 21 December 1817. *The Letters of John Keats, 1814-1821.* Vol. 2: 1814-1818. Ed. Hyder Edward Rollins. No. 45. Cambridge, MA: Harvard University Press, 1958.

Kickasola, Joseph G. *The Films of Krzysztof Kieślowski: The Liminal Image.* New York: Continuum, 2004.

Kieślowski, Krzystof, and Krzysztof Piesiewicz. *Decalogue: The Ten Commandments.* London: Faber and Faber, 1991.

Nussbaum, Emily. "Captive Audience." *New York* 9 August 2004: 52.

Porter, Lynnette, and David Lavery. *Unlocking the Meaning of* Lost. Naperville, IL: Sourcebooks, 2006.

Stok, Danusia, ed. *Kieślowski on Kieślowski.* London: Faber and Faber, 1993.

Tasker, Yvonne, ed. *Fifty Contemporary Filmmakers.* New York: Routledge, 2002.

Contributors

John Caruana is currently an associate professor of philosophy at Ryerson University in Toronto, Canada. He is also affiliated with the Arts and Contemporary Studies Program and the Graduate Program in Communication and Culture (Ryerson and York University). His publications include articles on Adorno, Freud, and Levinas. He has published in such journals as the *Continental Philosophy Review* and the *Journal of Religious Ethics*. His present research explores the intersection of philosophy, religion, and cinema.

Paul Coates is a full professor in the film studies department of the University of Western Ontario. He has taught at McGill University and at the Universities of Georgia (Athens) and Aberdeen, and his books include *The Story of the Lost Reflection* (1985), *The Gorgon's Gaze* (1991), *Film at the Intersection of High and Mass Culture* (1994), *Cinema, Religion and the Romantic Legacy* (2003), and *The Red and the White: The Cinema of People's Poland* (2005).

Sarah Cooper is a senior lecturer in film studies at King's College London. She is the author of *Relating to Queer Theory* (2000); *Selfless Cinema? Ethics and French Documentary* (2006); and *Chris Marker* (2008). She is also editor of "Levinas and Cinema," a special issue of the online journal *Film-Philosophy* 11.2 (2007). Her current research focuses on the relationship between film and philosophy, with particular reference to the work of Emmanuel Levinas.

Charles Eidsvik is a professor of film and drama at the University of Georgia (Athens), where he teaches film history, theory, and production. He is also a working filmmaker, having sold a number of short films to cable networks, including Bravo and Cinemax. His previous published critical work includes "Mock Realism: The Comedy of Futility in Eastern Europe," in *Comedy/Cinema/Theory,* edited by Andrew Horton, and "*Decalogues 5* and 6 and the Two Short Films," in *Lucid Dreams: The Films of Krzysztof Kieślowski,* edited by Paul Coates.

Georgina Evans is teaching and completing a PhD at the University of Cambridge, on synaesthesia in contemporary French narrative cinema. She has a particular interest in the films of Kieślowski, Haneke, and Claire Denis.

Marek Haltof is a professor of film in the English department at Northern Michigan University in Marquette. His *Historical Dictionary of Polish Cinema* was published in 2007. His other recent publications include *The Cinema of Krzysztof Kieślowski: Variations on Destiny and Chance* (2004) and *Polish National Cinema* (2002; translated into Polish in 2004 and into Japanese in 2006). He has also published several books in Polish, including *Australian Cinema: The Screen Construction of Australia* (2005) and *Author and Art Cinema: The Case of Paul Cox* (2001).

Joseph G. Kickasola is an associate professor of communication studies at Baylor University and Director of the Baylor Communication in New York program. He published *The Films of Krzysztof Kieślowski: The Liminal Image* in 2004.

Renata Murawska is a lecturer in media, film, and PR at the Department of Media at Macquarie University, Sydney, Australia. She has a BA in psychology and semiotics (University of Sydney), an MA in international communications (Macquarie University), and a PhD (2005) on Polish (post)transitional cinema (Macquarie University). She is a contributor to *Senses of Cinema,* an online film journal and magazine. She has published a range of articles on Polish cinema, including "Of the Polish People's Republic and Its Memory in Polish Film" in *KinoKultura,* special issue 2 (2005).

Sean O'Sullivan is an assistant professor of film and literature at Ohio State University. His research interests include British film, the British novel, narrative and the visual arts, and serial fiction across media. He has published articles on British television drama, *Deadwood,* and Charles Dickens. His book on Mike Leigh is forthcoming from the University of Illinois Press.

Emma Wilson is a reader in contemporary French literature and film at the University of Cambridge. Her publications include *Sexuality and the Reading Encounter: Identity and Desire in Proust, Duras, Tournier and Cixous* (1996), *French Cinema since 1950: Personal Histories* (1999), *Memory and Survival: The French Cinema of Krzysztof Kieslowski* (2000), *Cinema's Missing Children* (2003), and *Alain Resnais* (2006). She is currently completing a project on the films of Atom Egoyan.

Steven Woodward is an associate professor of film and literature at Bishop's University, Canada. His most recent publications include "Urban Legend:

Architecture in *Lord of the Rings*" (with Kostis Kourelis), which appeared in *From Hobbits to Hollywood: Essays on Peter Jackson's* Lord of the Rings, edited by Ernest Mathijs and Murray Pomerance (2006), and "The Arch Archenemies of James Bond," which appeared in *Bad: Infamy, Darkness, Evil, and Slime on Screen,* edited by Murray Pomerance (2003). He is currently working on a book about cringe comedy.

Index

Page numbers in italics refer to illustrations